DIARY OF AN EROTIC LIFE

DIARY OF
AN EROTIC LIFE

———◆———

FRANK WEDEKIND

EDITED BY
GERHARD HAY

TRANSLATED BY
W. E. YUILL

BASIL BLACKWELL

English translation copyright © Basil Blackwell Ltd 1990

First published in German as *Die Tagebücher: Ein erotisches Leben*
edited by Gerhard Hay © Kadidja Wedekind-Biel and Athenäum Verlag
GmbH, Frankfurt am Main 1986

English translation first published 1990

Basil Blackwell Ltd
108 Cowley Road, Oxford, OX4 1JF, UK

Basil Blackwell, Inc.
3 Cambridge Center
Cambridge, Massachusetts 02142, USA

British Library Cataloguing in Publication Data

A CIP catalogue record for this book is available from
the British Library.

Library of Congress Cataloging in Publication Data

Wedekind, Frank, 1864–1918.
[Diaries. English]
Diary of an erotic life/Frank Wedekind:
edited by Gerhard Hay; translated by W. E. Yuill.
p. cm.
Includes bibliographical references.
ISBN 0-631-16607-6
1. Wedekind, Frank, 1864–1918—Diaries.
2. Dramatists, German—20th century—Biography.
I. Hay, Gerhard. II. Title.

PT2647.E26Z46913 1990
838'.803—dc20
[B]   89-27724 CIP

Typeset in 11 on 13 pt Sabon
by Wyvern Typesetting Ltd, Bristol
Printed in Great Britain by
T. J. Press Ltd, Padstow, Cornwall

CONTENTS

TRANSLATOR'S PREFACE

THE present volume is for the most part a translation of the original German publication *Frank Wedekind. Die Tagebücher. Ein erotisches Leben*, edited by Dr Gerhard Hay and published in 1986 by the Athenäum Verlag, which includes practically everything that survives in the way of Wedekind's diaries and personal notebooks. This English version also contains, however, a certain amount of material that is missing from the German edition. In particular, the German editor has chosen to reprint a previously published account of incidents from 8 to 10 September 1893 and to leave out the corresponding pages 97–123 of the manuscript Paris diary. The previously published version is included here as an Appendix. The German edition also omits brief entries for 2 February 1890 (Munich) and 5 May 1892 (Paris), as well as two manuscript pages from the entry for 11 December 1892. Three sentences are missing from the entry for 11 January 1894, and there are some other minor omissions. I differ here and there from the German editor in my reading of Wedekind's – rather difficult – handwriting, and I believe I have managed to decipher some words which apparently defeated Dr Hay. The few remaining illegible words and phrases are indicated by . . . and those passages in the manuscripts that have been deliberately obliterated are indicated by —. A number of pages have been excised from the Paris diaries, probably by Wedekind himself. It was not until 1986 that the manuscript and typescript texts were released for publication by Frank Wedekind's surviving daughter, Frau Kadidja Wedekind-Biel, and we must be grateful to her for making them available.

The exact provenance of the texts comprising the diaries is given below.

The 'Autobiographical Note' was first published in January 1911, in the magazine *Pan*, vol. 1, no. 5, pp. 147–9.

The diary from Lenzburg Castle (9 February–25 March 1887) was published in a collection of Wedekind's writings, *Die Fürstin Russalka* (*Princess Russalka*), Paris, Leipzig, Munich, 1897, pp. 104–19. The original manuscript has been lost.

The Berlin and Munich diaries (24 May–4 July 1889 and 5 July 1889–4 February 1890) are printed from corrected typescripts nos. 5 and 6 under the archive reference L 2933 in the 'Monacensia' manuscript department of Munich City Library. It was probably Wedekind's intention to publish them, but they never appeared in print. There is no trace of an original manuscript.

Two exercise books containing the Paris diaries and the first three entries relating to Wedekind's stay in London are deposited under archive number L 3502 in the 'Monacensia' collection. His description of a visit to the Middlesex Music Hall in Drury Lane was published as 'A Fragment from my London Diary' in the magazine *Mephisto* edited by Julius Schaumberger (vol. 1, no. 10, 28 November 1896).

The brief notes from Berlin and Munich (21 December 1905–1 July 1908 and 16–23 February 1918) are taken from notebooks in the 'Monacensia' collection (archive no. L 3504). The poem to Tilly Wedekind (p. 249) comes from an undated pocket diary (archive no. L 3476/6/4).

Writers and thinkers from German-speaking countries and communities have made many major contributions to the cultural and political life of the twentieth century: political institutions in large parts of the world are unthinkable without the influence of Karl Marx, the ideas of Sigmund Freud in more or less garbled form have achieved remarkably wide currency, and it was probably Franz Kafka more than any other writer who expressed the malaise of urban populations suffering under the bureaucratic stress that is now regularly associated with his name. The same kind of pervasive influence could hardly be claimed for Frank Wedekind, but he may perhaps be given credit for being the first writer in any language to identify another obsessive feature of twentieth-century urban society: the part played in the consciousness of that society by sex and sexuality.

It was at the turn of the century that Wedekind began to explore this theme, and it is to his treatment of it in theatrical terms that he owes both his initial notoriety and the enduring reputation that keeps plays like *Spring Awakening, Earth Spirit* and *Pandora's Box* on the international stage today.

Spring Awakening, written in 1890–1 but not performed until 1906, is based, according to its author, on his own experiences at school and was written spontaneously and independently of any theatrical model. 'I started to write,' Wedekind tells us, 'without any sort of plan, merely aiming to set down whatever appealed to me. The plan emerged after the third scene and was compiled from my own personal experience or the experiences of my class-mates.' The action of the play features the suicide of a pupil who fails to cope with the exacting academic standards of his school, and the death of an innocent schoolgirl at the hands of a back-street abortionist, the victim of her own ignorance and her mother's prudery. *Spring Awakening* shocked the contemporary public, and it may well still startle audiences today because of its frank representation of adolescent love – both hetero- and homosexual – and of the sexual practices of young men deprived of female company. The play was banned in Berlin in 1912, but its supporters found an unexpected ally in an enlightened judge of the Administrative Court who lifted the ban, and whose assessment of the play's merit is still valid, although the social circumstances which gave rise to it may have altered radically. 'The play,' he wrote,

shows how the forces of real life affect innocent young people at the age of puberty, with particular reference to their own incipient sexuality and the demands made on them by life, and especially by their schooling. They perish in the ensuing conflict, because their appointed mentors, their parents and teachers, in the author's view, fail to guide them with proper understanding, because they are prudish and lacking in worldly wisdom ... Looked at in this light, and taking into account its overall tenor and subject, it cannot be denied that the play as a whole is a serious work: it deals with serious educational issues, and it seeks to state an attitude towards these issues.

The originality of the play's theme is matched by the novelty of its fluid dramatic idiom which places Wedekind alongside Georg Büchner as one of the most original playwrights of his nation. Turning away from the distinctly academic tradition of the German stage, and in particular the pedestrian Naturalism of the 1890s, Wedekind evolves a style which is flexible and capable of moving easily from one mood and one level to another – from sentiment to farce, from the vulgar to the poetic, from realism to fantasy. His sovereign handling of the drama as a spectacular performance medium is best explained by Wedekind's familiarity with the circus and by his experience as actor and cabaret artist.

The originality of Wedekind's approach to the drama is strikingly epitomized in the Prologue to the twin dramas *Earth Spirit* and *Pandora's Box*: the Ringmaster, traditionally armed with whip and revolver and often acted by Wedekind himself, spurns the 'domestic pets' represented by the characters of the traditional drama, with their metaphysical or social problems. Instead, he presents the audience with his heroine Lulu, 'the true, the wild and lovely beast'. Lulu is the very personification of sexuality and she makes her devastating way through a world where men and women are bound together only by lust, or else by the cash nexus. She emerges from a *demi-monde* of circus acrobats, criminals and confidence tricksters to wreak havoc in bourgeois society, destroying in one way or another her lovers of all ages and both sexes – only to fall victim herself to a figure who embodies the sexual urge that has been perverted by the pressures of society, Jack the Ripper.

The action of this 'monstrous tragedy', as Wedekind calls it, is bizarre and explosive, punctuated by apoplectic seizure, suicide and any number of murders, but there emerge from it certain striking truths – specifically about the exploitation of woman's sexuality and its implications for her place in society, but more generally about the inability of individuals to understand their own motives and the motives of others – an inability that has come to be known as 'alienation'. This phenomenon was identified and expressed by Bertolt Brecht in his early play *In the Jungle of the Cities* even before he came to interpret it as a consequence of economic development. But where Brecht's Shlink observes that men are so isolated from each other that they cannot communicate even by way of conflict, the Countess Geschwitz in *Pandora's Box* goes even further and comments despairingly on man's estrangement from his own nature which leaves him at the mercy of his physical appetites: 'Men don't know themselves – they don't know their own nature. Only someone who is not himself human can fathom them. Every word they utter is untrue, a lie. They don't know that, for they are this way one day, that way another, depending on whether they have eaten, drunk and made love, or not.' It is the unnerving representation of this ultimately irrational nature of human behaviour, on the one hand, and his emancipation of the theatre from the tyranny of illusion, on the other, that constitute Wedekind's originality – and hence his contribution to the literature of Germany and of Europe.

Wedekind's *Diaries* may perhaps best be left to speak for themselves: they are a plain record of a life largely devoted to social intercourse. It is indeed remarkable how unliterary they are as compared with the diaries of most professional writers. Wedekind very rarely writes about his current literary preoccupations in any detail. As he himself points out, the diaries had a kind of clinical function as a record of his responses to everyday experiences. They were intended to be a self-portrait, and this they certainly are to an almost embarrassing degree, portraying their author, piles, gumboils, false teeth and all. Given the emotive nature of many of the incidents described, they are remarkably dispassionate and objective. On one occasion only – following an encounter with the egregious Marcel Herwegh – does Wedekind seem to have lost control of himself and to have suffered a brief nervous breakdown.

Apart from recording Wedekind's emotional and intellectual responses, the diaries seem to have served another purpose: the careful recording of social environment and behaviour, particularly evident in the graphic descriptions of café society in Munich, Berlin and Paris. At times Wedekind seems to share that passion for pedantic note-taking for which he disliked and satirized the Naturalists, but it is evident that such observations are mediated and amplified in his literary works so as to make the necessary impact on an audience. The Paris diaries, which obviously provided a factual background for *Pandora's Box*, are nothing like as lurid as corresponding scenes in the drama. Indeed it may strike us as surprising that the life of Parisian prostitutes was as normal, economically secure and idyllically domestic as it is represented in the diaries.

The surviving diaries – whether in print or in manuscript – are discontinuous and at times fragmentary, but they do have a kind of fortuitous continuity as a series of mirrors reflecting the phases of the author's development from the juvenile erotic skirmishes and fantasies of Lenzburg, through his years in Berlin and Munich, where he seems to have hovered diffidently on the brink of sexual adventure, to his time in Paris, where he celebrated his sexual coming of age. In Berlin and Munich, according to Wedekind's observation, prostitution seems to have been a furtive fringe activity pursued by waitresses from the beer cellars, but in Paris Wedekind found a coherently organized and publicly acknowledged *demi-monde* that drew his attention to the powerful influence of sexuality in society and inspired the plot and action of *Pandora's Box*. The brief entries from Wedekind's later years in Berlin strike us by way of contrast as a kind of melancholy epilogue to a life that had been so exuberantly erotic in its prime. Plagued by professional cares and, it would seem, by the kind of jealous pangs suffered by Lulu's more elderly lovers, Wedekind had apparently little time or inclination to continue his detailed observations of himself and the world around him. The record closes on the same sombre note with the poem addressed to his wife Tilly and apparently written on the eve of the operation that was to cost Wedekind his life. It is a poignant and premonitory farewell from a man we have come to know through his personal diaries as sane, humane and full of the joy of life.

INTRODUCTION

AT the conclusion of Wedekind's comedy *Children and Fools* (published in 1891, and in a revised form under the title *The Young Folk* in 1897) a marriage is salvaged after it has threatened to break down because of the propensity of a Naturalist author, Meier, to take notes of everything around him:

ALMA: It was quite simple, really. Whenever he kissed me, he used to have a notebook in one hand while he took notes with the other on my facial expression. I was jealous of that notebook. I kept thinking, he only kisses you in order to see what sort of face you make (*in tears*) and – and –

ANNA: Well?

ALMA: (*weeping*) I stopped putting on any sort of expression. So then Meier reproached me and said I was behaving in an unnatural way, I was affected and hadn't the least trace of naturalness about me. It made me so unhappy to think that I, of all people, was unnatural, that I burst into tears and begged Meier on my bended knees to convince himself of my natural responses. And instead of answering – Oh, I'll never forget that day as long as I live . . .

ERNA: (*caressing her*) Just tell us, Alma. That's why we've met, so that you can tell us all about it.

ALMA: Instead of answering, Meier simply took out his notebook and started writing down what sort of look I had on my face . . . If I asked him, 'How did you sleep last night?' he wrote that down in his notebook. If I told him a child had been run over, he wrote that down in his notebook. If I begged him to stop taking his goddam notes, then he wrote that down in his notebook as well. In the end I used to think, if only one or the other of us were no longer in this world, I or his notebook . . .

OSKAR: And Meier wrote *that* down in his notebook.

MEIER: I don't wish to reproach Alma for a moment. But when I did my naturalistic studies on Alma, she became unnatural. If I made studies of some other object, then she became jealous of that object. So in the end the only alternative left to me was to carry out my naturalistic studies on myself. And that was what finally did for me!

ALMA: In the end I gave Meier the choice: either he should kill me out of hand, so as to be able to write a great novel about it, or else we should get divorced! . . .

MEIER: (*bursting into tears*) Oh, my friends, my friends!

KARL: (*taking his hand*) Come, then, dear friend! Your realism has driven your poetry quite out of your head. But it's your poetry I have to thank for the most precious thing life has given me so far. And you, too, should be grateful to your poetry. The true poet doesn't create his poetry by hanging round and spying on people, but by taking a pure delight in them. (*Leading him over to Alma*) Here's your muse. (*To Alma*) True poetry has never stood between lovers. After all, a poet only writes because he's alive, because he's in love, because he takes a delight in just being. Are you prepared to try again with our friend, on that basis?

ALMA: (*through her tears*) Yes. Yes. – But without – without –

KARL: That's the prime condition: without a notebook!

The dénouement of his comedy shows that Frank Wedekind was fully aware of the problems involved in fiction on the one hand, and truth to life on the other: 'So in the end the only alternative left to me was to carry out my naturalistic studies on myself. And that was what finally did for me!' This concluding scene may be merely a jibe at Naturalism, but Gerhart Hauptmann's notebook mania during his time in Erkner is in fact testified to in Wedekind's diaries. Wedekind, too, felt the need to make notes about himself, in a very different form, of course – and he, too, kept notebooks and diaries.

This kind of personal diary has been cultivated ever since the eighteenth century, when the Age of Enlightenment began, with its promotion of individualism, the psychological approach and the cult of personality. Diaries are written either with a potential readership in mind, or else exclusively for private, introspective perusal. They are dialogues of the ego with itself, and range from attempts at self-treatment to addiction to the drug of vanity. Like the letter, a writer's diary may assume a fictional character, and hence turn into literature. How great the discrepancy between letter and diary can be may be illustrated by an example from Wedekind. It is the account he gives of the fiancée of his friend Heinrich Welti, the singer Emilie

Herzog. In a letter to his mother which is dated 11 June 1889 she appears as a thoroughly lovable personality:

At any rate, Frl. Herzog would be not only an agreeable but a positively dear friend, as far as you are concerned. She is altogether unassuming, a thoroughly sound performer with a touch of genius, even. She is pleasant and cheerful, sensible, and beyond any doubt the best of souls ever to walk God's earth. In appearance, she is a shade on the diminutive side, but her voice is almost supernaturally fresh. People in Berlin are obviously delighted with her. I've never heard her sing without her getting the lion's share of the applause, which is all the more astonishing, since she is unlikely to stir the onlooker's soul by her acting. Her soubrette parts she acts in a manner so devoid of coquetry that, as far as my feeling goes, she seems at points even a bit silly. It looks as if she can't help it. In company she's utterly unaffected and straightforward, so there's no doubt you'd be absolutely delighted with her.

How very differently she is to figure in the diary notes for that same month of June!

Wedekind's surviving diaries are presented here for the first time in their integral phases. They fall into two parts: firstly, the diary entries published – and hence revised – in Wedekind's lifetime, that is the entries from Lenzburg Castle in the Swiss canton of Aargau, made in 1887, the Parisian sketch 'Les Halles' from 1893, and a London episode of 1894; secondly, the diaries from Wedekind's time in Berlin and Munich (1889–90), which he himself thought suitable for publication but which have never appeared in print, together with the record of his stays in Paris between 1892 and 1894. These texts, denoted by Wedekind as 'diary' or 'memoirs' are supplemented by the scanty entries in his pocket diary for 1918, the year of his death.

It is precisely from the discrepancies between these different texts – those written for purely private reference and those intended for publication – that the modified style, the professional writer's craft, clearly emerges. The general tone, however, reflection in the form of hindsight, becomes apparent in the text, as compared with the bald, matter-of-fact statements in the actual diary:

Why should I narrate in the third person something that happened to me in the first person? The reader may feel like crossing himself in the presence of such a narrator, but that is still better than having him yawn. What's more, the story is not all that out of the ordinary. There are plenty of people to whom the same thing has happened and who are in a position to check whether I'm telling the truth. For some of them, this is a crucial issue, for others, it isn't. What it means to me, I can't yet tell.

It was last night, while I was settling my bill in the restaurant, that I counted out my resources. I still had one louis d'or and a number of sou pieces. I worked out how long that would last. Four days at most. And then? – Behold the lilies of the field, I said to myself. They sow not, neither do they reap, but our Father in Heaven feeds them all the same.

Should I go back home? – What was I to do? – Earn money! But anything I earned couldn't possibly have arrived before my louis d'or had run out. I was in excellent spirits, by the way. I felt so invigorated and free. So I decided to go looking for adventure. I walked across the Pont St Michel to the Opéra Comique and watched the audience pouring in to listen to *Carmen*.

It is true that the third-person narrator is restyled into a first-person narrator, but how confidently this 'I' writes as a matter of course in the narrative past tense. He means to keep his distance, to sustain the fiction, however factual it may be. A striking feature is the direct relationship with the reader. In his diaries Wedekind reflects directly or indirectly on the diary form. After reading through the first volume, he notes: 'The overall impression seems to me to be distinctly psychopathic. If I were not convinced that my inner life is by and large very disciplined, these notes might alarm me' (21 June 1889).

As far as this most controversial dramatist of our century is concerned, the diary is a kind of check on his psychological state that can only be expressed in written form. Writing is his vocation, even when success is still lacking. Its therapeutic function is acknowledged: 'For my part I mean to persevere with these notes, since they exercise such a beneficial influence on my state of mind. Others have recourse to a girl, I stick to my diary, Joseph that I am! Paragon of virtue! And to think that I'm proud of it. Oh, irony, strange are thy ways!' (31 January 1890).

Wedekind knows that the diary is a substitute – life is the true diary. At the end of an excerpt from the Paris diaries which he published, he reflects:

Reading through these lines again, I suddenly notice something about them. The odd thing about such leaves from a diary, if they are genuine, is that they contain so little in the way of actual events. The moment events intrude on life, then the pleasure, the interest and the time for a diary all evaporate, and the human individual rediscovers the spontaneous innocence of the child or the animal in its wilderness.

But life and work are nevertheless a single entity, as these diaries also confirm: here we witness the struggle to pull the dramas *Children and Fools*, *Spring Awakening* and *Fritz Schwigerling* into shape, and the inspiration for the *Lulu* tragedy materializing on a Paris boulevard. It is in Paris that 'Joseph' Wedekind turns into a 'lover', it is here that fantasy turns into life, without a mental censor's scissors preceding the act of writing. Diary! Wedekind, whose favourite author was Casanova, finds himself and has the courage to write it all down, to turn it into words. In this respect the diaries are certainly exceptional. In his autobiography, *My Twentieth Century*, Ludwig Marcuse noted, for example, in a spirit of self-criticism: 'The last thing I dared do was to write down the social history of my flesh: the impact of the flesh at ten, twenty, thirty, forty . . . on men, women, on aristocrats, the middle class, and maidservants. This impact (or, rather, the idea of it) is one of the most powerful motive forces in any life.'

In Wedekind's diaries Eros, in highly diverse forms, plays a dominant part, and it is a theme that Wedekind took up in all of his plays. It is the anti-theme of the age he lived in, often treated as tragic, but also often seen in a comic vein. It is in his diaries that Wedekind the student and, later, the literary tyro emancipated by financial resources, turns into a dramatist who dominated the contemporary stage and freed himself from the prudery and the suppression to which his age subjected the libido. In Berlin and Munich Wedekind is still something of a voyeur; it is not until he gets to Paris that he experiences true sensuality and accepts it gratefully. To put it briefly: Wedekind *lives* the themes of the literary *décadence*.

But even in those years in Paris he was aware of responsibilities in matters of love. This ethical attitude is expressed in an excerpt from a lost diary of 1892, lover's lament and a search for identity at one and the same time:

Chin up! Chin up! Don't discard the mask in front of her. She's in love. Sad, but true! When I listen to her talking in those thrilling tones, then it seems to me that my way of talking might be the awful pretext. The spirit has won the day. It will pay dearly for its triumph. Chin up! To gain time is to gain everything. Any old excuse, just to gain time. Chin up! I'm not looking for X. I'm in search of woman. Glad to find her in any shape whatsoever. The veil must be rent sooner or later. I don't count for less than the others. I count for more than them. X represents a whole dimension of life for me; diplomacy, not love, is the leitmotif. She's a victim, not a deity. She fulfils her vocation, and passes on. Don't let go of the reins. Stay in command of the situation. Govern the elements – and don't do anything stupid. I'm in search of woman . . . I've been exiled by her for the past eight days. She tore me from my solitude, fell upon me, and I went to the devil. I thought I would enjoy the course of instruction, and would return a hero. That won't work. My only hope will be to come back to her in a moral sense. That's when the life or death decision will be taken.

'I'm in search of woman.' From his diaries it is evident how Wedekind was torn between Eros and wedlock. Marriage and children turn up at an early stage as a projection of the libido, and yet he is well aware of the perils of matrimony for a writer of his type: 'For a writer, marriage would spell ruin. And if, what's more, I were to marry for love, come to terms with the world, then I might as well be buried straight away' (1 March 1887).

It was in marriage with Tilly Newes, the mother of his children, that Frank Wedekind found blissful sexual fulfilment within a triangle of forces representing Eros, family and vocation. And, after all, his very last written words were addressed 'To Tilly'.

Gerhard Hay

ACKNOWLEDGEMENTS

The illustrations on the following pages are published with the kind permission of Kadidja Wedekind-Biel and the Manuscript Department of the Munich City Library: pp. 3, 65, 101, 118, 119, 123, 125, 126, 127, 131, 152, 169, 175, 214, 229, 239, 240, 243, 246, 247, 248.

The photographs on pp. 135, 164 and 242 were provided by the Archiv für Kunst und Geschichte, Berlin.

Permission to reproduce the other illustrations is acknowledged as follows: p. 8: Photoglob-Wehrli AG, Zürich; p. 56, 107: Munich City Archives; p. 23: Ullstein Bilderdienst, Berlin; p. 158: from 'La Vie parisienne' 1 June 1889; p. 188: from an original in the Musée d'Albi; p. 227: Langen Müller Verlag.

The translator would like to record his thanks to the staff of the Manuscripts Department of Munich City Library, and in particular to Frau Weber, for their assistance in dealing with the Wedekind papers.

AUTOBIOGRAPHICAL NOTE

WEDEKIND wrote this brief autobiography in 1901 to serve as a basis for an essay which Ferdinand Hardekopf planned to write. It was not published, however, until 1911, when it appeared in the magazine *Pan* (vol. 1, no. 5, pp. 147–9). Judging from Wedekind's diaries, amongst other evidence, his account of his travels with the Herzog Circus and his friend Rudinoff seems somewhat improbable. His employment in London as secretary to the artist and art dealer Willy Grétor is also of rather doubtful authenticity.

BORN 24 August 1864 in Hanover.

My father, who came of an old East Frisian family of civil servants, was a much travelled man. He was a doctor and spent ten years travelling in Turkey as a physician in the Sultan's service. In 1847 he returned to Germany, and in 1848 sat as a substitute member in the Frankfurt Parliament. In 1849 he went to San Francisco, where he lived for fifteen years. At the age of forty-six he married a young actress from the German Theatre in San Francisco who was precisely half his age. This fact strikes me as not altogether devoid of significance. My mother's father was a self-made man. He had started life in Hungary selling mouse-traps, but at the end of the twenties he established a chemical works in Ludwigsburg, near Stuttgart. In 1830, together with Ludwig Stein, he organized a political conspiracy, and the pair of them were imprisoned in the fortress of Asperg. As may be gathered from the relevant entry in the encyclopedia, it was there that my grandfather invented the phosphorus match. After his release he set up a chemical works in Zürich and in 1857 he died, totally insane, in the Ludwigsburg lunatic asylum. His name was Heinrich Kammerer. Ten years ago the citizens of Ludwigsburg erected a monument in his memory. He was musically extremely gifted. Anything that my sister Erika and my humble self may possess in the way of musical talent is quite certainly inherited from him.

In 1864 my father came back to Germany, lived in Hanover for eight years, and in 1872 purchased the castle of Lenzburg in Canton Aargau, Switzerland, one of the most lovely spots I have ever seen on this earth. It was there that I grew up as the second eldest of six brothers and sisters, of whom the third youngest is my sister Erika. I attended the local school in Lenzburg and then the cantonal grammar school in Aargau. In 1883 I took my school-leaving examination. For some years I worked as a journalist with the *Neue Zürcher Zeitung* and various other Swiss papers. In 1886 the Maggi soup cube factory, which has since become world-famous, was founded in Kempthal, near Zürich. When the firm was first established Maggi appointed me to run the advertising and press department. At that time I used to associate mainly with Karl Henckell, to whom I owe my appreciation of all our current trends and aspirations.

Besides Henckell, Gerhart Hauptmann and Mackay also belonged to our circle. And then Zürich was also frequented by pretty well everyone who had any reputation, or who hoped to make his name on the contemporary literary scene. In those days Zürich was a prominent intellectual centre with a significance it has altogether lost since the repeal of anti-Socialist legislation.[1]

In 1888 I spent six months touring as secretary to the Herzog Circus, and after it was disbanded I went to Paris with a friend, the celebrated fire-painter Rudinoff, subsequently accompanying him as his assistant on tours of England and the South of France. In 1890, I came back to Munich with Rudinoff, and it was there that I wrote my first book, *Spring Awakening*. Then, as my father had died in the meantime, I returned to Paris and ultimately became secretary to Willy Grétor, a Danish painter and art-dealer who was also known in Berlin, and for whom I worked in London for about six months. It was during my stay in London that Dauthendey first introduced me to the new Symbolist literature of Germany, which was just beginning to flourish at the time. The winter of 1895/96 I spent back in Switzerland, giving readings under the stage-name of Cornelius

Frank Wedekind as he appeared with the Munich cabaret 'The Eleven Executioners'.

Mine-Haha. In this capacity I used to recite scenes from Ibsen's plays in Zürich and other Swiss cities. My *pièce de résistance* was the recitation by heart of *Ghosts*, including elaborate descriptions of each stage setting, with myself generally acting the part of whichever character happened to play the lead in any given scene. To this period also belongs the plan for the establishment of a travelling literary cabaret which, as I once wrote to you, I discussed with Bierbaum and a number of young ladies.

In the spring of 1896 I went to Munich for the inauguration of *Simplicissimus* and worked for two years on its political staff. In the autumn of 1897 Dr Carl Heine founded the Ibsen Theatre in Leipzig and engaged me as secretary, actor and producer. When acting in his company I used the name of my grandfather, Heinrich Kammerer. We toured all over northern Germany and returned to Leipzig, via Breslau and Vienna, in mid-summer 1898. We performed *Earth Spirit* in Leipzig, Halle, Hamburg, Brunswick and Breslau, with the play running for ten performances in Leipzig.[2] As the company was then disbanded, I moved to Munich and became literary manager, actor and producer in the Schauspielhaus there. There then ensued the *Simplicissimus* trial,[3] the immediate consequences of which I temporarily evaded only so as to gain six months time and the leisure in which to write a play. The moment I had written the concluding lines of the *Marquis of Keith*,[4] I surrendered to the court. In the fortress of Königstein I wrote the novel *Mine-Haha*, which is currently being published by the Insel publishing house. Since my release I have only rarely appeared on the stage, twice at the Rotterdam Municipal Theatre, and five times as the 'Kammersänger' at the Munich Schauspielhaus.[5] I am currently appearing every evening with the Eleven Executioners Cabaret, singing my own poems to guitar accompaniment composed by myself.

LENZBURG CASTLE

9 FEBRUARY–25 MARCH 1887

9 FEBRUARY 1887

I'm so frightfully bored that I have recourse to my diary, which I haven't kept for the last ten months.[1] Wilhelmine comes to lunch, and as Karl and I escort her down from the castle hill I keep wondering how I might best talk her into an exchange of affections during the winter. She has actually turned out quite charming, with her dark eyes, her pretty little head, her plump, pretty arms that she flaunts for all she's worth. Although she's already twenty-seven, she has evidently only just reached her prime.

12 FEBRUARY 1887

Wilhelmine lets me know that I may take her to the ice-rink and that she's head over heels in love. The moment I enter her boudoir she thrusts a cabinet photograph into my hand: that's him. While I'm studying it, she plants herself firmly in front of me with her album in her hand and recites some doggerel verses she has addressed to him, accompanying them with hair-raising gestures. At the ice-rink, as we skate hand in hand, she takes the photograph out of her pocket again, ogles it, shedding a skate every ten paces. The same gambit is repeated on the way home. In my room she smothers the picture with kisses and slides it slowly in and out of the envelope, so as to relish its various charms in detail and by degrees. She would be happy if only she could go on tour with him for a month: he is in fact a celebrated tenor. She would give the rest of her life for six months together with him. I can't blame her: her life has been pretty boring and dismal up till now and will probably continue to be so in the future. While we're playing the piano four-handed, she plants a kiss on the adored features at every crotchet-rest. At the end of the Étude she relapses into utter sexual ecstasy, sinks back into a corner of the sofa and allows me to caress her without offering the slightest resistance. Only every now and then she stammers in languishing tones: Oh, you're so nasty, so nasty!

God bless you, divine tenor. I hadn't really imagined that things would take this turn. It seems as if I'm not going to be so frightfully bored after all.

13 FEBRUARY 1887

Wilhelmine receives me with open arms. She wouldn't have been able to sing her aria that evening if I hadn't put her in the right mood. The fact is, the St Cecilia Society is proposing to put on *The Armourer*.[2] She asserts that my lips are too soft and effeminate. Old fathead that I am, I run through my old comic routines. She insists, incidentally, that love between us is out of the question. I don't give a hang what's in or out of the question. If her mouth existed only for the purpose of speech, I'd sew it up. The cloudburst of her emotions gives me no chance to take the offensive. I prefer to proceed calmly and seriously in matters of indulgence. After ten minutes, thank God, she declares she is satisfied. She has written a poem to me, which, however, does deal with love after all. Evidently she does not have sufficient command of the language to avoid the word. She then proceeds to tell me how and where she learned to kiss, a tedious, tearful tale with neither ups nor downs, from which I gain the conviction that she still has every right to bear her maiden name. Suddenly she asks me where I learned to kiss, but, taken so abruptly by surprise, I shroud myself in sombre silence, being heartily ashamed of my first teacher, good old Auntie Helene.[3]

16 FEBRUARY 1887

After lunch I go to fetch Wilhelmine to supper. She says everything between us must cease, as from today. I reply that I haven't even started yet, was she losing patience, I wasn't in any hurry. She has written no fewer than six poems, variations on her decision. She fetches her revolver, pushes me on to the sofa, rams her chin against my chest, and, with the cocked revolver aimed at my forehead, reads me her poems. Shaking in every limb, I ask her to desist. Suddenly she throws a white silk scarf over my head, falls on my neck and kisses me through the cloth, then, flying into a temper with herself, flings her slipper in my face. Then she implores me to write a poem to her, for once. I string three short verses together, rhyming 'fume' with 'Sodoom', which offends her deeply.

During the evening, in the window recess on the balcony, she confesses that she had merely wanted to find out what kissing was like, and had then got hooked on it. She wanted to stop, though, before she was cast aside. Then she asks me, too, to be utterly frank with her. I ask her if she knows what the most dreadful thing in life is. She replies: Desire without satisfaction. I shake my head and whisper in her ear: Boredom. She feels profoundly sorry for me.

At supper the question is raised whether the pathway to the lips passes through the heart, or whether the pathway to the heart passes through the lips. Opinion is divided and the discussion grows lively. Mother defends the pathway via the heart;[4] Wilhelmine speaks very decisively in favour of the pathway via the lips. Karl, who has been chopping wood from morning to night for the past week in order to calm his nerves, reckons that the pathway to the heart doesn't pass through the lips but through the ears, and the way through the lips doesn't lead to the heart but to the stomach. Wilhelmine wishes to recite my poem, but can't, because she's lodged it in her bosom. Mother says it's a purely private party, but my dearest one replies that it's too far down. At these words Karl casts his eyes down and blushes.

After supper Karl and I light a great bundle of brushwood in the hall fireplace. Then we fetch the trunk with the Turkish costumes from the loft above the dungeons. As we carry it across the courtyard, brilliant sparks are streaming from the chimney over the hall and vanishing amid the stars. Karl says, that if the roof catches fire, we haven't even got water, as the pond is frozen over. I reassure him: what would it matter if the whole castle went up in flames: all this splendour wasn't going to last much longer anyway.

In the hall the whole company gets dressed up in Turkish costumes. Mother puts on a cloak of Genoese velvet with gold braid that reaches down to the ground. In this outfit she dances a *samaqueca* on

Lenzburg Castle, Aargau, about 1880.

the Smyrna carpet with incomparable verve and suppleness. Wilhelmine, Karl, the two little ones and I sit on sofa cushions round her drinking coffee. Karl plays the accordion and I accompany him on the guitar. Then Gretchen and Elsa dance a *pas de deux* that mother has rehearsed with them. Then she tells us about the experiences she had once had on the stage in San Francisco and Valparaiso, about life on the haciendas, and about her first husband, who had gambled away by the end of each concert everything he had taken at the box-office when it started. He had been condemned to be shot no fewer than three times in his life, once during a rising in Venezuela, once during the Commune, and finally in the Russo-Turkish war. He is currently acting as master of ceremonies at the Palais de Glace in Paris. I look forward with infinite pleasure to making his acquaintance. Suddenly Gretchen, with her penetrating gaze, detects a blood-red mark on my neck. I find it hard not to burst out laughing. Accompanying Wilhelmine down the hill, I suggest in a roundabout way, as a consolation, that she isn't the only one, but merely a representative: that precisely what intrigues me is to view her primarily as a type, and only then as an individual. I tell her that people so often thought they were the only specimens of their kind, as men do when they think they're suffering from imagined illnesses. If only they realized that it happens to almost everyone, then the illness would be cured on the spot.

17 FEBRUARY 1887

I go to see Wilhelmine between two and three. Her sister is at home. When she goes off to her Women's Guild at last, we are both glad to watch from the window as she departs. There are folk you prefer to see from behind rather than from in front, who cause you pain when you see them from the front, and pleasure when you see them from the back. I explain to Wilhelmine that this is the basis of Greek love. She cannot understand how a mind like mine which aspired towards the ultimate extreme could even reflect on such a serious matter. Then we talk about top-hats. If I ever want to cool her ardour, then I need only come to her wearing a top-hat. We would get married in an artist's slouch hat, and divorced in a top-hat. As we part she begs me, if I have the smallest spark of feeling for her, to write her a poem by tomorrow. We intended to go to Aarau, and I should read it to her in the railway carriage. Gretchen comes for her piano lesson. Wilhelmine pushes me into the next room without a word and strangles me, so that I turn red and blue, then she returns with the maternal composure of a Madonna to the music-room, while I slink out of the house on tiptoe.

After supper I hunt through all my poems but can't find anything suitable. I lie down full-length on the divan, but don't manage to concentrate my thoughts on her. I fall asleep.

18 FEBRUARY 1887

The big day. After breakfast I slip a blank sheet of paper into my pocket, in the hope that something will occur to me on my way down the hill. At the station Wilhelmine rushes up to me, where is my poem? I tell her I can't read it to her here and lead her to a secluded bench in the park. There I hand her the folded sheet of paper, which she proceeds to open, her face radiant with pride and joy. When she finds nothing written on it, I say that I must have mixed up the pages at home. Her eyes sparkle with fury and she slaps my face. Thank God, the train comes in a moment later. In the compartment I keep on kissing her hand and assuring her of my sincerest love. In Aarau I manage to calm her down completely over a glass of beer in the Zum Wilden Mann tavern. On the way back we sit in the coach immediately behind the engine, in a compartment directly over the axle. At the first set of points we are flung off our padded seats and I hold her in my arms, just as I held the little redhead, Delilah, three years ago, on the same stretch of line, possibly even in the self-same compartment. It was during my last year at the Aarau grammar school: and we, Delilah and I, used to travel together to and from school every morning and evening. In the mornings we repeated our lessons to each other, and in the evening we smoked cigarettes together. Now she's a teacher somewhere or other, teaching little girls to be moral and virtuous. But there is a considerable difference all the same. In one case blissful surrender, here still a timid bashfulness. But in both cases the identical silly incidental remarks. In spite of the dim flickering light I can make out the down on her cheek interspersed with a couple of brown moles, two wrinkles beside her eye, everything as if magnified five hundred times under the microscope. And I wonder whether the most delicate of complexions would stand inspection at such close range. I make no attempt to start up any further conversation, since I can see that she is sufficiently preoccupied with herself, and I see her home in total silence.

19 FEBRUARY 1887

Wilhelmine comes to lunch and afterwards indulges in a siesta on my divan, sinking instantly into a profound sleep. On waking up she explains to me that she is, on the one hand, too young, and, on the other hand, too old for me; I really ought to have two women, one aged sixteen, and another aged forty-six. Then she asks me to go to her sister, the Chief Magistrate's wife, to tell her that she, Wilhelmine, can't come to the coffee party tomorrow, because she has to give a piano lesson at the Town Clerk's. Trembling with delight, I make my way to the Chief Magistrate's residence. I knock, Elisabeth opens the door and offers me a friendly hand. This is enough to turn me into her most devoted suitor for the entire evening. Elisabeth is fifteen years old, just a little gawky, with the ample bust and delightful hips that are sometimes peculiar to that age. Neither her hands nor her feet are small, but she has an agreeably staid and measured gait. Her features are generous and florid, if a little too demure, her big dark blue eyes framed a little sombrely by blond hair. Her appearance disconcerts me, and I cannot help being sorry that I didn't say a friendly word or two to her. Her mother receives me in the drawing-room. I haven't set foot in this house since the time when it had just been built, and finding it so thoroughly lived in makes a strange impression on me. The younger brothers romp round the house, busy removing a large heap of ashes. Elisabeth's mother talks about her husband with pride and pleasure. The old man comes in and still pinches his wife's arm by way of greeting. On my way home I have the most vivid fantasy about marrying the pretty little creature as soon as ever possible, leading her out into the wide world on all sorts of travels and escapades, while retaining a splendid Buen-Retiro[5] in our castle. I dream of the venerable Chief Magistrate as my father-in-law, I dream of Elisabeth as my spouse, as a mother, as a matron by my side, surrounded by a troop of sturdy children and grandchildren.

I MARCH 1887

In a light snowfall I take Wilhelmine out along the road towards Seon and into the woods, where she imagines she is walking in the footsteps of her father, who went out hunting about noon. The solemn silence, the peace of inanimate nature inspire us to talk interminably of love. If I were a painter I would marry her today. For a writer, marriage would spell ruin. And if, what's more, I were to marry for love, come to terms with the world, then I might as well be buried straight away. She longs to love passionately once more, but not now, later, as late as possible. She asserts that, even if I wanted it now, she would not consent. I then start to boast for all I'm worth. A mere half hour, the distance from here to home, and she would be madly in love with me. She turns away and sobs into her handker-chief. I say I need only give free rein to my idealism; its effect on her would be all the more infallible since she has known me only as an idle fellow. She asks me to take her home. I say it would call for no sort of master-stroke on my part. These resources were at everyone's disposal, physical in some cases, intellectual in others. I return home much invigorated. Everything is quiet at home. I go to bed early and long for Paris.

9 MARCH 1887

Wilhelmine is preaching a moral sermon; she feels she has forfeited something, she's not at one with herself, she tells herself every now and then that it isn't right. She starts up joyfully and asks me to say on my honour what she means to me. – What did she want to know that for? – That was none of my business. – I say, after all, I might tell her a lie. – She lowers her head: that was just the sad thing: that was how I always had the upper hand. – I ask her why she had suddenly started up like that, why had she asked the question at all. – She says she would feel less constrained if she knew for certain. – I say: Supposing she was nothing but a plaything as far as I was concerned. – She looks right past me: for her, I had been an agreeable interlude. – Perhaps a treasure trove as well, a sort of encyclopedia? – I had practised vivisection on her, she says, as on a captive rabbit. – But what was all this about, then? – She felt freer. – I ask her whether she didn't think some deeper feeling had not perhaps taken root within me after all. – Oh, no never! She was simply asking for her own sake. – Parting, with endless embraces. Under the railway bridge, as luck would have it, I run into little Elisabeth. She salutes me with a friendly nod, which gives me a delightful sensation all the way down to my little toe. I return her greeting in as dignified a manner as possible. I think it better not to smile. I'm frightened of the keen gaze of innocence. She has, incidentally, magnificent lips and eyes of a deep dark blue. At home I spend an hour strolling on the bastion, enjoying the mild spring air in a mood of exaltation. The blackbirds have started to sing. Along the Black Forest and the Jura the carnival bonfires glow. Boring evening in the hall.

20 MARCH 1887

After having breakfasted for the first time in a fortnight, I go down to watch the gymnastics examination at the girls' school. The second year cherishes in its bosom one single pretty girl, extremely delicate features, a complexion like milk, dark eyes, dainty nose. Little in the way of expression, apart from a hint of mischievousness lurking beind the mask. A dainty foot and very bad posture. In the third and fourth years, who do their gymnastics together, there is also one girl worthy of note, but she is indeed a prime specimen, my Elisabeth. She has her place right in front of us. An exuberant physique, a healthy face, fresh, sober and not stupid. Exemplary posture and a pliancy of movement dictated by a certain plumpness. Absolutely charming is a baton dance performed by the girls to the old-fashioned strains of a minuet played on the fiddle by their old teacher.

25 MARCH 1887

After lunch my Orsina comes up.[6] She has once more written a whole stack of poems addressed to me. I feel incapable of listening to them. Wilhelmine is deeply offended. I comfort her, making clear that I understand her grief. She is sensual in a homespun sort of way. At coffee-time I am so overwrought that I fling a plate of bread and butter at Gretchen's head. She bursts into tears and shuts herself in her room. I then go to listen to the examinations in the girls' school, sit down directly opposite Elisabeth and pull up a second chair to lean on. As I do so, I assume a disgruntled expression, partly to keep the other visitors at arm's length, partly so as to be able to stare at her the more openly. In any case no one shows any inclination to address me. The gentlemen of the education committee move round the tables with unbelievably ludicrous self-importance, opening and closing the large exercise books and trying to cope with the central heating without losing their dignity. Elisabeth shows no sign of embarrassment whatsoever, although she cannot have failed to notice my behaviour. She knows her lesson perfectly, as, in fact, they all do. In general the examination procedure makes an extremely disagreeable impression on me, especially the practice of holding up a finger, which, in the case of some girls, is accompanied by venomous looks. I pick up Elisabeth's composition exercise-books and, since I happen to have a pencil in my hand, write down my feelings in the form of marginalia. Her exercise-books are none too neat, the style is peculiar in places. I read an entire essay about a holiday trip. I then make, as it seems to me, an effective exit; although it's all the same to me, in fact. In the adjacent hall I look at her geometrical drawings, which are none too geometrical. I am already looking forward to fooling her as well. All thoughts of marriage have vanished. The old Chief Magistrate has lost all the attraction he once had for me, and so has she, as my revered consort. In the evening I work in my turret room. Along comes old Bautz, the cutie, Pussie, and mews at the door. I reply. As I don't open the door straight away, she begins scratching at it. Yesterday she did the same thing. When I let her in then she went straight up to my wall cupboard and tried to open it with her paw. I let her in, she goes up to the cupboard, clambers cautiously on to the bottom shelf, settles down comfortably on my manuscripts and poems, and purrs. I leave the door slightly ajar so that the light does not fall directly on her. After a while she begins turning and twisting. She groans and purrs, bends over backwards and licks herself. Then comes a stiff, regularly recurring tensing of her body. Now and then she snaps at the poems stacked up beside her. Then she uses her mouth to guide out the first one. I hear her eating something and see her vigorously chewing. The procedure is repeated five times. The confinement lasts a good hour. After she has licked her young properly all over, they start squeaking. I fetch my mandolin and play Brahms's 'Cradle Song' for their benefit. It is half past three by now. A moist, refreshing breeze wafts in at the open window. All over the castle, doors and window-shutters bang to, and there is a rustling like distant surf in the ancient lime-tree.

BERLIN

24 MAY–4 JULY 1889

24 MAY 1889

I cannot close my eyes to the fact that, whereas Welti's fiancée has developed, both inwardly and outwardly, under the influence of her happy state, he has more or less stood still in his ideas.[1] Her ill-temper is nothing but an expression of her annoyance with the host of unspoken condolences on his account that she can read in people's faces wherever she goes. She is, of course, too proud to defend herself or justify herself, much less to complain, in public. She is capable of expressing these feelings to Welti himself, if she happens to have an inoffensive tone handy. When she's alone she's probably admitted it to herself often enough. I'm heartily sorry for Welti, but he cuts too comic a figure for me to be able to take his part. As they are leaving, she hands me her shawl and objects when I try to pass it on to Welti.

The editorial staff of the *Tägliche Rundschau* consists of very amiable gentlemen who are dog-tired from their daily labours and who fill me with a kind of surreptitious dismay. After the company has dispersed, Julius Hart conducts me to the Café Preinitz, where the vast amount of female flesh on offer causes me some initial embarrassment. Café Preinitz and Café National, the stock exchange for this commodity. Among all these articles only one with a slender figure and an intelligent face appeals to me. She walks down the room wagging the pointed end of her bustle: My bum! My bum! This is my bum!

With Julius Hart I act as if I were more artless than I really am, in the conviction that the city slicker won't take it amiss.[2]

25 MAY 1889

Pillars of Society at the Deutsches Theater.[3] Welti has not in fact made much progress since we parted in Munich. His reminiscences still culminate in his escapades at the cantonal school, how, for instance, he once slipped away half-drunk from a boozy party in Lenzburg and gatecrashed a St Cecilia dance in Aarau. It almost seems to me that he was at his wittiest in those days. He keeps on coming out with borrowed *bons mots* and is naive enough to sneak a sidelong glance at me each time to see what effect they are having on me. He seems to have lost all interest in observing life. He confines himself solely and exclusively to art. He wants to indulge in art all the time and feels out of sorts whenever this need is frustrated. I visit the Café National with him. All he has to say is that life there doesn't compare with Paris. What treasures Thomar[4] would have unearthed at this point!

26 MAY 1889

I ask a policeman where Erkner is.[5] – There was no such place. He himself didn't know. At lunch I get them to give me a timetable and travel out on the suburban railway. Halfway there a blind, but quite respectably dressed girl gets on the train, takes a tin whistle from her pocket and has just started to play, not much better than I would do, when she is sharply rebuked by the ticket-collector. In Erkner a level-crossing keeper directs me to the Villa Lassen. Some distance away I can see tall chimney-stacks looming up and I think of the pallid watchman and the lime-kilns from Hauptmann's poems. The road is endlessly grey and sandy, so that I find it very hard going. On the outskirts of the village lies the villa, a plain building with a grand, lofty raised ground floor and a squat upper storey, set in a garden that is homely rather than luxuriant. By the entrance I am approached by a husky dog who seems to know me. I can see straight away, however, that it isn't Hela. I find the company playing croquet behind the house. Gerhart Hauptmann receives me with open arms, leads me over to his wife and sister-in-law,[6] and introduces me to his friend Schmidt[7] and the latter's young wife. The croquet game continues, but I don't manage to get beyond the second hoop.

Everyone is obviously very pleased to see me again. Hauptmann invites me to come out really often, as he is frequently unbelievably bored. 'Papa Hamlet', by Arno Holz and somebody else, was an epoch-making work which showed that the drama, and the drama alone, was the art-form that matched reality.[8] The fact that it's by Arno Holz is supposed to be a secret. Julius Hart confided that to me on Friday, on the assumption that I already knew. Hauptmann is on the point of giving the game away, but fortunately manages to bite back the words just in time when he realizes that I already know. He asks after Karl Henckell and about Hammi's wedding,[9] whereupon I instantly feel somewhat abashed and on the verge of pouring my heart out once more. He asks what was talked about on Friday evening. I can't recall any details. In fact it was Karl Henckell who formed the first topic of Friday's conversation. After that Dr Lange asserted that mountains restrict the horizon, whereas it is extended by a plain or by the sea. He then launched into a defence of the word 'shit', thinking himself lucky to have such a word in his vocabulary. Then the whole company raved about the puppet show as something belonging to their finest childhood memories. When I happened to use the word 'psychopathic' Dr Lange replied that they didn't understand what that meant here. The word 'psychopathic' was known only in Switzerland. Then the level of the conversation declined. The Café National and the Café Preinitz were stock exchanges. Did anyone know what 'You father, you!' meant as a term of abuse, and what the expression 'to go down into the salad cellar' meant? He, Julius Hart, had made enquiries. 'Father' was the term for a woman who was prone to lesbian love, and 'to go down into the salad cellar' meant using your tongue in a woman's vagina. The Germans hadn't adopted Realism from the French, on the contrary. Zola's aesthetics was based, sentence by sentence, on Goethe's views on art as these had been transmitted to France during the thirties. The fact was that people just didn't know the German Realists. I only had to read O. Ludwig's 'Between Heaven and Earth'.[10] I report this admonition to read 'Between Heaven and Earth' to Gerhart Hauptmann, who replies that at one time he had understood my saying that kind of thing, but if an expert like Julius Hart was saying it, then that was an alarming sign. During the croquet game I notice that Hauptmann's wife is pregnant once again, which I find all the more surprising, seeing that in Zürich he used to talk about his intention to use condoms.[11] She moves about only with some difficulty and mostly sits on a bench, but she is no less comical than before.

In his study G. Hauptmann reads us the first act of a play.[12] In response to 'Papa Hamlet' he has in fact discarded his novel without a second thought and written a drama in six weeks. He reads the play with all the emphasis that can possibly be put into a reading. The study is very tastefully decorated with busts, pictures and antiques, without being overladen. The desk stands between the heads of Socrates and Herodotus, which wobble alarmingly on their pedestals whenever anyone stamps hard on the floor. Above the desk hovers an eagle with outstretched pinions, holding an open Chinese parasol in its talons. After the reading and a brief stroll in the garden we are summoned to supper. The table is set with three kinds of fish, two kinds of meat, four sorts of stewed fruit and a stodgy rice pudding. Frau Hauptmann has premonitions. She has had a premonition that I didn't travel here from Switzerland by myself, which causes her to blush a deep red, and that there is some hitch or other in connection with my American citizenship.[13] To promote digestion we proceed to the garden, where a swing has been erected for the children, on which the master of the house makes himself as comfortable as possible. The ladies sit on chairs in a circle, some of them smoking so as to drive the mosquitoes away. Gerhart H., incidentally, looks the very image of a lunatic, with his grotesque, rather stupid profile, with his close-cropped head, dressed in thick, dark nut-brown woollen garments that hang round his figure as if they had been turned out by some village tailor or other. The ladies are most tastefully turned out. Frau Gerhart in black silk, her sister in white wool. During the digestive interval the question as to the most convenient mode of suicide is ventilated with the liveliest concern. I come up with a declaration by Frau Hilger, who warmly advocated jumping down a ventilation shaft. The sun has already set as Gerhart and I escort the Schmidt couple home. The way leads through magnificent plantations of Scots pines. The sky flaunts a vivacious medley of colours against which the dusky trunks stand out brilliantly. Frau Schmidt is a slender, striking figure, somewhat hard-featured, with a large mouth and big blue eyes beneath straight, masterful brows. The sight of an express train hurtling across the road at top speed ignites in her something like a flare of ardour. She looks at me as though seeking the same response, and I feel myself crumble to ashes. Herr Schmidt, incidentally, knows Welti from having met him in Munich, but he doesn't seem to think very highly of him. He gives the impression of being by nature dry and matter-of-fact. My mood is profoundly affected by the way in which the handsome young couple make their way through the seclusion of the woods, engaged in quiet conversation, as we turn to go back. Gerhart H. thinks that perhaps I am not altogether deficient in love, he considers me capable of self-sacrifice, etc. That I readily grant him, but for me such feelings denote weakness rather than strength. They would not reinforce my moral fibre, but undermine me.

After I have taken leave of the ladies and been obliged to pocket a couple of oranges, he sees me to the station. I say goodbye, feeling agreeably touched, indeed well-nigh exhilarated by the sight of his unalloyed happiness. I envy him, but only with the most altruistic emotions, and am painfully moved, in spite of all this, by his fear that he might be burgled that same night. I have no desire to call on Welti. I stay in the Café Bauer until nearly two o'clock.

When I asked Gerhart H. how his health was, he replied he had feared all winter that he was suffering from tabes dorsalis.[14] I reply that I have encountered few young men of our age and in our circumstances who did not fear that they were suffering from tabes dorsalis. He is barely able to conceal his satisfaction at this.

27 MAY 1889

Diem perdidi.[15]

28 MAY 1889

Daughter of the Regiment.[16] Herzog hasn't the faintest trace of aesthetic feeling in her legs. She invariably plants her feet in parallel and at least 12 inches apart. On the other hand, her drumming is brilliant. I like her singing, too. Welti tells me how Dressler gained her title of *Kammersängerin*, and how he composed an epigram which he pushed into various overcoat pockets in the Café Viktoria. The epigram is remarkable for its crudity. It reminds me of the following lines of verse:

> The chamber-singer, so the rumour goes,
> Has only half performed her duty: Heaven knows,

The chamber's just her thing,
But she don't know how to sing.

Welti is very undemanding as far as wit, comedy and social accomplishments are concerned. He's bad for me, because he imbues me with overweening self-confidence. He's no longer what he once was to me. But he clings to me with boundless affection. I simply can't bring myself to throw him over. Indeed, I positively decide privately *not* to throw him over.

29 MAY 1889

On Friday evening a dapper little Jew told the story about the chaste family. Else says to her brother Fritz: My goodness, dear Fritz, Mama always says you can do it better than Papa, but I certainly don't agree.

Towards evening I lose my way and end up in the Tiergarten [Zoological Gardens], where a host of memories of Hanover are aroused.[17] The flamingoes strut in the water with measured, stagey strides. Their gait on land, too, still has something histrionic about it. The polar bears lie under the electric lights by the bars at the front of their cage in a feverish, restless slumber. Every so often they start up, scratching themselves or drawing groaning breaths, as if troubled by bad dreams. The spectators march and counter-march between the two bands. Few pretty faces and commonplace attire.

I go into the Café Bauer and then on to the Elysium, where the waitresses, a number of pretty girls among them, have the job of entertaining their customers. Each of them has a row of six tables, with six places at each table, which makes thirty-six customers or seventy-two hands which she must at all times willingly permit to fondle and squeeze her four limbs, especially those parts of her anatomy designed by nature for sexual indulgence and for the bearing and rearing of children. If a customer doesn't start doing this himself, they are in duty bound to draw his attention to the liberties to which he is entitled by sitting down beside him, starting up a conversation and pursuing it until the individual in question has grown sufficiently ardent. This is beyond any doubt one of the most basic forms of exploitation to which a resource employed for a specific purpose can be applied, for these girls are earning money both actively and passively at one and the same time. Their performance consists in waiting on the customers, and at the same time they have to let themselves be performed upon on the side, in order to raise the rate of output. They boost the business not only by the strength inherent in their bodies but also by the outer configuration of the same. In the case of a handsome carriage-horse, supposing it is rented out, the same relationship does not hold, in so far as the horse's fine appearance, albeit paid for, is not systematically consumed. Of course, the girls cannot stand this mode of life for long. But this needn't worry the proprietor of the business, seeing that he doesn't need to buy them but only hire them. Whether one girl lasts thirty years or whether thirty last only one year apiece makes no difference to his balance-sheet, especially in a city like Berlin, where the supply still far exceeds the demand. The proprietor, in a manner of speaking, is simply investing a certain amount of other people's capital in his business, paying interest on it, at the regular rate in fact, until the capital has been written off in the course of trading. In particularly heavy labour, like road-building etc., there is a similar rapid consumption of horse-flesh. All the same, the difference remains, that in this case the animals have to be purchased, hence the capital as such is expended. No horse-dealer would dream of hiring out his stock for undertakings of this kind.

I go into the Café National and sit down at the table in the middle in order to have a view of the entire establishment. For the most part the faces are the same as on the previous occasion. Opposite me sits a white-haired old gentleman with a full white pointed beard, with his hands folded on the marble table-top and his well-nigh soulful eye roving restlessly round. His expression clearly manifests the most ardent desire not to miss anything that is going on. He scans every woman who enters from head to toe and back again. For a brief spell his gaze may linger on this or that physical feature of the woman in question. In a window bay two high-school lads are sitting with feverishly glassy, staring eyes and wrinkled brows. All the time I'm there they don't exchange a single word. Nearer the front, a slim, dandified young man is dancing attendance on a lady sitting next to him on a divan who must weigh at least 250 pounds. She has a strongly marked, but by no means repellent Jewish face with a square bulldog chin sagging on to a colossal bosom. And to go with it a waistline like a barrel, so that I really can't imagine what brought her here. There is in fact something maternal about the cheerfully animated expression on her face. She looks to me more or less like a boarding-school matron among a crowd of her charges who happen to have a free period. As I'm leaving the café, a girl calls after me that she has seen my parasol at the World Exhibition in Paris. I go into the Café Preinitz, where I find nothing but trash, not a single passable face. A girl with a distinctly sheeplike face but a most elegant costume is sitting with her legs apart tickling her private parts. To save embarrassment she has spread a handkerchief over her hand. Her neighbour, who apparently finds this indecent, strikes her on the hand with her fan, and a teasing conversation ensues, to the amusement of both parties. Most of the girls have a bottle of cognac in front of them.

30 MAY 1889

Don Giovanni. Herzog's voice definitely pleases me most. Don Octavio bellows like a bull and waters down all his consonants. He's an Italian. Donna Anna's tremolo wobbles into a whinny. Donna Elvira, with a voice as keen as a knife, is boredom personified. She acts as if she had no eyes in her head. Don Giovanni is the perfect rat-catcher. He is paid 700 marks per evening, incidentally. I can't help thinking that Herzog's acting is silly. Welti decides that he ought at last to take up something creative. He has a comedy in mind, the first act to be set in the Kletzengarten.[18] But he can't think of a way to get his characters out of the Kletzengarten. I advise him to make them found an association. – Oh, no, there's nothing in the whole world he detests as much as an association. – That's just the point. – Hm, hm, there's something in that. – He defends himself against the charge that he has lost touch with life. It's just that he feels towards more recent trends in art – he's reluctant to utter the word but would do so just the same – towards these new trends he feels an implacable, almost Olympian equanimity: You do as you like, behave any way you can, when the time comes for us, we'll be there.

31 MAY 1889

Evening in the Tiergarten. Dismal atmosphere. Go home round about eleven, the first time since I've been in Berlin that I go home and write until dawn. Letter from Minna.[19]

Berlin, Potsdamer Platz, about 1900.

1 JUNE 1889

Towards evening in the Tiergarten. A great many tasteful dresses, with the absence of bustles pleasing me particularly. And yet at one time I was very keen on the bustle. I simply wasn't familiar with any other fashion. I feel a sense of relief, like someone who has had his esteemed spouse snatched away from him. Two pretty brunettes in sky-blue strolling in the crowd who underline an absence of bosom by means of a diagonal strip of cream lace. In the animal house four or five young lions share a cage with a large bitch who acts as their foster-mother. They treat her in exactly the same way as we used to treat our nannies, i.e. utterly *en canaille*.[20] They let her caress them, gambol round her legs and crawl underneath her belly without showing the slightest trace of affection in return. On the contrary, they keep themselves entirely to themselves. It's to their credit, no doubt, that they don't eat their nurse alive. At the same time they go in for a great deal of ill-natured howling, giving every sign that they are well aware of the indignity of their imprisonment. The keeper climbs into their cage to tickle them and rid them of vermin. He calls them his dear children and dear little ones, and says: What d'you want, then? I can't very well cuddle you, can I? That's enough now, yes, yes, you go to sleep. Their foster-mother is called Minkel. He

23

turns to her, she'll have to go walkies soon. The young lions have large heads, disproportionately hefty legs and paws and slender bodies. The royal tiger leaping up against the bars in the adjoining cage is addressed by the keeper as: You lout, I'll teach you a thing or two, what with your bad manners and all. An elderly gentleman watching the royal tiger being watered remarked to the crowd round him: Just like mine! Exactly like mine! The keeper reckoned, however, that dogs didn't know how to lap nearly as nicely.

In the Café Bauer until two.

The insufferable heat and a host of distractions of every kind have prevented me from putting pen to paper in the past fortnight. In the evenings I generally go to the Tiergarten, where I am well able to devote myself to my own thoughts amid the surging throng of fashionable folk. My thoughts revolve round sketches and newspaper articles, but come to rest all at once on a scene in a boarding-house.[21] The second and third act take place four years later. In the fourth act, when a further two years have elapsed, the last survivors of the Association for the Abolition of Wedlock are finally provided for. During the next few days I am fascinated by my background reading. A pamphlet by Helene Lange on university education for women threatens to put me out of humour.[22] It is written in a lucid and simple style and through the description it gives of English institutions it evokes in me a momentary enthusiasm which runs counter to my purpose. I then pick up Michelet's book *L'Amour*.[23] One fine morning Gerhart Hauptmann and his friend Schmidt wake me up. In spite of the atrocious heat the day passes in a very lively manner. The climax is reached in a wide-ranging gossipy conversation about Thomar and Henckell in the Café Passage. The creative exuberance of these two friends I find most refreshing, as opposed to the barren, almost arrogant and frequently myopic criticism that pours from Welti's lips on every occasion. Then Uncle Erich from Hanover turns up.[24] He's the biggest child I ever met at his age. He immediately starts cross-examining me about Papa's death and goes on from there to the issue of our financial circumstances. I would find that understandable, he reckons. Papa was his brother, indeed he might say, his favourite brother. When we cross the street he grasps me convulsively by the arm, for fear of being run over. In a barely audible whisper he induces me to admit that Berlin is nothing special, and in equally *sotto voce* tones dwells on the Berliners' tendency to brag. He whispers almost inaudibly in my ear that the Kaiser has a brutal cast of features. He keeps on gossiping all the time. As soon as he has dealt with one topic he simply reverts to a previous one, repeats everything he said before and tries to squeeze something more out of it. In this way the three or four subjects of his conversation have to be resorted to hour after hour, like the teats on the udder of the cow in a fairy-tale. He has come to Berlin to visit his eldest son Eduard who is a boarder in the Protestant St John's College in Plötzensee. Until four in the afternoon he drags me from ale-house to ale-house, constantly trying in vain to make up his mind where the beer is better and where it's worse. He has no thought of lunch; instead I have to accompany him to the Nordlandpanorama. Remarkable is the urbane nonchalance with which he evades the obvious temptation to spend money on me. At four o'clock he gets on to a tram and leaves me with the most unpleasant headache. I make my way to the Belle Alliance Theatre and watch a genuine Berlin farce, *Kyritz-Pyritz*,[25] a supreme piece of nonsense which to some extent restores my self-esteem; in conclusion I listen to a duet from the *Mikado* performed by a gigantic Dane and a daintily diminutive female compatriot. The Danish lady has a soft, agreeable voice, and during the bar-rests she strikes the most charming poses with a large fan which every now and then is noisily deployed at the fresh entry. On my way home across Belle Alliance Square I am struck by the fact that all the benches are occupied by workmen spending the night there. Where do they all take shelter when it's raining? All the way up to the Spittelmarkt I follow a pretty girl who is strolling casually along the street. I would give a great deal to know for certain whether she is a 'priestess'[26] or not, and am not sure which of these alternative certainties would be the more welcome.

On Easter Monday I go to visit Uncle Erich in Plötzensee. Cousin Eduard is mentally and physically very backward. He has a broad, bony Mongoloid skull with ears that stick out and, judging by his physique, would seem to be no more than ten years old, although he is actually fourteen. Uncle Erich starts up again with his old twaddle. He takes me to have coffee with Pastor Dummrese, a conceited parson who is so narrow-minded that he is incapable of sustaining the most rudimentary conversation. He has a sly, transparently pallid wife and a dreadfully ill-conditioned lout with a sharp intelligent gaze. From the way he talks he seems to think the entire Creation was undertaken for his sole benefit. Nevertheless, his horizon extends no further than the diminutive pine-trees he has planted in front of his house, and the adjoining kitchen-garden.

At half-past four a so-called people's party is celebrated in a pine coppice in the college grounds. Among the sparse stunted trees eight benches have been set up and coffee and beer are served on either side of them. On a mound at the front there is a rostrum with a crude pulpit, and behind it a long table for the governors, where the parsons and their wives take their places. The crowd consists of humble folk, mostly from Moabit, who have turned out complete with wives and children. First of all a sermon is preached by Pastor Kirstein, the principal of St John's College, who obviously has no talent whatsoever as a speaker. He speaks like a fidgety schoolboy who is afraid of failing his examination. Then the head of the nearby Magdalene Institute for fallen women mounts the pulpit. He is clean-shaven, has clean-cut features and wears his hair rather long. At first sight he strikes me as better suited for the part of Franz Moor than for a cure of souls.[27] However, as he speaks, a fire of fervour is kindled in his eyes which convinces me that all his fallen females must be in love with him. Between the various addresses soporific chorales are sung to the accompaniment of a ruthless brass band. The next item on the programme is an interval for refreshments, and the children are marched off singing and led by a banner to a playground. Then the second part of the programme begins. Frau Dummrese has invited me and Uncle Erich, as the institute's guests, to sit at the governors' table, where, incidentally, a number of very pretty girls have turned up and are doing their level best to join in the singing of the hymns. To open the second part a chorale is played on the trumpet, and a lad of about ten years old is announced from the pulpit as having become separated from his parents. The Pastor heaves him on to his shoulder, he has a huge slice of bread and butter in his mouth and is howling for all he's worth. It is announced that he'll be kept at the governors' table until the parents in question have made themselves known. Then the hero of the day, Court Preacher Stoecker, gives his address.[28] He is thickset, has a broad skull like a mastiff, a delicate straight nose and sharp, intelligent eyes quite devoid of fervency. The impression he gives is by no means disagreeable. He speaks in Berlin dialect, catechizing the children who have gathered round him at the front of the rostrum with no sign of constraint, half attentively and half contemptuously, as though they were by no means entirely of the same persuasion as himself. Some of the children start to quarrel during the sermon, others listen with half an ear, pensively picking their noses. At the conclusion of his address Stoecker goes off into ill-stressed ranting, which is evidently meant to suggest the presence of the Holy Spirit. After he has finished, deathly silence reigns. He steps back to the table, dons his lightweight summer overcoat as rapidly as possible, and doesn't join in the singing again until he has moistened his larynx with a full glass.

Supper at Pastor Dummrese's is somewhat scanty, but by no means the more congenial for that reason. While the others behave with restraint and decorum, the old man guzzles like a pig, helping himself from the serving-dishes. When his boy says he is sorry not to have heard Stoecker, he retorts that he hasn't missed anything: after all, he had heard his father preach that morning. After we have bidden farewell to a very pleasant elderly lady von X., and an even pleasanter Sister Emma, Uncle Erich accompanies me through the sandy wastes out of the college into the street, utterly dismayed that his Eduard is entrusted to such an egoist as Pastor Dummrese. He asks me to visit the boy every month, to take him an orange, and to pay my respects to Pastor Dummrese. It was pathetically comic to see how Uncle Erich danced attendance on the various parsons and their wives with a sort of hangdog courtesy: hardly had he turned away from one, hat in hand, before he was already circling round the next with the same gesture and no end of bowing and scraping. On Tuesday morning we meet in the Café Bauer. Following my example, he orders lemonade. Yes, I can tell you, my dear Franklin, this is the only proper drink for this time of year. But we'll have a pale ale afterwards all the same. He keeps on claiming that lemonade is the only proper drink for this time of year until he has to stump up 50 pfennigs for it. The 50 pfennigs seem to cool him down rather more than the lemonade.

After that we go to Hilsebein's Beer Hall, right opposite the station. It is eleven o'clock and his train goes at twelve. The moment we've sat down Uncle Erich has an attack of travel nerves, which grows more acute from moment to moment. In his excitement he recalls our Alpine walking tour of five years ago, reiterating one memory after another. He speaks with the lugubrious sentimentality of an expiring lion, but still can't get over the fact that we turned left instead of right going up the Hörner Grat. In the Friedrichstrasse station he checks his platform with all the railway staff in turn, and when the train steams in he runs up and down its entire length like a hunted rabbit, until a guard shoves him by force into the nearest compartment. He's hardly sat down before he starts asserting he's come too late, we shouldn't have sat so long in Hilsebein's, now he hasn't got a corner seat. At last he steams off, having once more shouted from the carriage window all the catchwords of our conversational topics. Coming out of the station, I find all the passers-by in the Friedrichstrasse in a state of undisguised panic. The sky is a dirty grey, and the view towards Unter den Linden[29] is shrouded in a murky haze. Everyone is looking for shelter. I go into the Monopol for something to eat and wait until the storm has passed. It leaves behind it a very pleasant coolness, and I resolve to start working as from today, but don't manage to do a stroke all week.

Not the least of my distractions the moment I enter my room is my charming opposite number on the floor below. Apparently she acts as a domestic help, or something of the kind, has to look after two or three children, and is busy from morning until night. She has a pretty, delicately pink little face, fair hair, a slender, but not too slender figure, and a dainty white hand. I can't help thinking that I must be an object of detestation to her because of my incessant curiosity, especially as I usually appear at my window in my shirtsleeves. To get at the truth of the matter I watch her for longish periods from a corner of the window, hidden behind the curtain, and observe, it seems to me, that she looks out at my empty window just as often as I used to look down at her. Once, when the children are being put to bed in the adjoining room, and she's drawing the curtains, she laughs quite openly in my face from between the curtains. After the children are in bed, she comes back, sits down to her work, and keeps on working until about eleven o'clock. Then she disappears again and returns with a thick book, apparently a reader, but devotes herself to its contents, it seems, with rather less than undivided attention. A little later she finally goes into the next room and places the lamp close by the curtain. Through the gaps in the curtain I can see her slip fall to the floor. Then I can see a dainty white foot, with slender fingers being passed one by one between the toes. In the depths of my soul thoughts of marriage begin to germinate. I go off to the Café Bauer and don't come back until almost two o'clock. I haven't seen the sweet girl for two days now. Through the open window I can see her empty work-table as well as her little low bed, also empty, which stands close by the window and is untouched from morning till night.

The entire family seems to have gone away on their summer holiday. Only one old maidservant has stayed behind. She sits in the kitchen, bent over her ironing-board and fast asleep. One evening Welti started to talk about his friend Öhler, and told me about Öhler's fiancée Anna Spichart, who had been engaged to him for seven or eight years. In the course of their engagement he hadn't once spoken to her in private because of her mother, a crazy old woman, and the Philistines of Frankfurt. Öhler had given her all sorts of things to read, had trained her up, until he finally broke off the engagement, imagining that his income as a doctor would be inadequate. Thereupon Anna had come to live with Emilie in Munich;[30] in a state of utter nervous disorder, Anna had had fainting fits every day, but had nevertheless gone to the Festival in Bayreuth, being an incorrigible Wagner fan, and had returned totally distraught. On the day she left Munich her fiancé had arrived in a similarly highly strung state, morose, unpredictable. They then met in Heidelberg, had a long talk, and since then they had been exchanging letters within the walls of Frankfurt and understanding each other considerably better than ever before. The following day he tells me that Frl. Anna Spichart will be coming here in the next day or two in order to introduce herself to a theatrical agent. She was in fact a budding vocalist, and Emilie was trying to put her on her feet. When I next called on Frl. Herzog I was introduced to Frl. Spichart. She has an imposing figure and the face of a governess. The conversation turns to artistic reproduction and she advances with supreme persistence the proposition that an individual can reproduce anything that is dormant in him, irrespective of whether it had actually emerged in real life. While she's putting her view she generally lowers her eyes, sits bolt upright on her chair as though on pins and needles, and plucks with both hands at her handkerchief, which she has twisted round her fingers as tightly as she can. In the evening over a beer Welti tells me he has after all reduced her case *ad absurdum* by quoting all sorts of examples from the whole human race. I would appreciate, he says, that even the most stubborn of creatures could not keep her end up in the face of these facts. A few days later Frl. Herzog sends me a ticket for *The Lady from the Sea*.[31] Going into the theatre I mention to Frl. Spichart the matter of her defeat, which, however, she refuses to admit on any account. Welti digs me in the ribs and asks me in a whisper not to refer to the subject again. With *The Lady from the Sea* I have the same experience I once had in Munich with *Torquato Tasso*.[32] What seemed to me on reading the play to be muddled, obscure and tedious, emerges on the stage as organic, artistic truth. On the way home I arrange to meet Anna Spichart in the Museum the following day. Frl. Herzog joins us. Anna Spichart in ecstasy over the Pergamon Altar, which Welti has spoken of in disparaging terms.[33] She declares her intention of making her view plain to him and is vigorously seconded by Frl. Herzog.

The following day alone with her in the National Gallery. At the sight of Feuerbach's *Symposium* I promise her the Reclam translation.[34] She hadn't said anything to Welti, Herzog had been in a bad temper at lunch, so that there was no call for her to pour oil on the flames.

At tea on Monday afternoon the atmosphere is very strained. Frl. Herzog is insufferably restless, and Welti is more stolid than ever. As we're escorting the ladies to the theatre, Anna Spichart pours out her heart to me. He would always remain nothing but his wife's husband. It was all the more deplorable, since she wasn't content with that, but kept on rubbing it in. At table it was sometimes intolerable. Heinrich was always having to leap up and fetch this or that. At the same time, however, he dwelt on every slight slip on the part of the maid, which wasn't a particularly manly trait either. It was simply that he lacked any sort of chivalrous instinct, but after all she was only running herself down when she ran him down. On the way home the first thing she says is that she had spoken to her quite frankly, and that Herzog had said she was quite right. I object that this is a one-sided way of dealing with the situation. All she would do would be to weaken Herzog's power of resistance, and once Herzog submitted to him she would be done for, because his fondest dream was to get her off the stage. I ask her whether she doesn't intend to point this fact out to Herzog. She replies that she can't do that. I go on a pub-crawl with Welti until nearly one o'clock, only slightly discomfited by the awareness that I'm plotting against him behind his back. As I'm handing Anna Spichart the *Symposium* she confesses that someone once gave her Demosthenes' Olynthian speeches to read.[35] And she had read them, but it had been awful. As Welti told me later, this 'someone' was her fiancé.

Welti is sitting at his fiancée's desk writing a postcard. The two ladies are sitting on the balcony with me opposite them in the doorway. They are engaged on a very delicate piece of embroidery for a handkerchief box. Anna Spichart tells me it's for the doctor, but he'd been given to understand that it was for her, Anna, so that they could work on it without interruption. He would no doubt be very pleased with it, remarks Herzog. I had noticed for some time, however, how her knees kept shaking, and I see that she's frightfully worked up again. Welti catches these words over his postcard and calls back: For Heaven's sake, put that confounded embroidery away! Can't you just talk quietly for a moment? Herzog suppresses her anger with a great effort, while I try to placate Welti. After he has gone, Anna Spichart says they really ought to stop the embroidery for a while, since all his spleen would be vented on her. This remark, which shows Welti's tactlessness in its true light, seems to me precisely calculated to rekindle the glow beneath the ashes in Herzog's case. It's difficult to discuss this disagreement with Welti. In Herzog's case it is essentially merely a question of her behaviour, which one may well venture to find fault with. With Welti it's a matter of his personal worth. It would involve a most severe emotional disturbance in his case. In my mind's eye I can already see him once more laying his dark poodle's head on my shoulder and bursting into burning tears, as he did five years ago in the Schwabinger Allee in Munich after the performance of *Zenobia*.[36] Frl. Herzog had told him that very morning that she was engaged to be married.

17 JUNE 1889

During the morning Frau Pansegrau brings me a letter from Mama which has a depressing effect on my mood for the entire day.[37] Donald is on his way back to New York.[38] He has borrowed money from Mrs Fleck, Obenanders and Heralds. Mama has paid it all back. But that's the end of it. Willy goes drinking in the Krone.[39] His fiancée is welcome. I start the first scene with great caution and little confidence. In a way I'm afraid to finalize anything. In the Tiergarten until three. Occupied with Michelet's *L'Amour*. Then to lunch in the Karlsbad. After lunch I buy Stendhal's *De l'amour – Physiology of*

Love, the title page of which I like very much.[40] I sleep from six until eight. After supper I write to Hammi regarding recruits[41] and meet Welti in the Karlsbad between eleven and twelve. The relationship between Welti and Herzog has a great deal in common with that between Sadi and Mieze.[42] Except that the circumstances are much more serious here.

18 JUNE 1889

Dreamt about Papa. After lunch I have myself measured for a suit, getting extremely flustered. I shuffle out of the shop door like a poor sinner, not daring to put on my hat till I get into the street. At the same time it strikes me that this sort of behaviour doesn't do much to improve my creditworthiness. After supper I go for a stroll through the city and meet any number of pretty priestesses. But I haven't got the time at the moment. Later, later. Once a sense of well-being has set in and I can put my mind to the matter. And yet, even in these reveries, the investigator comes to the fore. The price of flesh is falling. I can feel myself growing more devout, more harmonious day by day. Today I even resolve to write to Mama once a month from now on. That was, by the way, just after supper, and my elegiac mood was merely a side-effect of a placid digestive process. But I mean to carry out my resolve all the same. I go to the Karlsbad and eagerly await the arrival of Welti. It's odd how artlessly Welti dwells on Henckell's unhappy engagement: after all, he's stuck in the same swamp himself, only a few yards deeper. He complains about the curse of having to earn one's daily bread, but without any sort of Titanic pride or rage, and without a trace of gallows humour. He doesn't complain like a Pegasus under the yoke, but like a pack-mule hearing the 'Marseillaise' from afar. His deepest concern is the rise in the price of beer. For my benefit he works out that in Munich he had drunk a litre and a third of good beer for 42 pfennigs, while here he gets only a litre and two-fifths of the most wretched Berlin brew for 55 pfennigs: if he wanted to drink as much beer here as in Munich it would cost him one mark and ten pfennigs per day. At times he couldn't stand it, he felt he had to have Munich beer at all costs. But then he was annoyed the whole time he was sitting there drinking it. He then tells me the story of his boils for the third time. He mostly had them on his testicles, great lumps he'd had, and now he was getting one on his head. He had smeared them with lanolin, but now the skin was peeling off by the spoonful. As I observed, his fiancée shows the most lively concern for her beloved's boils. After all, she's got no choice! All the same, it's not exactly to her taste. And he makes such a frightful fuss about it. He actually seems to set great store by his boils. When he offers her his arm to escort her home from the theatre, and she presses him to her heart, then he lets out a groan, as if she'd landed on his mortal wound – the ass!

19 JUNE 1889

A letter from Uncle Erich, in which he once more recapitulates the four or five topics of our conversation. Not a single word that is new. At my tailor's I manage to put on a rather more casual air. Even before lunch I find I can't help thinking about tabes dorsalis. The possibility that I may be suffering from it myself doesn't actually worry me all that much. But my thoughts keep coming back to it. When I've finished at my tailor's I am suddenly seized by the feeling that someone is looking for me at home. I think, it'll be Welti bringing me a ticket for *Figaro*. I hurry back as fast as I can, barely taking time to pick up *Women's Rights* from the bookseller's. I keep hoping I may run into Welti on the way back. I don't meet him, however, and there is nobody at home. As though compelled by some inner urge, I pick up Niemeyer's *Pathology* and read five pages on tabes dorsalis. As I said, I'm not particularly worried about my own health, but I am reassured all the same to find that I have no obvious symptoms. Just before teatime Frau Pansegrau tells me that Gerhart Hauptmann has been here round about noon – once before lunch and once after lunch, having missed me at Bischoff's. In the lavatory I make the unpleasant discovery that I'm suffering from piles, although there is no bleeding so far. I immediately take a dose of pulvis pectoralis liquiritii compositus haemorrhoidarius Curellae vel Hufelandii and work until eleven. Then I make my way to the Café Bauer, where I spend two hours waiting in vain for labour to begin. About two o'clock I go home, still labouring under the oppressive feeling that I am suffering an injustice through no fault of my own. During the silent hours as dawn is breaking the catastrophe erupts.

20 JUNE 1889

After a somewhat wearing night I feel very frail all day. At noon an intoxicating hush prevails in the Tiergarten. It had rained just previously, so that the air is uncommonly refreshing. Apart from the waiter at dinner, I don't exchange a single word with anyone.

21 JUNE 1889

During the morning I complete the first scene and write to Mama. At lunch a simply dressed young man with fair hair cut short, a beard and a callow, expressionless face sits down next to me. He orders a large plate of vegetables and drinks seltzer with it. He eats crouched over his plate, holding his fork limply and shovelling large helpings into his mouth, which he scarcely opens. On more than one occasion he's on the point of falling asleep, but pulls himself together each time, every now and then belching like a suction pump. After he has finished his vegetables, he pulls out his purse and counts the contents on to his knee, a couple of coins falling on the floor during the process. One of them he pushes under my chair with his foot, without taking the slightest notice of my presence. He then orders a 'sweet', which is the name given in these parts to a dish of blancmange, but has barely got it down before it comes back up the same way. He pulls out his handkerchief, wipes his jacket and catches the remaining dollops as they come up.

In the meantime I have been trying, in a tentative manner, it's true, to enter into conversation with him, but without the slightest success. Now I feel an urgent need to take him by the arm and lead him out of the restaurant. On the other hand, my vanity rebels at the idea, because I'm afraid that the other customers and the waiters will think he's a friend of mine. The fact is, I have a holy terror of waiters, against which I constantly battle in vain. In the end I point out his condition to one of the waiters who has had his eye on the wretched man for some time. He orders him pretty sharply to go and get cleaned up, and then asks me if the gentleman has been sick: when I tell him he has, he says it's incredible that a fellow wouldn't feel it coming on beforehand. I try to placate him, pointing out that the poor man after all feels rotten, and ordering a coffee. But then I can't stick it any longer. What do I care about the customers and the waiters! It's true that the poor chap, contrary to my expectations, had walked upright and fairly steadily through the restaurant, but no doubt he had instantly collapsed outside and was perhaps writhing helplessly on the dirty concrete floor of the urinal. I've not even got as far as the door when I experience a grand sense of satisfaction, familiar to me from past experience, at my forthcoming role as good Samaritan, and I can scarcely refrain from smiling. To my disappointment the urinal is empty. Apparently the patient is sitting in the toilet. Accepting this circumstance as sufficient reason to feel my presence superfluous, I return to my seat with my ardour somewhat damped. It occurs to me, incidentally, that the young man, obviously a student, may not be suffering from anaemia and overwork, but only from a monumental hangover, an assumption which I repudiate, however, as not entirely honest on my part. A few minutes later my neighbour comes back in, obviously somewhat relieved, but still deathly pale. I advise him to take a bitters, which suggestion he repudiates pretty ungraciously. He settles his bill, the waiter thanks him with a certain degree of reserve, and he departs without deigning to wish me farewell. The waiter prances round the table for a bit and says he had looked very pale from the outset. I pay for my coffee with the most urbane air of nonchalance I can summon up, reckoning it a great honour that all the waiters, in contrast to my ill-fated table-companion, call a farewell after me.

I go back home through the Tiergarten and write to Mali.[43] At intervals I dip into the first volume of my diary with some satisfaction. The overall impression seems to me to be distinctly psychopathic. If I were not convinced that my inner life is by and large very disciplined, these notes might alarm me. My flirtation with Minna strikes me as infinitely trivial, a wretched abortion born of conceit and randiness, apart from the few moments of subjective embarrassment, which are, however, less productive than with any grammar-school boy. At ten o'clock I go into town, intending to visit a cabaret, but after standing at the entrance for some time I can't summon up the nerve to go in. I curse my solitude. I haven't exchanged more than a couple of words with anyone all day. I decide definitely to join the literary society, if it is at all possible. I must associate with young people, the younger the better. Welti himself is old, he's ten times older than I am. In the literary society I have a chance to meet very young people indeed. I finally go into the Café

Bauer but even here I have no chance to immerse myself in my thoughts, so I return to the Karlsbad in the hope of meeting Welti, or the Harts,[44] or both. I find no one, and after a few moments I am the last customer, so I gulp down my beer and set off home with a light heart. A young girl in a grey dress, without an overcoat, wearing a straw hat trimmed in white, steps out of a dark doorway and strides purposefully, if a shade timidly, across the road. She walks as if driven by some inner urge. I pass close by her and try to catch her eye. She doesn't appear to notice me, however. Turning round, I see her stop by the garden opposite and, with outstretched arm, throw a dark red rose across the little garden on to the open verandah of the ground floor. As calmly as she had come, she walks back across the street and lets the heavy door fall to behind her. In her serene, unwavering gaze there seemed to me to be something ineffably feminine, a certain doleful determination, as though at that moment she felt herself to be no more than the victim of an ineluctable destiny.

22 JUNE 1889

I am oppressed all day by a sense of loneliness. Towards evening I go to my tailor and request him not to send me the suit tomorrow but a few days later. He understands what I mean straight away and says, just as I wish. I expected him to say, it didn't matter, he trusted me implicitly. That's why I hesitate for a moment and say, about Tuesday or Wednesday, then. I toy with the idea of drinking a coffee in the St Helena, but buy a copy of *Don Quixote* instead and read it in the Tiergarten until eight. Get back home and hear that Welti was there and intended to take me to the theatre. I meet him about twelve in the Karlsbad and heave a sigh of relief to be facing another mortal after three whole days. I tell him I intend to go to Erkner next day. He tells me his fiancée is expecting me. Anna Spichart is going back to Frankfurt on Monday. I shouldn't let that stop me, however.

23 JUNE 1889

The glorious weather encourages me to go out to Erkner. Gerhart Hauptmann received me with the news that he's expecting the little mite to arrive any day now. To my rather doleful enquiry about her health his wife replies: Pretty well, she couldn't help laughing. She was still appearing in public now and again. Hauptmann and his brother[45] mean to buy property and settle in Pankow.[46] Holz and his friends would also take up residence there for the summer, I should come as well. I inform him that I have found someone else suffering from tabes dorsalis. His wife reckons it is better, after all, for someone to think he is suffering from the disease and to be in fact healthy, than to think he is healthy and to have it. After we've had a cup of tea Gerhart and I go to Fangschleuse to fetch his friend Schmidt to supper. On the occasion of a burglary in the neighbourhood Gerhart had reported to the local magistrate that he had seen a whole suit of clothes, together with a shirt and other accessories lying in the woods.[47] The magistrate had bawled him out and demanded to know why he hadn't brought the suit with him. He had responded to this in very agitated tones, and was still labouring under the unpleasant impression that the incident had made on him. We turn off the path through pines and undergrowth and at last find Schmidt at the edge of the wood, behind an easel with a half completed study on it. Hauptmann does everything he can to induce me to give my opinion of it. I reply that I know nothing of such matters, especially as the picture is only half finished. We accompany Schmidt back to his quarters, a little cottage by the weir, where he has one room and a couple of little closets. The room is artlessly rural, simply furnished. Against the longest wall stand two very comfortable low beds. Schmidt's wife is still in Berlin, where she's been having treatment for a tapeworm. She was suffering from dilation of the stomach.

During our walk Gerhart Hauptmann told me, incidentally, how a friend of his had become a reviewer on the *Deutsche Rundschau*. It is actually a secret, but he declares he simply can't keep it quiet. His friend was short of money and had taken one of Rodenberg's books to the secondhand bookshop. While he's in the act of selling it, it occurs to him that he might actually write something about it. And so he does. A few days later he's invited to call on Rodenberg.[48] Rodenberg assures him that he had always considered him a great writer. Wouldn't he take over the review columns in the *Deutsche Rundschau*? They would discuss the details shortly at the editorial offices, or, better still, he should come to Rodenberg's home. In Schmidt's room is another, larger painting, also unfinished, in connection with which an argument starts as to whether it's in order and not at odds with the truth to introduce a baroque element. In front of the house a farmer's wife is standing with her daughter, who, because it is Sunday, has been wearing shoes and has rubbed her heel raw. I advise her to put oil on it after she has washed the sore place, and then to bandage it with a piece of linen. Schmidt speaks quite firmly in favour of arnica. The farmer's wife says she has already put 'Provencal oil'[49] on it. Gerhart Hauptmann asks me for a piece of paper, notes something down and puts it in his pocket. I can only imagine that he's going to let the woman have some arnica, and I'm on the point of passing some complimentary remark, when he comes back to the 'Provencal oil'. Often you searched and searched for that sort of blunder. And all you found was crap. That's the way it was. There was no other word for it. That's why he had written it down straight away.

On the way back he tells me about Henckell, how he had once sent a manuscript to Arno Holz, asking him to go through it. Holz had changed it here and there, but in the end had advised him not to publish it. In the manuscript there was, amongst other things, an effusive poem addressed to Holz himself, and when Holz got the printed copy all the gushing passages had been toned down, and even at some points turned into the opposite. By way of a joke he had written in the original passages. He had shown the poem to Hauptmann and to Schmidt. The whole business doesn't seem quite plausible to me. As for Böcklin,[50] Schmidt finds fault with him only because he doesn't produce paintings with any sort of everyday atmosphere, but is always striving for something out of the ordinary. As far as he is concerned, the intellectual content of Böcklin's paintings is non-existent.

After dinner experiments in thought-reading are carried out. I happen to be blindfolded when two young gentlemen enter.[51] They have read *Promethidenlos* and Hauptmann's short story in *Die Gesellschaft*,[52] and wish to make his acquaintance. The conversation promises to get very literary. Hauptmann suggests a game of croquet, which I actually find a relief. The two youths summon up an admirable show of keenness. In the meantime Frau Hauptmann concocts a strawberry punch. I am delighted to observe that I am more a member of the household than the two newcomers. I even manage to improve my proficiency at croquet, although I still cheat for all I'm worth on the side. The conversation over strawberry punch revolves round Karl Bleibtreu whom the young men reckon to be the leading German writer.[53] True, they haven't read Büchner, but he's nothing compared with Bleibtreu.[54] Hauptmann gets excited and defends his opinion warmly, but in moderate terms. Schmidt and I confine our attention to the punch, while Frau Hauptmann repeatedly draws her sister's attention to our empty glasses. Otherwise, the ladies play a passive rather than an active part. Suddenly Schmidt bursts out, speaking calmly, it's true, but in the plainest of terms. Bleibtreu had positively slandered Leixner's wife, and that was simply a vile thing to do. The young men then retreat under cover of various concessions, and the conversation quietens down. The spokesman for the couple is a pale, gaunt student who can be identified at a glance as a literary gent, largely on account of the fair whiskers round his chin and chops, which, although far from luxuriant, are distinctly casual in style. He speaks with a South German accent,[55] and instantly recognized me as a South German. The other, a former painter now applying himself to music, is generally silent, although there is no reason to suspect him of hiding his light under a bushel. He has a plump, swarthy pug-face, wears a pince-nez and is smartly dressed. When he opens his eyes wide, a very faint rakish glint is undoubtedly the only thing that suggests an artistic soul. Some time after ten Schmidt and Hauptmann escort us to the railway station. Hauptmann promises to come to Berlin next day. In the compartment I talk to the literary man about Lausanne, where he studied last term, associating almost exclusively with German students. It doesn't occur to me to ask about Cousin Theo. He had gone to old Secrétan's lectures,[56] but hadn't spent much time at the Academy otherwise. He had grown very fond of the countryside there, and states that he often had a painful longing to go back. The two young bloods get out at the Silesian Station.[57] Before they turned up at Hauptmann's they had already been to call on another German writer, who lives in Grunewald, but whose name was unfamiliar to me and remains so, although they did mention it. A boy aged about ten, with a remarkably pale, handsome face, comes in from the adjoining compartment. Round his slim shoulders he is wearing his mother's black shawl: it is embroidered with shiny beads and comes down almost as far as his knees, so that his short black trousers are completely covered. His elegantly shaped legs in their white stockings appear below the shawl. On his head he is wearing a white handkerchief knotted at the corners. He stretches out on the seat opposite me and instantly falls asleep. His little sister comes in from the same compartment and tries to wake him but is prevented by his father, who appears in the background. To my regret, the whole company alights at Alexanderplatz. I make for the Café Bauer, and set off home about one in a pleasantly elated frame of mind.

24 JUNE 1889

Gerhart Hauptmann doesn't turn up. I feel in urgent need of some effective stimulus to get on with my comedy.[58] I decide to go and see *Romeo and Juliet* at the Deutsches Theater, but oversleep at home and wander round town for a couple of hours in the evening, missing Welti and coming home in a pretty vile temper. I am obsessed by totally sincere thoughts of matrimony. My intended is the younger daughter of Widmann in Berne. I've never set eyes on her. I only know that she's pretty, vivacious and on the buxom side. I have a vision of her in a pink cotton dress. I imagine a roving, Bohemian life in her company, from Berlin to Rome, from Rome to Switzerland, etc. When I think of our first son, my heart almost bursts with joy. I walk past a ground-floor flat where Wagner is being played and think that she doubtless has an understanding of music. She wouldn't need to perform much. After all, she need only have a pleasant voice, so that we can sing a catch or a folksong in two parts when we're bored. I believe this daydream harks back to the two comfortable beds by the wall in Schmidt's quarters.

25 JUNE 1889

Go to the museum before lunch. I'm dying for inspiration. As far as my work goes, I see myself standing at the foot of an insurmountable mountain. I stray through the various galleries without my attention being caught anywhere for any length of time. Facing Titian's daughter, I am overcome by a feeling that any affinity with reality is lacking. What I have in front of me is a varnished canvas. Only when I have been granted the chance to study the original in all its details will these works once more acquire a three-dimensional quality for my eye. At the moment the effect is merely that of dreams that inspire yearning, dissolving into nothing the moment you stretch out your hand to grasp them. By virtue of a renewed contact with reality they will once more turn into those soothing ideals which I perceived and revered in them when I was in Munich. If a man is not conversant with life, then, in the long run, he will find art barren as well. Exclusive indulgence in art fosters a taste for all that is unnaturally exaggerated, feverishly far-fetched. A refined taste in art can stem only from a zest for life. To my shame, I find myself drawn to the martyrdom of St Agatha, and look round eagerly for French paintings of the rococo period. What in fact captivates me more than all these pictures is an unaffected young girl serenely engrossed in her painting. She is copying the portrait of an old lady. I sit down on a couch behind her and absorb myself in watching her movements. But even as regards the young painter, I am afflicted by a sense of the profoundest shame that drives me from the spot. The Dutch painters fascinate me, it's true, but they distract me at the same time. I quit the building without having found what I was looking for. With true reverence I read what Michelet has to say about the influence of wedlock on pages 267, 268 and 269 of his book on love. As I'm leaving my room for a moment in the course of the afternoon, I see a policeman standing in the doorway and instantly guess what's afoot. He asks me to accompany him to the police station, where they demand a certificate of nationality. The distress the incident causes me, however, I immediately divert into my work, where I soon find the right approach after briefly casting around. In the evening I go to Kroll's, and then to the Karlsbad, where Welti is much dismayed by my fate. I look up the fare to Munich in the railway guide straight away. If they pester me in the same way in Munich, then I'll go to Venice. But I'll return, just as surely as I'll come back to Titian's daughter, otherwise my life's not worth a fig and I need have no misgivings about settling down to earn my daily bread. Anna Spichart has gone away to Frankfurt and sends me her greetings. Welti says he was scolded because he hadn't told me she was travelling on Monday evening.

26 JUNE 1889

Letter to Anna Spichart. After lunch I go to Frl. Herzog to ask for her address. Herzog is much more genial than usual. Nevertheless, she plays with Welti like a cat with a mouse. She spares him no humiliation. She inspects his footwear in my presence and keeps on trying to find fault with me. At home I find a letter from Mama, who says she can't get her shoes on any more. But she's afraid to go to the doctor. If you once started, then there was no end to it. The letter upsets me very badly. Willy's fiancée has arrived.[59] Mama draws a very detailed, but not exactly flattering picture of her. While I'm at supper Welti turns up and I read extracts from Henckell's poems to him. He can't help being considerably impressed. We go to the Karlsbad together and talk a great deal about my departure. Welti does indeed seem to be deeply affected by my fate. I expect to steam off to Munich in the course of the next week or two. Mama has sent me a letter of recommendation from Auntie Plümacher[60] to Frau von Hartmann. I'm still not sure whether to use it or not. I haven't made a scrap of progress with my comedy.

27 JUNE 1889

While I'm working I'm constantly worried by the news of Mama's swollen legs. And I can't help thinking over and over again about that truncated porphyry column. I wonder whether she didn't herself tempt fate. But that idea cuts no ice. At the moment I'm above mysticism. In any case, the causal connection is undoubtedly the other way round. By and large, such anxieties are of a thoroughly egoistic nature. In any case, I'll put the matter in Hammi's hands. – I'm beginning to look forward to Munich, after a fashion.

28 JUNE 1889

A quiet day, when I acquire *Des Knaben Wunderhorn*[61] and make some progress with my ideas. In the evening a jar of Hofbräu, which levels out my frame of mind. Until twelve in the Café Bauer. I dream about Munich.

29 JUNE 1889

About noon I meet Welti in the Karlsbad, from where we go on to the Spaten in town. Welti makes strenuous efforts to smoke a Virginia cigar, but he hasn't got the puff. It goes out every five minutes, which makes him very cross. He says I've changed a great deal. I've become more serious-minded and less irresponsible, although I'm still pretty giddy. As we proceed to our second glass I remind him that he once said to me on the Maximilianbrücke in Munich that a strong character must be capable of doing something wicked from time to time. He doesn't recall saying it, although I remind him of the occasion that prompted the remark. This was an anonymous letter concerning the rumour of an engagement between him and Frl. Herzog that he had got his cousin in Rio de Janeiro to write to the parents of a man who was engaged to Herzog at that time. We come back to his statement, and I happen to use the expression 'lecture'. He obviously feels touched to the quick. He well knew that this was an old failing of his. He certainly didn't mean to 'lecture', and far be it from him to presume to do so. Doubtless he had felt at that time that I was superior to him in many points, particularly in dialectics. But at the same time he couldn't help noticing that all these points were of little substance. I was the exact opposite of him. And that applied to my social manner as well. Frl. Herzog had said, if only Wedekind would just be a shade more genial! She always felt I thought she was a silly goose. I made the sort of conversation you could tell was just being made. People had the impression that I was making fools of them. By my excessive politeness, even. The overall effect was spurious. When I object that I always tried to be as unaffected as possible, and that I fancied I had always behaved in a very unaffected manner towards Herzog in particular, he suggested that I hadn't succeeded, since Herzog was artlessness personified, and that therefore I was always the one who was fooled in the end, because people involuntarily withdraw into their shells in my presence. For instance, Herzog had told him I had asked her not to play fast and loose with him so mercilessly. I surely couldn't be serious, knowing their relationship as intimately as I did. I find it pretty hard to keep my composure at this turn in the conversation, at the same time doing everything I can to make my remark seem as innocuous as possible. In spite of everything I would never have suspected Herzog of such slyness. It's more reminiscent of Isa in *L'Affaire Clemenceau*.[62] No wonder she was so upset by the play. If you take into account that her rational faculties are obviously somewhat limited, then everything in the picture fits together. And my good Welti reckons that all this, trait by trait, constitutes artlessness. The landlord makes his appearance in the restaurant, pointing out that it's nearly three o'clock. I say, now they're going to chuck us out. We've got to say goodbye some time, he replies with a winning smile.

43

In the street it's already broad daylight. We go into the Tiergarten, with Welti still expatiating on my abortive social calculations. It was to be hoped that I might still discard my perverse nature. As I was at the moment I could only cut a ludicrous figure in grand society. I was thoroughly *au fait* with social manners, but I overdid it at every turn. I reply that I always felt inferior in any company, even if it consisted of no more than two persons, whereas I always imagine that I totally dominate anyone with whom I find myself alone. This remark stops him momentarily in his tracks, but he soon gets back on course and goes on to discuss the case of Anna Spichart.

On the bridge in front of the Lehrter Station we watch the sun rise over Berlin. It climbs up uncommonly slowly and barely forces its way through the dense mist that lies over the Spree. The streets are still absolutely empty, apart from the occasional cab with a bleary-eyed company of revellers. In the Lehrter Station we drink coffee, and I reduce Welti to despair by asking him what he thinks of Schiller. We plan to purchase a variety of cooked meats and have a knife-and-fork lunch in my digs. We've barely left the station, however, before Welti begins to back out. I see him home, going via the Kurfürstenstrasse so as not to fall foul of the police. In bed I read some more of *Des Knaben Wunderhorn* and fall asleep around seven.

30 JUNE 1889

Nursing a fair hangover, I go round to visit Herzog after lunch in order to say goodbye. She's frightfully busy. Welti is sealing her stocks and shares, which are to be deposited in the Reichsbank. We agree in deploring the fall in interest rates. I accompany Welti back to his lodgings, and while he's packing I read him Fleixner's article on the musical life of Berlin. Then we take dinner together in the Dessauer Gardens and stroll down to the theatre. I express my feeling that, even if one didn't personally have much in the way of good fortune, it was nevertheless interesting to watch all those threads one had seen knotted together being spun out, waiting to see what would happen to all those personalities who had striven shoulder to shoulder with oneself towards the same goal, to trace the development of those individuals whose career one had witnessed and whose antecedents one knew at first hand. At the same time, it was comforting to bear in mind that the whole business would hardly last longer than sixty or seventy years, and that a good third of that seventy had already been accounted for. Welti reckons that a man could still suffer a good deal of misfortune in seventy years. He doesn't show the slightest understanding of the other points I made in my observation. *Der Freischütz* is a welcome treat.[63] I'm exceptionally well pleased with Herzog, even with her acting. She also looks very handsome, which, it's true, may have something to do with my lack of opera glasses. Leisinger stalks across the stage like a horse in the *dressage*. The last act moves me almost to tears, while I follow the scene in the Wolf's Glen with the greatest interest, turning my attention mainly to the grotesque infernal apparitions. It is the last performance before the holidays. I take farewell of this temple of the muses accordingly.

Received a letter from Mali.
Address of Frl. Herzog jun. in Munich
        19 Herzogstrasse, Schwabing
Bennat's address
        6. III Theresienstrasse
Heinrich Hart's address
        18A Karlstrasse, Berlin N.

1 JULY 1889

Get up at eleven and settle up with Herr Pansegrau. He's not prepared to let me off a single penny of next month's rent. I buy *Don Quixote*, 2 and go off with it to the Tiergarten, then to lunch, and back to the Tiergarten, where I end up at a children's playground. Nannies come with their charges, by whom they are addressed as 'Fräulein'. They obviously agree to meet here, take their needlework from their bags, chat, and every now and then make sure that the children don't say 'mich' where they should say 'mir',[64] and don't say 'Stöckern' instead of 'Stöcken'. In the case of the children I am once more immediately struck by the difference between the aristocratic and the common. I take a fancy to a girl of about six because of her clever face, her pretty head, and the sedate manner she has of placing her feet. In her posture, too, when she is standing and watching other children, there is a kind of unselfconscious nobility. She has a rather younger brother with her who looks exceptionally stupid. Her playmate is a loudmouthed brat, not ill-favoured either, but without the slightest mark of distinction in her appearance. At any rate she's a good deal more vulgar in her mentality. She takes her friend by the arm, leads her over to three other children, a girl and two boys, and, pointing at them as if they were freaks, says, that girl says 'wasch' instead of 'was'.[65] She said 'wasch' this very minute instead of 'was'. The three children stand stock still, as if they didn't belong here. All three have a wary, brooding, almost dour look about them. They seem to me to be the children of some petty official who has worked his way up into a new sphere and who doesn't find life easy. One of the two boys, who doesn't in fact look stupid, looks to me as if he might one day leave the entire company behind, aristocrats as well as plebeians. Now two very well dressed little lads of about seven to ten years old come along, and the two girls start to play with them straight away. They are obviously both very well bred, and the elder is distinctly handsome, doubtless a legacy from his mother. He is slightly built, has a round, healthy little face and clear blue, if rather expressionless, eyes. Both of them wear their hair combed down over the forehead and cut straight across, with a flat white straw hat with a brim all the way round and a white satin ribbon. The older of the two brothers goes straight up to the cheeky brat and says: You don't know how to spell, Gretchen. You always miss out the 'e' in 'lieber'. Then he plays exclusively with the girl with the clever face, the handsomely shaped head and the sedate way of putting her feet down. His brother, who seems to be a little delicate, stays with the others, who are brought into the game by the cheeky brat.

I make my way to the Friedrichstrasse Station, where I find that Welti and Frl. Herzog have already arrived. Welti entrusts his fiancée to me, because he is travelling third class. I manoeuvre her into a 'ladies only' compartment and say goodbye. But then I have to convey various messages to and fro between the pair of them. Finally, they both look out of the window, she in the second, he in the third class and nod 'au revoir' to each other. Incidentally, she has instructed me to tell her sister in Munich that Welti is still in Berlin. Herzog calls me back, I'm to tell Heinrich that they have to get out and wait in Hanover, a message he receives with the greatest delight, because he can then be together with his Emilie for a while. He instructs me to tell her he's in the very next carriage, close by the door. She gives me a friendly nod for this report. At last the train rumbles out.

I go home for supper, feel very much alone, sleep after supper until

46

about eleven, then go out for a jar at Pschorr's. On the way back I see a couple of cute girls coming out of the Spaten in a pretty merry state. They stop by an old beggar, and as I'm walking past they come up to me and ask me to give the old gentleman something. A number of gentlemen following me are also stopped by them in the most charming manner with just a hint of a slur. The old man is overjoyed and keeps on stammering: I'm a Berliner, born and bred. I'm a Berliner, born and bred. Everyone who is stopped pulls out his purse, and in return takes home a pleasantly novel impression.

2 JULY 1889

Despondent mood, did no work, slept mostly, oppressive dreams, in the evenings a session of Munich beer. I feel so positively insecure that I decide to clear out as soon as may be.

3 JULY 1889

Letter to Armin, to Gerhart Hauptmann, to Mama.

I have it in mind to enquire at the *Tagblatt* offices about my short story,[66] but I don't get round to doing it. Coming home after lunch, I find the story together with a polite printed rejection slip. Late in the afternoon I go through the Tiergarten to Charlottenburg,[67] in the hope of seeing something in the way of a palace, a grand garden, or something of that kind. Since there is nothing to be found, I take the tram back, a splendid journey through interminable avenues of hundred-year old trees. At supper Frau Pansegrau surprises me by criticizing women's liberation. She's been skimming through *Women's Education*.[68] Who's going to darn the socks, then, if women go in for reading books? Our Excellency's wife darns all the socks herself, often until late at night. And, after all, she's got seven maids and two man-servants, and His Excellency never interferes. Her Excellency tells each of them what they have to do, and then she checks to see whether it's been done. Now she's off to our part of the world for the summer. She doesn't go to a spa. She goes to her estate in Upper Pomerania. Do I know His Excellency? – No, I only know Court Preacher Stoecker. – Yes, I heard him once. It wasn't just hot air, either. – His Excellency is the Minister of Education, Baron von Gessler. He actually came from Upper Pomerania himself, where folk are stupid enough to think that people in Berlin are as stupid as they are. And that was the reason he was against better education for young girls. When I tell Frau Pansegrau that in our country girls even go to the university, she says, well yes, they'll have their own separate apartments. When I say it's not so, she replies: Well, that would just be the last straw here, where everything's in an unholy mess as it is.

It's actually because of Frau Pansegrau that I'm sorry I have to leave Berlin. As soon as she's gone, I start packing and get one case half filled. Then I go to the Panoptikum until two o'clock, where I see a very pretty priestess in the company of two gentlemen. I don't manage to get a seat from which I can have a clear view of her, however. I immerse myself in the railway timetable.

4 JULY 1889

Packing suitcases from eleven until two. Then to lunch, when I manage to find my express in the timetable. I go off at once to the baggage office in a cheerful frame of mind at the prospect of the journey, since everything is going so smoothly. At home I nail up the packing-case with Herr Pansegrau lending an incredibly clumsy hand. Say goodbye and carry my suitcase to the station myself, feeling no end of a hero. I was afraid Herr Pansegrau would offer to do it. I would have had to give him a tip, and couldn't very well offer him less than three marks. That would have been one-third of the ready cash with which I'm supposed to start a new life in Munich. At the sight of the Anhalter Station I'm afflicted by a strong sense of shame when I think with what bold spirits I arrived here in the glorious morning sunshine six weeks ago. To the right of the station I notice the basement cobbler's shop where I bought a pair of boot-laces on that occasion and first heard the Berlin dialect. I wouldn't have dreamed that my stay here wouldn't outlast the bootlaces. I do actually need a new pair: both of them have broken. But I have to economize, and if I tread carefully they can still be tied for a while yet. The bootlaces are, by the way, not the worst of my problems. But the soles, the soles! They're as thin as paper and, as usual, my only pair. I've been walking on them ever since Hammi's wedding. For more than a fortnight now I've been anxiously steering clear of any sharp stones in the road, and at night, wherever possible, I walk on the soft asphalt of the carriageway. It used to cause me a downright pang of anguish when I saw ten-year-old urchins in the Tiergarten scuffing the ground with their footwear and wearing a supercilious air, as if they were about to master the world. On these occasions I used to recall instantly that morning in the Zürich Botanical Gardens when the gaping lateral wounds on my only pair of shoes were suddenly complemented by the protruding soles. I may admit to myself, however, that I could watch the ten-year-old urchins without resentment. I found the sight of them somehow gratifying, by reason of the contrast.

I go into the Spatenbräu and partake of a tankard of Munich beer and a sausage to go with it. My neighbours at table are two elderly gentlemen in their sixties, one of them obviously married and speaking only Mecklenburg dialect, the other a retired major in a slightly shabby genteel outfit, with more of a Berlin twang, in the cheerful company of a tart whom I consider rather skinny but otherwise pleasant, and who is drinking cognac with seltzer, i.e. first knocking back the cognac and then washing it down with the seltzer. I buy myself some cigars and some sliced sausage and make for the station. The train is packed. There are four of us in the compartment, and two of the gentlemen are saying interminable goodbyes, one of them smartly dressed with a red nose, grey hair and podgy hands, to his wife, the other, a hulking great brute, to his wife and children. The grey-haired one promises to write to his wife from the Adler in Nuremberg. You know the place, too, asks the brute. Oh, I know where there's good grub. – Good cuisine, good table d'hôte, Regensburg sausages. I'm not all that keen on them. – Parboiled with sauerkraut. Not fit to eat, cold. – Yes, parboiled, parboiled, you're right. As the train pulls out, the fat man calls his grey-haired companion back to the window. Won't you wave goodbye again? Your wife is still waving. So back he goes to the window, and the pair of them wave their handkerchiefs. After the train has left the station they agree that the right thing to do is to say goodbye at home.

I'm sitting next to the stout gentleman, who is groaning with might and main because he can't stretch out. This is because a quarter of our compartment is obstructed by the lavatory. The grey-haired gentleman makes himself comfortable straight away. In Leipzig he leaves us, and the stout man takes his place, so as to be able to sleep, but wallows about on the narrow seat, the arm-rest of which reaches no higher than his backside, like a hippopotamus in a bath-tub. I lie quietly until one o'clock, then eat my sliced sausage with great relish, lie down again and sleep until six. It was on this anniversary of the American Declaration of Independence that I had to quit Berlin on account of my American citizenship.

MUNICH

5 JULY 1889–4 FEBRUARY 1890

5 JULY 1889

In Landshut I buy the *Neueste Nachrichten*, which I read from cover to cover, and am so impatient I can hardly sit still for the last hour. At last, just beyond Freising, the towers of Munich come into sight.

At first sight Munich strikes me as a one-horse town. The streets dirty and narrow. In a cigar shop I see the same window display that I saw there three years ago. I go into the Franziskaner, which disgusts me with its grimy appearance, both inside and out. Then the search for an apartment. Find charming digs, which are not vacant until the 1 August, however. I finally rent a room at 41, IV Adalbertstrasse with an old lady who wants to be paid in advance. After I've explained my circumstances she no longer insists on that. I take a pound of cherries into the Englischer Garten, the atmosphere of which affects me strongly, as compared with the Tiergarten, and go on to the Café Luitpold. Then to Bennat, whom, unexpectedly, I find still at home.[1] He has just been writing a card to Baumgartner and he adds a greeting from me. At eight in the evening he's going to the Hackerkeller with Hilpert[2] and his wife and Feurer. As it's only six o'clock, I go to the station to collect my suitcase. On my way down the Luisenstrasse I catch sight of Paul Heyse sticking his Apollonian head out of the window.[3] I carry my suitcase home, feeling rather proud of myself, get myself more or less spruced up, and on my way out see a pretty young lady in the kitchen whom I take to be my neighbour, the painter. However, it turns out to be my landlady's daughter, the manageress of Schütze's shop in the Arcades.

I find the whole company assembled in the Hackerkeller: Bennat,

51

Herr Hilpert, who finds I've changed for the better, Frau Hilpert, who doesn't find I've changed for the better, Fritz Hilpert, an impertinent young lad whom I reckon to be twelve, but who is in fact sixteen. Also old Feurer with his young wife, and her sister, Frl. Klingenfeld, the Ibsen translator,[4] then a cousin of Hilpert, a young girl, not ill-favoured, who prides herself on her wit, and feels an obligation to entertain the company, and various other ladies and gentlemen not known to me. The conversation is extremely lively, and I feel very much at ease, the glorious evening, the grand view and the balmy air contributing not a little to my mood. Rural bliss, compared to Berlin.

On the way home, the female cousin is snatched from me by a male cousin, but old Hilpert joins me and proceeds to curse the German Emperor up hill and down dale. Bennat interrogates me closely about the Berlin cabaret scene, whether it really is a Sodom.

6 JULY 1889

After an excellent night's sleep I set off to call on Dr Muncker,[5] but on the way feel the most urgent need of a beer. Dr Muncker lives at daggers drawn with his landlady, who, by way of reprisal, contrives a muddle instead of announcing my arrival. He receives me very graciously, looking like a young curate, both his rooms spotlessly clean, lined with bookshelves, he himself tall and dapper, genially talkative, with dark hair, not much back to his head, blue eyes, prominent aquiline nose, sensitive mouth and a rather protruding chin. On my confessing that I'm working on a comedy, he becomes rather embarrassed. We say goodbye and arrange to meet tomorrow evening in the Hofbräuhaus cellar. I go to lunch in the Engelsburg, which has become very popular. The whole place is full of students and one-year conscripts.[6] I buy myself a pipe and some tobacco and go home, where I quickly fall asleep and dream that Thomar has come to Munich. I can scarcely credit it and hence keep on touching him here and there in order to convince myself that I'm not dreaming. Then I dream up a sentimental drama which unfolds before my eyes smoothly and uninterruptedly.

At eight o'clock I go to the Hofbräukeller for a beer and some smoked ham. I almost fear I won't be able to work in this utterly relaxed frame of mind. Faced with this beery mode of life, I feel as if

I'd been whisked back to an earlier century. It seems to me infinitely absurd how certain slogans were put about in our student days regarding the status of various artistic monuments, and how these catch-phrases were then passed on with a superior air by all and sundry. In the Café Luitpold until twelve o'clock. During the night a fearful brawl in the Nordendstrasse, not far from my place. Amidst the unholy din only one word can be heard: 'Out! Out!' The whole street is in turmoil and cursing the police, who fail to put in an appearance. One or two cabs drive up, evidently to take away the casualties.

7 JULY 1889

Before lunch I go to Schwabing, where I have something to eat. After lunch to Frl. Herzog Jun. in Schwabing. She lives with her sister in a little summerhouse in rural seclusion. Her sister soon takes over the conversational lead, telling us about her adventures on the stage. The wickedness of theatre managers, her colleagues' rakish way of life, and so on. She strikes me as being better suited to be a governess than an actress: she doesn't pronounce her consonants, her vowels are strangulated, and her voice is anything but ample, and besides, she's far from good-looking, not even ugly. She's got no figure at all, and an utterly nondescript manner. She appears to have no aptitude as an actress other than an inflated estimation of her own abilities, and the circumstance that her sister is a singer. As I get up to go, the ladies offer me a glass of wine, at which I can barely conceal my delight. So we tipple a little, and the conversation turns to literature. Frl. Herzog, the middle one, reads French and asks what she might read in French, whereupon I offer her Paul de Kock's *Mon ami Piffard*.[7] With startling suddenness Frl. Herzog Jun. asks me whether I know Goethe. After I have recovered from the initial shock I reply: Not personally, does she, perhaps, read him? – No, she hadn't read anything by him so far.

The most interesting thing for me was making the acquaintance of little Phylax, really an exceptionally pretty little hound. He rubs himself most confidingly against my knee and licks my wrists, as though he knew precisely where I come from. After I've spent nearly two hours there I walk home through the Englischer Garten and sleep until seven. Afterwards in the Hofbräukeller, where I meet Dr

Muncker in the company of three Jews, one of them a civil service probationer, the other two students, who are trying as hard as they can to crack jokes. The subject of conversation is in fact the Classical, i.e. Latin and Greek texts in the grammar school. The civil servant, Assessor Pariser, reminds me, in his wisdom and his manner of dispensing it, very much of the Sublime Porte. On the way home Dr Muncker is so sleepy that he walks past his own house. When Hafis was mentioned,[8] one of the students remarked that that was a fearful lark.

8 JULY 1889

I receive money from Hammi. My landlady asks me if I've heard about the railway accident. The train from Berlin, by which I arrived here three days ago, plunged down the embankment near Schleissheim this morning, complete with its two engines. I feel a peculiar thrill at the news. They say the entire station is full of dead ladies.

Before lunch I go to the exhibition of paintings, where nothing interests me as much as young Prince Rupert,[9] a handsome officer who seems to be interested in Böcklin. Three years ago he was still going around in mufti with his tutor. After lunch via the Englischer Garten to the Forsthaus. Evening in the Hackerkeller and the Café Luitpold.

9 JULY 1889

Woman's Future, by Frl. Meta von Salis-Marschlins is very stimulating.[10] I enquire about Frl. von Alten at the police station and learn that she moved to Dresden two years ago.

Afternoon in the Englischer Garten. Evening in the Unger baths. Then to Bennat's, but he has been away since Saturday. After that, to the Hofbräukeller, where I unexpectedly run across Dr Güttler,[11] and fritter away an hour in brisk conversation. On my way back, in a toilet on the Maximilianstrasse, I encounter an elegant bearded gentleman who virtually devours me with his eyes. He actually follows me a good way, but then gives up. I have a considerable struggle with myself to decide whether I shouldn't after all turn back. I reach a decision by telling myself: Later, later, when I've feathered my nest, when I'm sure I'm not a fellow-sufferer. In the Hofbräukeller there were two young men sitting opposite me talking about their year's military service. One of them tells how the sergeant-major had made it clear to them from the outset that he would accept nothing from them, neither cash nor provisions, but that he had a wife. They had taken the hint, and the whole time they were in barracks they had taken coffee in her house, paying double the normal price, had presented her with a ham at Christmas, and so on at every opportunity. When manoeuvres were over they had given him their field service allowance 'to look after'. He had kept on saying, I should remind the short-service gentlemen that I still have some of their cash, but in the end he had simply kept it, since no one asked for it back.

The waitresses in the Café Luitpold have three marks a month wages. Apart from that they have to rely on tips, but they have to pay out of their own pocket the girl who serves the water. They work from eight in the morning until half-past two the following morning.

On the way home I feel so merry that I burst out laughing and can't stop.

10 JULY 1889

Met the teacher Landgraf with his class on the home farm at Oberföhring. My daily beer consumption has risen to three and a half litres. Letter to Mama.

11 JULY 1889

Increasing heat-wave, hence a decrease in my diary entries. In the Gärtnertheater in the evening *Mme Bonivard* by Bisson and Mars.[12] The Gärtnertheater has improved a great deal. Met Dr Güttler and his friend Roth in the Hofbräukeller.

12 JULY 1889

I have my breakfast brought to me in bed at nine o'clock. In the kitchen my landlady keeps a pigeon that nests in a newspaper rack. She does have to trim its wings now and then. It lays eggs, she says, and is pleased with them. As long as the eggs are in the nest, she won't leave it. She can't hatch them, of course, because there isn't a cock-

The Hofbräuhaus in Munich before its renovation, 1896.

bird. When there are three or four eggs, they take them away from her. Later, when she doesn't lay eggs any more, they'll have to keep a closer guard on her. At the moment she doesn't venture beyond the balcony. There is in fact an iron balcony in front of the kitchen. When you go into the kitchen in the morning, she coos a 'Good morning'. She gives us a great deal of pleasure. Last night I went to fetch a drink of water. While I was letting the water run, a kind of cooing mating call came from the sink. I thought it was a cricket. Evidently it was the pigeon.

While I'm waiting in bed for breakfast in the morning I place my teeth on the bedside table for convenience. A dozen flies instantly pounce on them, browsing their way from one tooth to the next and obviously revelling in the process.

In the evening I make the acquaintance of the landscape painter Engelmann in the Arzberger beer-cellar.[13] He reckons the jury for the modern exhibition is biased, because they prefer the more recent school and don't appreciate anything from the older school. Böcklin he scarcely knows by name. The price of up to 500,000 francs paid for Millet's *Angelus* he reckons to be an art-dealer's trick. In any case, he has only heard the whole story at second hand. In 1848 he spent nine days in Dresden during the revolution,[14] and couldn't leave the house on account of all that revolutionary business. He, his wife and his children were on the point of starving to death when bread was handed out in some public place or other, and his wife went (only women were allowed to go) and brought home a large loaf. Richard Wagner and Semper had behaved atrociously at that time.[15] Semper had sketched barricades, and Wagner had wanted to persuade the King to abdicate and appoint him, Wagner, regent.

13 JULY 1889

Evening at *The Mikado*, where I was considerably bored. Afterwards in the Hofbräuhaus. The Hofbräuhaus renovated, it's no longer the classical pigsty it once was, but it's still very snug all the same. As soon as I enter I notice a young artist at the bar, with curly hair and incomparably more genius than intelligence in his face. My heart rejoices at the sight of him. Unfortunately, I lose sight of him. But I fervently long for someone like him to associate with.

Letter to Aunt Plümacher.

14 JULY 1889

A dull, sultry day. Slept the afternoon away. Evening in the Löwen-bräu. One or two cute priestesses. I'm reading 'The Equality of the Sexes' (in *Das freie Reich*) by Irma von Troll-Borostyáni.[16]

15 JULY 1889

Hofbräukeller.

16 JULY 1889

I go looking for an apartment, could move into one in the Amalienstrasse, with 'very high-class' service, as the sly old master tailor puts it, come very close to renting something in the Georgenstrasse, and finally find something suitable in the Akademiestrasse: up four flights of stairs, an elongated intestine of a room with alcoves, for 15 marks. The landlady, who reminds me very much of Frau Hilpert, doesn't seem to trust me quite, since I turn up rather casually with a paper bag of cherries. In the Hofbräu-hauskeller in the evening I spot Dr Muncker at the bar and hurry to join him in the hope of finding company for the evening. He says there are one or two other gentlemen of the party who might come in, at least he would know where I was sitting. He clearly has the gravest doubts as to whether I am worthy of his company. After a while the other gentlemen do in fact enter and sit down at the far end of the room. Dr Muncker sits down so that he has his back to me. It occurs to me that if he sees me still sitting there he might imagine I'm waiting for him, so I go on my way – to the Hofbräuhaus, where, the moment I go in, I notice old Stahl,[17] sitting in sequestered seclusion at a table right at the back. He looks to me to be in even finer fettle than three years ago, although he has suffered serious disorders of the stomach, bowels and kidneys since then. But when he'd recovered the doctor told him to look round for a good beer. – Which was a good beer, then? – Hofbräu. His verdict on the German Emperor is philosophical and dispassionate, we would have to wait and see.[18] On the other hand, he simply can't see why food should be cheaper in Berlin than in Munich. After we've chatted for half an hour or so, he abruptly asks me whether I mean to stay much longer, because if so he would just nip out to the toilet. I'm too much on the alert to take this at its face value, so I drink up as quickly as I can and take my leave, reflecting on how quickly you can lose touch with people.

17 JULY 1889

Before lunch I go into the Neue Pinakothek, where I'm particularly fascinated by Bonveret's *Maria*, and also . . . and Böcklin's *Play of the Waves*. Piloty's paintings leave me utterly cold.[19] In Feuerbach's *Iphigenie* I look in vain for the spirit that seemed to me to emanate from his *Symposium*.[20] As I'm raising the cloth covering an unwrapped blackish brown Egyptian mummy in the Antiquarium, a stout strapping lady standing next to me asks if that's an ancient Egyptian: I confirm that it is, although I very much doubt that she asked the question for the ancient Egyptian's sake. But since she actually seems to be interested in the subject, I tell her all I know about sarcophagi, hieroglyphs, etc. She seems to be particularly intrigued by the fact that the ancient Egyptians used to wear false beards. As we're leaving the premises she asks me to show her the way to the Deutscher Kaiser inn, and since the affair is beginning to interest me, I accompany her, after fetching her things from the cloakroom. There it transpires that she is married, because her husband's overcoat is there as well, and I have the honour of carrying it. She is the wife of a Leipzig art-dealer by the name of Weyer. Since she couldn't accompany her husband on his business visits, she had visited the Pinakothek. Her husband had recently purchased an original sketch by Lenbach for 1,500 marks, which is not all that expensive, considering that Lenbach so seldom lets anything at all go.[21] Apropos Lenbach, I mention the photographer Hahn, whereupon she agrees with me so hastily that I almost assume that her husband had got the Bismarck sketch from Hahn.

At Alois Denk's, where I go for lunch, the waitress sits down beside me and says: Now I've got to tell you something. Frl. Rosa says, supposing you were to ask, supposing the gentleman with the moustache who always sits here were to ask, who the two gentlemen are with whom she lunched yesterday, then I'm to tell you I don't know them. I have mixed feelings about this. On the one hand, I'm glad there's at least one fellow-creature who cares about me. On the other hand, the whole business seems a bit unreal to me. The waitress asks what she should say in reply. I say I can't very well send her my respects, since I don't know her. – Oh, you can send her your respects all right. She'll be only too pleased. I know her only too well, as far as that goes. – I send her my respects, then. But where on earth did she get the idea? – Well, she just thought you were in love with her, you know. Maybe she's a little bit in love with you, too. She's got an admirer across the road, and a couple here as well. – Frl. Rosa is a saleslady in a nearby draper's shop. She's tall, with a slim figure and a jolly face. When she speaks, her husky voice reminds me very much of Rothgang. So now here's a first-class opportunity to start something, but I feel anything but comfortable at the prospect. It strikes me that I was very stupid not to see from the waitress's manner at the very outset that she had already spoken about me to Frl. Rosa, seeing that I'd enquired about her the very first time I saw her. I look forward to the following day in something like fear and trembling.

18 JULY 1889

I move to Frau Mühlberger's. In the morning to the Alte Pinakothek, just to see people. But the sight of them is distracting. At lunch the waitress tells me that Frl. Rosa sends her thanks and returns my greeting. A load is lifted from my mind, I send her my thanks once more. The waitress says she'll arrive any moment now, won't I wait? I make myself scarce, however. A concert in the Hofgarten, where I'm struck by the ugly type of Munich female. Their faces have a wasted look, they have thick noses, unsightly necks, rotten teeth and complexions the colour of leather. If all the tarts in Munich aren't good-looking, then at least all the pretty girls are tarts. I'm less aware of my loneliness since my work is going ahead rapidly.

19 JULY 1889

Morning in the Neue Pinakothek. In the afternoon I get into conversation in the Englischer Garten with a young, simply dressed girl who sat down on my bench. She's reading an anthology entitled *Edelweiss* and doing crochet-work at the same time. She's learning a poem by heart so as to be able to recite it in company. Not long ago she had recited a Swabian poem and had done it very well; although she's Swabian, it's true, she had not been brought up in Swabia. She's from Regensburg, in fact. Last year she was in Switzerland and saw *Parsifal* performed in St Gallen. She didn't think the audience enjoyed it very much, however. While she was on Lake Constance in a gondola she had tried to change places and all of them had fallen into the water. Her uncle had fished her out. Her uncle comes from Stuttgart, in fact, and owns the Hirschberg Bazaar. She herself seems to me to be an out-and-out Christian. She has a hard struggle with herself, because she's constantly tempted to go on the stage. A few years ago she had been on the point of doing so, but various people had advised her against it. If you couldn't put up a first-class performance, then there was no point. She seems to have close links with the Gärtnertheater. She knows Dreher personally. He was a very serious-minded sort of man to deal with. She had already performed, incidentally, in the Catholic Social Club, in fact. She had always had leading parts, for instance in *The Last Window*, in *The Promise behind the Hearth* etc., and had always done well. The day after she couldn't help weeping to think that she hadn't gone on the stage. She went walking a lot by herself. A few days ago she had walked via Grosshesselohe, Pullach and Höllriegelkreuth to Grünwald, where a waiters' society was holding a dance. She had sat there in the crowd without knowing a soul. She preferred to be by herself during the day, but in the evening, after seven, say, in the

Englischer Garten, she was often very grateful if a gentleman offered her his company, since she was frightened otherwise. I bid her *au revoir* and stroll down to the Café Putzer under the Arcades, where I observe a fellow-sufferer in the form of a Great Dane. The dog is lying on his lead and obviously also suffering from his lack of company. He's extremely worked up, and at the same time evidently suffering from mental depression, as his facial expression shows.

20 JULY 1889

Bought a pair of shoes which are, of course, once more too small for me. In the evening I meet Dr Muncker, Dr Köppel, young Kaula and the medical student, Geise, with his brother, in the Hofbräukeller. The talk turns to Dr Wörner,[22] who gives lectures in New York wearing a black frock-coat and a white tie. Dr Muncker inadvertently says 'a white frock-coat and a black tie'. Laughter all round, like the cackling of young chickens. Then the whole company repeat the expression 'white frock-coat and black tie' one by one, each laughing at it in turn. And so it goes on all evening. So what? The Devil feeds on flies for want of something better. It's no wonder that I don't recoil from a spider like this Dr Muncker when I'm pretty well starving. And the spider is poisonous, into the bargain. On the first evening we met I had barely mentioned Dr Güttler when he served me up a rumour to the effect that Dr Güttler had at one time written the most vicious sort of articles for the *Fremdenblatt* – and this in angelically sweet tones. I must say I prefer Dr Güttler a hundred times over to this venomous babe-in-arms, this boyish hyena, Muncker. On the way home I'm foolish enough to let myself be drawn into a defence of higher education for women against the medical student Geise. And, sure enough, he treats the matter with all the sheer stupidity you could imagine, as was only to be expected.

21 JULY 1889

Letter to the *Fliegende [Blätter].*[23] Afternoon in the Café Putzer and in a Mohammedan café in the Müllerstrasse. Evening in the Café Italia, formerly the St Peter's Café, where once upon a time Poldi Fröhlich's Munich novelette with the fair Gretchen took place, when he went with her to see the *Gipsy Baron* and was so appalled by this artistic treat.[24] Now the St Peter is a cabaret with really good acts. What I actually like best is a charming tart in the company of some students, a consummate actress, haughty, gracious, aloof, yet affable. I've never seen vice in such a spiritualized form. There is a young man sitting in front of me, early thirties, smartly dressed, with thinning hair. In a manner that's totally at odds with his whole appearance he's ogling the admittedly rather pretty waitress with such a helplessly beseeching and hopelessly forlorn expression on his face that I feel sorry for him. He seems to me to be an utterly vacuous individual, who has suddenly fallen a victim in all his vacuousness. After the show I go to the Hofbräu, where I fall into conversation with some Swiss. On the way home I am strongly tempted to shoot myself.

22 JULY 1889

What a stupid thing I did again today! I leave the Café Luitpold and go into the Englischer Garten, unhappy because I can't get on with my E.[25] At last an opening comes into sight, a glimmer of hope that there may be a way through the impasse. I'm on the point of getting out my notebook when an open carriage drives up on the nearby roadway. A young lady gets out, takes the footpath to the path I'm walking on, and within a few minutes is walking on ahead of me. She is wearing a pale, striped overcoat, has an attractive figure and walks with easy, leisurely steps. I hurry on, so as to overtake her. As I do so, she glances at me with an unaffected smile, so unaffected that I'm in hardly any doubt that I'm dealing with a priestess of the higher class. I slacken my pace so that I'm walking a short distance ahead of her. On the right-hand side, a narrow path leads through the shrubbery to a bench that offers a prospect of open fields. I think, if I turn off here, she'll probably walk straight past, although it's probably on account of this spot that she came here. So I walk on, and she turns aside. Ass! I think to myself. Missed the ideal spot for a talk. In the meantime, her carriage has been following slowly, and now it stops opposite the crossing. I look back at the bench. She certainly hasn't sat down to muse, but is standing there, scraping the ground with her parasol as if searching for something. After I've walked on a few paces resignedly, I suddenly hear the horse's hooves close behind me. I look round, and, sure enough, my beauty is coming down the footpath. I hastily conceal my pipe, which I have only just relighted, put my hat straight, balance my parasol over my right shoulder, and curse the fact that I have neglected to shave. So I wait for her, sauntering more and more slowly, firmly determined not to miss my chance this time. She overtakes me, but this time she is looking down at the ground rather than at me, so that I'm once more taken aback. I decide at any rate that I'll address her as 'dear madame'. That would eliminate the possibility of any offence. The carriage has driven on fairly far ahead. My beauty is striding on briskly, so that I'm afraid she'll be out of range any moment. She's walking on the right-hand verge of the road, I'm on the left. Now I'm abreast of her again. I'm humming an aria, so as to give an impression of nonchalance. She looks as good as gold. I take heart now, thinking that 'take heart' is a very apt expression. The following conversation ensues: You left that lovely spot very quickly, dear madame. – I came here for a walk. – And no doubt also to be alone. – Indeed. (She speaks, by the way, with a most engaging smile.) – Then I must ask you to pardon me for interrupting you in your thoughts. – Oh, not at all! –

In spite of this curt reply, I still can't make up my mind to retreat. I fall back, but a mere seven or eight paces. I think, perhaps she'll have second thoughts. I wouldn't want to deprive her of the chance to make up for her over-hasty response. A cart drawn by two hefty oxen is coming down the road. A farmer and his wife are sitting in the cart. It's on the tip of my tongue to ask her: What do you think of this ox, Fräulein? I'm about to do so, but then I tell myself, it would be importunate on my part if I make the first move again. By the time I have overcome these scruples, the cart is already so far away that my question would be bound to sound just too silly.

Nevertheless, I hang on no more than a few paces behind her, on the other side of the carriageway. I can't bring myself to fade away gradually and without trace, so to speak. That would be tantamount to admitting my discomfiture. And yet I know that I'm utterly ruining the pleasure which the young lady hoped for when she came out here, obviously in order to be by herself. At last her carriage appears in the distance. It seems to me that she's quickening her pace. She waves. The carriage drives up. In the meantime I've dropped back a fair distance. She gets in and leans back, throwing me a casually curious glance as she drives past. I can't help following her with my eyes.

After she has disappeared I mutter 'Blockhead!' to myself a few times, without feeling any evident sense of relief. Doubtlessly, I tell myself, she left that secluded spot with the bench and the fine view, not because of me, but only because there was a cactus there. As a rule there is a cactus at popular vantage points of that sort.

I make for a bench in the nearby shrubbery, where I rapidly fall into a kind of trance. After I've jerked myself out of it I write a bit of the little play and turn back towards the city. I wonder whether I should submit my sermon to Buchholz and Wörner.[26] After tea, to the Hofbräuhauskeller, where the student, Giese, summons me to his table the moment I enter. Pariser is present, otherwise there is a young student from the Conservatory by the name of Weinhöppel,[27] and a grammar-school teacher from Hamburg who maintains a forbidding silence. I feel very much at my ease. On the way home I ask Weinhöppel whether he had perhaps known a certain Marie Gingele. Oh, yes, he had in fact been very intimate with her. She had told him he was stupid, whereupon he had retorted that he had a long way to go before he could match her in stupidity. He was telling me this just to show on what intimate terms he had been with her.

I dream about my father night after night these days. When I think of him during the day, I'm so overcome with grief that I get a lump in my throat. The day after tomorrow is my birthday, the first time that I can look forward to it in joyful anticipation of getting some news from home.

23 JULY 1889

At home nearly all day. Finished reading Troll-Borostyáni. Evening in the HBK [Hofbräukeller], met Dr Güttler, who treats me to a homily concerning our recent political discussion. It wasn't just that Roth was an East Prussian, from Königsberg, and married to the daughter of a civil servant, and, above all, an artist by royal appointment. He had done engravings of Moltke and Bismarck, and would have liked to get the Emperor as well. At one time he had had permission to do an engraving of Prince Wilhelm.[28] But when he applied through the embassy here to use this permit in the case of the Emperor, he was turned down. He had spent a fortnight in Berlin pursuing this aim, but to no effect. Since then, naturally, the Emperor's face has been a particularly sore point with him.

Eight of the 'Eleven Executioners' in the courtyard of the Munich restaurant 'Zum Hirschen'. Wedekind is standing at the extreme left.

24 JULY 1889

My twenty-fifth birthday. I wait all day in vain for news from Switzerland. It's possible that harassment at the border is to blame for the delay. While I'm working I dig out letters from Minna, Anny Bark, Oskar Schibler and Moritz Sutermeister,[29] and they provide me with an enjoyable day. In the late afternoon I'm in a sentimental mood as a result and hence feel the need to be by myself. I go to the Münchner Kindl, to a cabaret, where I'm moderately amused, mainly because you get a better view of the girls' legs there than in the Italia. At home I finish reading Oskar's letters and write to him. Bought

Ibsen's *Love's Comedy*.[30] It will bring about one or two developments in my plan.

25 JULY 1889

In the afternoon in the Englischer Garten in boots that pinch. Letter to Mieze. Frl. von Mink is at home as a lodger. A number of English ladies as well. Willy proposes to get married next week. He had actually intended that I should officiate as parson, but has now decided to follow a more conventional course. A very pleasant evening in a beer-cellar with Assessor Pariser, Kaula and Dr and Frau Seiss. Drank gin in Pariser's room at midnight and fetched something to read. He gives me Keller's *Legends* and Dóczy's *Last Love* to take away with me.[31]

26 JULY 1889

Letter to Minna. In the evening Westendhalle, a dreary selection, no faces, no voices, no calves. The audience unbelievably dunderheaded. In the Hofbräu until one o'clock.

27 JULY 1889

My landlady, Frau Mühlberger, keeps a little white dog and a couple of cats. She lives, drinks and sleeps together with these three companions. The animals live together in perfect harmony and are in the flat all the time. They fill it with a stink that would knock you flat on your back. When I ask Frau Mühlberger where the stink comes from, she says she has a cold in the head and can't smell anything, nor can she think where it might be coming from. She goes over to the stove where some potatoes are sizzling and lifts the lid off the pan. Then she looks through my laundry, and finally hunts through her pockets. When I pass her next time she asks me if I know of something she could use to put a cat down painlessly. She was very sorry, he was such a grand lad. Then she grabs the cat that is sitting stolidly in an armchair and lifts him up to her chest. He's a great skinny beast with a huge humped back. After she's kissed him ardently, she throws him on to the sofa where the dog is sleeping. The pair of them circle round each other a few times and then lie down together. When I remark that I'd been in a few households where cats were kept, but I'd never known a stink like there was here, she objects that she couldn't let him out anyway, because there are large dogs downstairs. He'd never been out of the apartment once, he'd have no idea how to use his legs if he were attacked. She'd meant to have him chloroformed, but he was such a good lad. And it wasn't that he was dirty. The animals had a pot of their own with sawdust in it, and it was emptied each day.

The work goes ahead desperately slowly, and that depresses me. Whenever I get bogged down, I'm overwhelmed with sadness, thinking of my father and what I did to him. Sometimes I also think of Donald and hope that I may at least be granted a chance to put him on his feet, to have him educated under my guidance. Last night I was haunted by a vile dream in which our home appeared in a most unedifying light. It had turned into a sort of cabaret, in which Mother and Donald were the principal figures and performed all sorts of tricks. I was sitting in the audience. Not infrequently I'm also plagued by doubts as to whether my work really is work, after all. This feeling comes over me mostly on Sundays, when I see everyone lazing about, which is something I can't do. My work isn't work in fact, when it proceeds at such a snail's pace. I spend a great deal of time doing nothing, idling away by far the greater part of each day. Work is actually something that multiplies of its own accord.

Piccolo is docile, as if he didn't exist.[32] I can't think what's the matter with him. Whether he's reached his ultimate stage of development, or whether he will some time or other rise up in hitherto unsuspected glory. There is a peculiar irony in the fact that it is actually the individual who aspires to evolve into a universal human being who lags behind the merest machine, however restricted its development, precisely in this most human of all functions.

I go to the Kletzengarten in the evening and run across Bennat and Skerle [harpist from Graz]. The Kletzengarten hasn't changed much. The green birch boughs by the doorposts have gone, and the beer is even worse than it used to be.

The waitresses are still as grubby as ever, and the landlady just as fat, although she's not called Frau Salchner any longer. She sits, armed with gold-rimmed spectacles, next to the stove, slicing turnips into a trough all evening. Skerle has become rather more stolid, and Bennat more irascible. The talk turns to politics, Wohlgemuth in particular,[33] and I notice that I'm unable to maintain the same sort of detachment as I used to. I came very near to getting heated. As a result I mean to adopt Dr Güttler's principle and never talk politics. Pariser gave me Keller's *Seven Legends*, two of which I read with great enjoyment: 'Eugenia' and 'Wicked St Vitalis'.

28 JULY 1889

First day of the gymnastic festival. It pours with rain all day. I can't help feeling a certain sense of satisfaction, although I'm thoroughly ashamed of it. Letter to Welti. In the Café Roth until one o'clock.

29 JULY 1889

After lunch I follow the procession and review it as it passes down various streets. Bought the *Physiology of Marriage* and lent it to Clementine Halm. Spent the whole day reading. In the afternoon a row with Frau Mühlberger because of her stinking brute. Evening in the Regensburg sausage kitchen.

30 JULY 1889

Evening at the stadium, where I feel infinitely alone. Go by a long roundabout route to the HBK and meet Pariser and Geise there. Animated conversation.

31 JULY 1889

Evening in the HBK with Pariser and Dr Xaver Hamburg. The conversation revolves round the question as to whether any ethical progress can be detected in the history of the world. Letter from Minna. Tuschel had put my letter in her bed and she had slept on it all night. Willy has got married, apparently in Zürich.

1 AUGUST 1889

Evening: *King Lear* in the new Shakespeare production. The play moves me profoundly. Afterwards in the Franziskanerkeller. Weinhöppel joins me between twelve and one.

As I labour upstairs after lunch, it seems to me scarcely conceivable that I may possibly look forward to this pleasure for the next thirty years. While I'm pursuing this thought to its conclusion, I suddenly find myself standing at the corridor door. I owe letters in all directions, most urgently probably to Willy, who sent me notice of his engagement and wedding, and to whom I haven't written a syllable in reply.

I would scarcely have believed how empty my life is at present. And yet I spent the greater part of my student years in this manner – a waste of time that could be atoned for only by ceasing to go along with it. Last winter I felt like a beggar, a hermit, and compared to today I was a Croesus then. What are all these learned men, civil servants, professors, lecturers lumped together, compared with two days like Uncle Wilhelm's funeral? Judging by outward appearances, they seem like inexhaustible treasure trove, where God knows what unsuspected hoards lie hidden. If you enter, however, you find yourself in the most wretched junk-store in the world, in a warehouse full of secondhand goods, an old clothes shop, not a single piece of living rock, nothing but garbage, trash scraped together, haggled over, begged and stolen from the archives, treasuries and workshops of world history. And yet you have to blush at every turn because you're not such a barrel of pickles yourself.

2 AUGUST 1889

Row with Frau Mühlberger over the stink of cats. Evening in the Regensburg sausage kitchen. Letter to Willy.

3 AUGUST 1889

Evening in the HBK, where I don't meet a single soul I know, afterwards in the Café Central. Letters to Mieze and Mali.

4 AUGUST 1889

Afternoon in the Moorish Café, then worked. Evening in the HBK and in the Café Central. Once again, I haven't spoken to a soul since Thursday evening.

5 AUGUST 1889

Midsummer Night's Dream. I have a rotten seat, and can't make out a single face, even with opera glasses. Mme Ramlo's voice seems to me to have deteriorated considerably during the last three years. With Pariser and Dr X. in the Scholastica after the show.[34] The subject of the conversation mainly Matthäi. Pariser tells us how he used to collaborate with Wörner, and how they criticized each other's work. Whole scenes had ended up in the fire. It's no good, it'll have to be rewritten by tomorrow. I speak in favour of going into print. Burning the stuff doesn't destroy it. The spirits of the victims lived on like those of incinerated heretics, and one's estimation of what had been burned became in the course of time suffused with a shade of optimism. Publication was the only real form of destruction. After all, it cost nothing, apart from one's reputation, but it was better to have a poor reputation than none at all.

6 AUGUST 1889

Made the acquaintance of Herr Eder, my next-door neighbour. He works as a restorer in the Pinakothek with a Professor So-and-so. He looks as stolid as a wine-waiter, but is first-class at his job, wins prize after prize, and is held in high esteem by his professors. In his room he has some pictures I like, especially an old peasant woman with eyes reddened by weeping.

My work goes ahead very slowly, I spend the whole morning thinking about yesterday's dialogue. It's getting on for evening before I find a solution, and I consequently get very excited.

7 AUGUST 1889

My excitement gets to the point where I draw a picture of a young girl. That is, the context is as follows: the teenager, Marguerite, is brought into the plot. In order to have a clear idea of her, I try to get her down on paper. This excites me beyond belief. During the evening in the HBK I keep thinking of Goethe's distich: Raise your legs to heaven, etc.[35]

8 AUGUST 1889

Marguerite is giving me no end of trouble, although she has precious little to say. I can't get that distich out of my head. Last night in bed I thought of the anecdote from Krafft-Ebing:[36] the Parisian prostitute with the bulldog. I visualize it all in detail, thinking how the girl enters, walking on her hands, and collects money by holding her legs slightly apart. Then she gets monkeys to undress her, the whole point being her total passivity. Then at least three or four bulldogs are driven in and beaten. The girl lives and sleeps with a bitch for the sake of her spiritual aroma. I spend the entire afternoon trying to draw the girl. On the way to the HBK I think of the girl as my own daughter, but only as regards the walking on her hands bit, that I would teach her myself, and in fact teach to all my children at as early an age as possible. A pity that the money-collecting bit doesn't go too well with my role as father. A pity there's a limit there, a pity the whole business encroaches on the area of sex, it would be so nice if it could be done with a proper gravity, with dignity and love.

In the gardens on the Isar island in brilliant moonlight. I think how I would punish my young son by tying him down and letting him lie there for four hours. Such thoughts well up from time to time, like a floodtide at sea. The whole business is like a high tide. Who would have dreamed of this sudden assault? Piccolo, otherwise somnolent, is suddenly painfully sensitive. He won't stand any nonsense. He's up and ready in a trice. Until one o'clock in the Café Central, where I study a midsummer night scene in Puck.

9 AUGUST 1889

The floodtide persists. I wake up thinking of how to punish my lad. After all, he might stick it for a whole day. How cordially I'll compensate him with my affection. My daughter shall learn to walk on her hands to perfection. First of all I'll lift up her legs in the way you play wheelbarrow with children. She'll be dressed in a jersey and short blue pants. Then I'll get her to stand upright with her feet in the air, and I'll put her feet backwards against the wall. In this way she'll get the knack of the thing. Then come the refinements, mainly extending the toes, flexing each knee in turn with weights attached to the toes. NB There is no punishment, only kindly encouragement with a slender switch that I draw across her abdomen. When I was quite small I saw that done once by an itinerant dog trainer who got a Pomeranian to walk on his forelegs by constantly tickling the poor beast's genitals. Then she won't just have to walk on the floor, but up and down a step-ladder, and finally on the table among the crockery.

71

Her sister will learn to walk the tightrope. During the morning I devise another version of the girl I sketched yesterday, then it occurs to me I could add another couple of sketches and make a revolving peep-show. At lunchtime in the Café Luitpold it strikes me that I could add dogs to my peep-show. A dog between each pair of girls. I hurry off home and try to draw the dog, but can't manage it for the moment. Then I do a third version of the girl, but that doesn't come off either. Now I think it's high time to put a stop to this feverish fit. I'm afraid I might go mad in the end. Odd, how it took me so completely by surprise and quite bowled me over. My solitary situation may have played no small part. I'm so defenceless vis-à-vis my work, I'm so spellbound by this idea that I roam aimlessly round the streets. I feel like a criminal as I scuttle past the houses. I can't bear to look anyone in the face. I'm surly and short-tempered with Frau Mühlberger and the waitress. I decide, therefore, to set myself a goal, and write my diary. In the middle of writing it, at the point where I'm describing this urge, it comes over me once again. That shall be the last occasion for some time to come, I trust.

Yesterday I saw Diefenbach's *Höllriegelsgreut*, a major painting.[37] Last night I thrashed the cat.

Power of attorney to Mama. Met nobody in the HBK. Cabaret in the Münchener Kindl with some very nice numbers. In the Café Central until one. At home afterwards worked on the *New Firmament*.

10 AUGUST 1889

Before lunch I have no idea whether it's Friday or Saturday. I've totally lost my bearings. Work on the *Firmament*. Over lunch I'm preoccupied with the idea of inoculating my daughter against anaemia etc., once she's reached the age of eighteen or nineteen: I'd advise her to get some labourer or manservant to come to her room. I'd supply her with a contraceptive, of course.

Only a little done on *Eppur*.[38] Towards evening, the walking-on-her-hands business recurs, but without obsessive force. My spirits have been positively raised by the cabaret in the Münchner Kindl. Once I've left the restaurant, these fantasies seem absurd. Alas, I'm already a shade tipsy. I drink two pale ales in the Café Luitpold, wishing most fervently that Hans Müller might enter all of a sudden.

I'm sure I'd kiss the ground from sheer joy. At home, *New Firma-ment*. All sorts of costume rehearsal.

11 AUGUST 1889

After lunch to the Café Luitpold, busy with *Eppur*, then to the exhibition, where I stay until closing-time. As I step back, immersed in contemplation of a picture, I stand on someone's corns, but can barely manage to stammer an apology as I turn round, because I'm laughing so much. The old lady is hopping round and round on one leg, saying over and over again: I beg your pardon, I beg your pardon. I came too near you.

I go to the Franziskaner for supper, where a young man sits down at my table. He has long, skinny, reptilian fingers, a strongly hooked, prying nose, a vacuous, scowling gaze, and an assortment of grazes on his face. He spends about five minutes cleaning the lid and rim of his tankard. Then he turns his attention to his knife and fork, and finally to his plate. He takes a broth, then orders a beefsteak. At intervals he goes off to consult the directory. He strides through the restaurant with a regular, slightly swaying movement of his elongated torso, placing his feet down noiselessly, as though walking on velvet. When his beefsteak arrives he objects that there are onions with it. He did in fact order onions and an egg with it in the first instance, and now, of course, the waitress has brought him both. After he has given way about the onions after all, he makes a deep cut in the steak and buries his nose in it for five minutes or so, simultaneously prodding the sides of the incision with his knife and fork. Suddenly he withdraws his nose, lays his knife and fork aside, and pushes the beefsteak into the middle of the table. Then he waits until the waitress is passing, summons her, and indicates the beef-steak with his open hand. She understands at once that it's not thoroughly cooked, and takes it away again. On her way to the kitchen she stops again, however, in order to collect some crockery; as she turns, she collides so violently with the apprentice waiter, who is also carrying a pile of dishes, that about ten plates, with or without contents, crash to the floor. 'There goes my beefsteak,' remarks my neighbour to me, not without a spiteful grin. Then he absorbs himself in the *Neueste Nachrichten*, obviously assuming that he'll have to wait a fair time for it. Studying him in this way, it occurs to me that he's even more of a crank than I am, and I'm inclined to respond to him, not without a certain smugness, as a warning and example. I am particularly impressed by the way he wears his thick dark hair so meticulously parted, without a trace of hair-cream, but all the more striking because of its impeccable correctness. The beefsteak returns from the kitchen more quickly than might have been expected, and when he turns it over, sure enough, he finds the old incision. I can't help remarking that it probably hadn't fallen on the floor after all, although I'm well aware how shaky this conclusion is. 'I'd better scrape it off all the same,' retorts the youth, with a sickly grin. In the meantime I've finished my meal with enhanced enjoyment and am looking forward more than ever to my pipe, since an obscure premonition tells me, if anything in the world can drive this man to distraction, then it's my pipe. I don't even give him time to finish eating. With the most elaborate circumstantiality I start my preparations in front of his very eyes, cleaning my pipe, knocking out the dottle and refilling it, then lighting up in the most ostentatious manner. Sure enough, he starts shooting venomous glances at me which I parry airily, as if I were nothing more than a steaming bowl of soup. Seeing that all this is of no avail, he decides to drive out the Devil with Beelzebub, takes out a posh cigarette, lights it, immerses himself once more in the *Neueste Nachrichten*, and starts spitting on the floor after every puff. I'm not to be put off, however, and now a battle for survival ensues between the pipe and the cigarette, a duel to the death. After my pipe has gone out, however, and he sees me instantly getting out my pouch, he reaches for his overcoat and leaves the restaurant, not without treating me to an extremely noble bow.

I go to the Münchner Kindl, where there is little new on offer. Frl. Scholz hasn't even got her white costume on with the long tresses.[39] She comes on, first all in black, and then as an adolescent girl. As I'm leaving the place, the tide surges up once more. I think I'd tie my daughter's legs together, so that she couldn't walk at all, except on her hands. I suffer infernal torments. I resolve that my fate shall depend on whether I meet a female or not. At every street corner I survey the next stretch of pavement in hectic apprehension. I'm quaking with fear, like any young girl, precisely because I would go along without question. But I don't find anyone, and finally fling myself into the Kletzengarten like a shipwrecked mariner at a rock, and meet Bennat there, together with two other gentlemen. Boring small-talk about dramatic art and painting. After we've parted I'm so agreeably aroused that I hope to do some work when I get home. Once I've got there, however, this arousal changes its character, to the effect, indeed, that I have recourse to certain abominable practices. I fall asleep with the beginning of a satirical song for Frl. Scholz in my head.

12 AUGUST 1889

After lunch I lose my way in the Munich suburbs under an overcast sky and end up in the Pfarrauen.[40] Across the river, in Au,[41] a crowd of girls are sitting in front of an apartment house, each with her knitting, and singing 'Stand I in the Darkest Midnight Hour'. In the broad bed of the Isar a couple of slim girls are larking about with a great brute of a dog, sending him into the water and then being pretty well bowled over by him as he brings back the branch they have thrown. Close by the bridge, under overhanging willows, some barefooted lads are engaged in gymnastic antics, leaping over each other's arms and legs, or making 'crabs' by linking their limbs together. In the end I leave the last of the houses behind, and there in front of me, on an embankment that's taller than a house, a church in neo-Gothic style looms up.[42] I go in, glad to have found a place to rest. I esconce myself in one of the two side-aisles, where I'm totally undisturbed. Devout worshippers can see me only if they go all the way up to the high altar. I take out my notebook and carry on with the cabaret number for Frl. Scholz. The chorus runs: 'The golden mean'. Not long after I've entered, a young man sits down opposite me, in the other side-aisle, and doesn't budge from his place as long as I'm in the church. His devotions don't seem to amount to much either. At least, the slovenly way he has slumped down on the seat suggests as much. I suspect he has sought out this snug corner in the house of God so as to be able to pursue his thoughts undisturbed – and to masturbate.

Some students appear in front of the high altar and move in my direction. As I don't turn a hair, they come right up to me, then they walk on. A father leads his two children up to the altar steps, but when he spots me sitting in my corner he sends them back to their pew. A convalescent with a bandaged foot keeps on reciting interminable prayers at one of the side-altars. Finally, an old lady comes in with two handsome children. She leads them from altar to altar, from one Station of the Cross to the next. All three of them kneel down in front of each picture, with the woman in the middle, cross themselves, say a brief prayer and pass on, having once more genuflected before the altar. As I leave the church, a gentle drizzle once more sets in. A steady, mild breeze is blowing across the ridge, and kites may be seen rising here, there and everywhere among the gardens. I walk back to Haidhausen across the rise, and thence via the Quaistrasse and the Maximilianstrasse back home, where I finish my cabaret number. About twelve o'clock at night I meet Bennat in front of the Residenz and accompany him to the Kletzengarten, then back to his apartment. After that I go to the Central for a bare hour.

13 AUGUST 1889

I write in exquisitely polite terms to Frl. Scholz, sending her my composition in the firm belief that she will welcome this contribution. As I do so, I can already imagine myself sitting in the audience. I have invited Bennat to come with me, Bennat having a taste for such unnerving experiences. I have put on my top-hat, so as not to discredit the object of my adoration – adoration is not the right word, it is only her art that I worship – let us say, the lady who enjoys my support. If she were a member of the Court Theatre, I'd leave out the top-hat. But one can't simply ignore the legitimate claims of the relationships one aspires to. So there I am, sitting with Bennat among cobblers and tailors (although the better sort of folk go there, too, incidentally) and revelling in inward ecstasy, without showing the slightest outward sign of it. Frl. Scholz has already performed the number a few evenings previously, so that the regular customers know it by now. And sure enough, after she has performed 'It's Not Just That' and 'It Must Be Just Too Charming' to moderate applause, the cry for 'The Golden Mean' is raised, tentatively at first, in distant corners of the hall, but quickly spreading to the entire audience. The applause swells into an ear-splitting roar, interspersed again and again with that unanimous shout. The entire reaction has something elemental, to be frank, something brutal about it. Bennat turns to me with raised eyebrows and a curt nod: this is going to be hot stuff. He has taken his cigar out of his mouth and knocks the ash from it with an air of infinite superiority. And now she comes on in front of the footlights once again, in her scanty white girlish outfit, with a red sash, long red stockings and a little red hat, making each point just as I had visualized it in performance. The applause positively brings the house down. After it has died down, I turn to Bennat and whisper as casually as possible, indeed, with an incredulous smile: That was by me, actually. My excitement commits itself more or less spontaneously to paper in the form of a young female with sturdy legs holding a large mastiff by the collar. It's only after my blood has simmered down somewhat that I notice that the large mastiff, in relation to the sturdy legs, is actually a little dog, while the girl, thanks to the sturdy legs, is actually a young lad in girl's clothing.

In the Kletzengarten I meet Bennat with a bookseller by the name of Foth, a North German, and an unprepossessing little baron. I watch the play of the billiard balls in the Café Central until after midnight. My interest in the walking-on-her-hands act has much abated.

14 AUGUST 1889

A dull day with light drizzle. After lunch I stroll along the Sendlingerstrasse, which appeals to me especially because of its relatively materialistic appearance. It is positively the busiest street in Munich. Here, the priestesses are out making proselytes, even in broad daylight. All of a sudden I find myself in the South Cemetery. The vast family graves strike me as excessively vulgar. At the entrance to the colonnades a coffin is just being borne to its last resting-place. I push my way nearer just in time to hear the closing words of the blessing. As it's just starting to rain again, I refrain from paying my last respects. As the procession from the mortuary to the grave is forming up, one of the mourners, obviously a close female relative, pushes a young girl – who does in fact look slightly moronic – a few rows further to the rear, swearing at her in the coarsest terms: didn't she know where she belonged, she belonged there. She scolds the girl as if she were within her own four walls. I have scarcely emerged from the colonnades when I spot a second cortège moving down the central avenue at the far end of the cemetery. I quickly join it and arrive together with the mourners at the grave, a family tomb that has only a shallow excavation. After a small coffin has been lowered into the earth, the priest reads out the deceased's particulars. It's an illegitimate child, born to the daughter of a baker and property-owner, that had died only a fortnight after birth, but had undergone Christian baptism, and was hence in a state of innocence. I stand some distance away, doing my honest best to do justice to the ceremony. The priest recites a series of prayers, pausing at intervals in order to cast a shovelful of earth on the coffin, to sprinkle it with holy water, and to swing a censer over the grave. After he has withdrawn, the mourners round the grave throw in wreaths of white flowers, each of them following this up with a shovelful of earth. The ritual act thus looks exactly like a process designed to pickle the white flowers. A little boy of about five with an unhealthy, stupid face is led up to the grave by his mother, so that he can throw in his wreath along with the others. This he does so clumsily that his little sexual organ sticks out through his flies. Evidently the little lad is an uncle of the deceased child. The woman leading him by the hand is in floods of tears. Her husband, presumably the master-baker and property-owner, in his black overcoat and top-hat, having turned away from the open grave, is composed and smiling.

15 AUGUST 1889

Unbelievably vile weather. In the morning I get a letter from Mali, which horrifies me with the news that the bastion is to be demolished.[43] Late in the afternoon I feel very unwell, but nevertheless go to the Residenztheater to see *Nora*.[44] I feel as if I'm going to faint at various points during the performance, and spend the whole of the second act sitting on a folding chair in the foyer. Afterwards in the Kletzengarten.

16 AUGUST 1889

I have a fearful bout of gastric flu, spend the whole day sleeping. Evening in the Kletzengarten all the same, with Spalato. In the course of the following night I read up my case in Niemeyer, and am much comforted thereby. I read the account of Cholera asiatica with sheer delight, being particularly amused by the rice-water stools.

17 AUGUST 1889

Roam round the city until four in the afternoon without eating or drinking a thing. Then I drink a chocolate with supreme relish, stroll along the Maximilianstrasse, and drop in at the Italia late in the afternoon, where I am particularly amused by a nigger dance. The people around me find it outrageous, because the girl, an extremely pretty and very intriguing figure, keeps on leaping into the air at the conclusion of each number, so that her legs, clad in black tights, can be seen all the way up beneath her knee-length skirt. But that's German taste for you. Dirty stories of the crudest kind can be sure of applause. The moment they're faced with something a bit more subtle, the audience are filled with feverish anxiety. They yearn to get back to something sentimental. Three Alpine milkmaids with their sentimental yodelling are greeted with relief, although they sing so off-key that listening to them is enough to give you a sore throat. On the whole I feel very much at home in the cabaret.

18 AUGUST 1889

I've asked Frau Mühlberger to make out my bill, and my money hasn't come. I work all afternoon.

19 AUGUST 1889

I write to Hammi a second time.

20 AUGUST 1889

Frau Mühlberger proves to be very reasonable. I put her off until tomorrow.

21 AUGUST 1889

Still no money, I write a third time. Letter from Minna, in which she maintains she's suffering from an infantile fever. The remittance arrives in the evening.

22 AUGUST 1889

I buy a tie and an umbrella and in the afternoon I go to visit Frl. Herzog, with whom I spend a couple of hours in cosy chat.

23 AUGUST 1889

Evening in the Scholastica, where a very pretty waitress does the honours.

24 AUGUST 1889

Evening in the Monachia. Grand cabaret. Hermaphrodite as a young girl.

25 AUGUST 1889

Evening in the Residenztheater, *A City-dweller. Un Parisien.* I've completed the first act.[45]

26 AUGUST 1889

I dream of Matthäi all night long. He's leading a mysterious life in the sewers and swimming-baths of Munich. I'm searching for him across all kinds of narrow gangways, wading through water at times, and always in pouring rain. I very nearly caught up with him once, in a dilapidated changing cubicle, but he'd just moved on to a café close to the water's edge. The door opens, and a porter brings in a travelling rug and a holdall. Half an hour later Welti arrives. As I lie in bed he washes and tells me that old Rauthenstein has died after having turned childish, that the monastery at Muri has burned down and the Catholics from Freiamt had stood by with their hands in their pockets. – Oh, yes, they were devilish fellows up there. – And that his sister had got engaged to a prosperous industrialist. We toast the event together in cocoa. While he was standing stripped to the waist at the washstand, I could scarcely bring myself to look at him, for fear I might detect something he'd rather I didn't detect. I recalled that he'd always had a marked aversion to public bathing-places. But now I could hardly go on staring straight past him, that's just the sort of thing that would really offend him. So I try my very best, more or less to look through him. And in doing so, sure enough, I notice a lopsided crop of pitchblack hair on his chest, just like Hermann Eichenberger has on his back. What with all this, incidentally, I quite forget to ask after his boils. After he has taken his leave, in order to enfold his fiancée in his arms, I spend the whole morning sitting at my desk in an elated frame of mind, playing the flute. A strange feeling of happiness creeps over me. Not even the thought of the irony of fate can put me off my playing. It seems to me, all at once, as if I weighed only half as much in body and soul. I go off to lunch in this mood, and then to the Café Luitpold, where I don't even dream of picking up a newspaper. At home, I revise the first half of the second act. I feel I can't go on building until the foundations are well and truly laid.

Towards evening Welti arrives with the news that he has to go to the theatre with his fiancée: since he hasn't had a chance to tell Matthäi of his arrival, I eagerly volunteer to go and look him up. So I bolt my supper and set out along the interminably long Hessstrasse. I've forgotten the number of the house, but I do know that it's the last one in the street. In front of me the towers of the artillery barracks loom up against the evening sky. The dreadful noise of someone strumming on a piano comes from a tavern on my left. Seeing it's the last house in the street, I go in.

The beershop is situated in the lobby. The staircase is pitch-dark. Halfway up I bump into a young girl, apparently of slight build, who asks me who I'm looking for. She informs me that Herr Matthäi lives three flights up, on the left. I carry on up and grope my way to the door indicated. After I've rung the bell, the door opens, and a voice from the darkness enquires, who's there? Matthäi has gone out. When he'll be back, the voice doesn't know. That varied a great deal. The voice doesn't know either where he's likely to be found. When I ask if I may leave him a note, I'm admitted to his room, and in the glow from the clear evening sky I can just make out a little old lady with white hair and a round, by no means unprepossessing face. As I look round in vain for a candle, she goes off to fetch a light and comes back with an unlighted lamp, carrying the shade and chimney in her other hand. She hadn't been able to find the matches. I light the lamp at once, and can now take in the narrow, cramped room at a glance. No washstand, no bedside table, no desk, no sofa. Nothing that would offer the least degree of comfort. Only a bed that seems to have practically nothing in the way of blankets, as low as a pallet, a couple of chairs with clothes lying on them, and shelves along the walls with masses of old books. In one corner, next to the window, stands a small table with writing materials very neatly arranged on it. In fact, however, I can find only one hard-black pencil, with which I write my message on a visiting card. I do my very best to contrive a staid but unpretentious style, although I fear in the end I have not expressed myself with sufficient politeness. I scan the card quickly once again and find some mistakes in spelling. No wonder. The landlady is standing right next to me the whole time, holding the lamp and staring at my fingers. What's more, the discordant sound of the piano comes up from the bar, as if it was actually being played in the room. What infernal torments the man must suffer daily in these circumstances!

As the door and the window are both wide open, a brisk draught blows over my head, which is still heated from my rapid walk. I find this so unpleasant that I don't manage to grasp the full import of the penury around me, and subsequently feel ashamed that I've been so preoccupied with myself. After I have spoken a few sentences, the old lady asks me if I'm a Prussian. She had guessed so from the way I spoke. She seems to be thoroughly familiar with Muncker's[46] circumstances. As I learn later from Welti, Matthäi has been travelling around with her for the last ten years, and entrusts all his material concerns entirely to her common sense. She strikes me as being a thoroughly good, stout-hearted woman who would be well worthy of such a position of trust. She knows all there is to know about his friends. Welti she knows, of course, and reckons the theatre management are crazy not to allow Frl. Herzog to get married. After all, Herzog is anything but a raving beauty. As she said, she doesn't know where Matthäi is to be found. If he had been at the theatre he would generally go to the Franziskaner with friends, in order to write a review of the show. I ask whether he writes for a Munich paper. Not for Munich papers, but for papers in Berlin, Hamburg, and so on. She is almost offended by my question. He was very rarely at home. he very often spent the evening with Elias,[47] frequently he went to the Kletzengarten for supper. (Not so badly off after all, then, I think to myself.) He was probably with the family tonight. If he came back early, she would give him my message, but she doubted whether he would come now. Tomorrow was Tuesday, he ate with her then, so that I would no doubt find him.

I take my leave and stroll back along the Hessstrasse as slowly as possible, in the hope that I might still meet him. But since it's barely past eight o'clock, the prospect is pretty remote, and in the end it starts to rain. I'm not inclined to go home, and simply can't think which way to turn. In the end I make for the Scholastica. There's a young girl serving in the Scholastica in whom I recognize the water-sprite from Goethe's 'Fisherman'.[48] Features that are the sheer image of rippling waves, a voluptuous, shapely figure, and a ringing laugh that betrays a certain lack of the profounder sentiments, une certaine froideur du coeur. In fine weather she serves in the garden, wearing a black skirt and a blue cotton bodice with sleeves down to the elbow, a turn-down collar and lace trimmings. She has a lovely, erect walk, and swings her hips ever so slightly. I thought it admirable how she manages to remain so brisk and sprightly until long into the night. Her regular customers, including a number of bald-headed officers, she treats with unflagging joviality. Towards others she behaves in a strictly business-like way. She has a younger sister, incidentally, who works alongside her, is dressed in the same style, and bears a strong family resemblance to her. But in her outward appearance she represents the merest shadow of her sister's splendour, and serves more or less as a foil to her. I take a seat in the middle of the restaurant, order a tankard of beer, and begin to make eyes at my beauty. The girl may well be accustomed to this sort of thing, and, as I notice after a certain time, she decides to bestow her favours on me. When my neighbour wishes to settle his bill, she begins to get confused and is quite unable to add up. He's an old soak, and belongs to the Discharged Prisoners' Aid Society. They'd had very good results with those they'd persuaded to emigrate, he tells one of his acquaintances. A young man and a young girl had been released here in Munich at the same time, in fact, and had emigrated together. They had already got to know each other in prison. They had got married in New York, and were now a prosperous couple. The results with those who stay here are less good. In Haidhausen the Society has its half-way house, where they can stay for a week following their release with absolutely free board and lodging, provided they are back home by eight o'clock in the evening. As soon as they have found work, they can stay out until nine o'clock. They can have free lodgings there for three weeks. Suddenly the old soak is seized with a violent fit of coughing, which reveals that his lungs are full of sputum. He goes as red as a lobster and can barely pull himself together, as the fit is repeated several times over. He gets up to leave as quickly as he can, saying there's too much of a fug here for his liking, says goodbye and goes off.

The waitress finds his beer-mug half full and asks me if the gentleman has gone. I reply that he has settled his score, and suddenly sense that her question was after all nothing more than a mark of her favour. Then I see how she pours the contents of the old consumptive's beer-mug into her own tankard at the bar. She seems to have a healthy thirst, as it is. She has recourse to her mug every couple of minutes or so. But this isn't something that upsets me unduly. It makes the situation somehow more homely. It cuts out sentimentality. No abstract phantoms intrude between my gaze and that admirable bosom. Is the bust genuine? I recoil from this thought with a grimace. Mind you, if it is genuine, then it's truly adorable. The upper contour in particular is as gloriously domed as the Hagia Sophia.[49]

I order another half, and the girl brings me a full measure. That seems to be her way. She did exactly the same with the old stalwart from the Prisoners' Aid. I invite her to join me in a drink. She doesn't like to drink the froth, but she's prepared to stretch a point. For all its beauty, her face no longer has a pristine freshness. I reckon she's about twenty-six. Her name is Fanny, a real water-sprite's name. What are Waltraute, Woglinde, etc., compared to Fanny.[50] Fanny has something sturdy and yet something delicate about it, something naturalistic, it suggests a slender, swift-footed young doe, in a bright, sunlit glade, but at the same time it indicates something of a delicacy. Fanny is a child, and she will remain a child all her life, but a child who will nevertheless play the woman's part with astonishing ardour, when that is what is called for. Fanny is always jaunty, either cheerful or fickle. She is not hot-blooded, but she is sensual. He who holds her in his arms will shrink from any obscenity. One has the feeling that one is inseminating one's own body. At the same time one is constantly concerned that the lovely voluptuous limbs might be nothing but some magical hocus-pocus and might suddenly melt away into nothingness.

In the Kletzengarten I come across Welti in the company of Hahn and some other gentlemen I don't know.[51] Matthäi hasn't come. He [Welti] tells us that the orchestra here is better than in Berlin, but that the drama is better in Berlin. He didn't like the new Shakespeare production any more than the photographer Hahn did. They both declare it's no good, without giving the least reason. He thinks Bonn's Fool is too whining. I remark that the Fool was whipped, to which he can find no answer, without for that reason being inclined to change his opinion. I ask Hahn about the art-dealer Weyer from Leipzig, whom he claims not to know. He says that no doubt Weyer had told me any number of evil things about him. After midnight Bennat stalks in and joins us, and Welti tells us once more, for Bennat's benefit, that the drama is better in Berlin, but the orchestra worse. The trouble was that they had had to play too much ballet music under Kaiser Wilhelm I. Betz was still an excellent singer. It was well known with what degree of objective detachment he, Welti, stood above a work of art during its performance, but when Betz sang the hermit in *Der Freischütz* he had been on the verge of tears. Bennat behaves very calmly, in spite of their prolonged separation. Ultimately he remarks that it was just as if he, Welti, had never been away. No wonder, their friendship in fact has never extended beyond the limits of a table in a tavern.

On the way home Welti tells me that Frl. Herzog would like me to come to tea at five o'clock next day. The Kletzengarten beer has given him heartburn. As I have no bicarbonate of soda, I give him some hydrochloric acid to drink. As a result his heartburn gets so acute that he scarcely knows what to do. I take him across to his room and keep him amused as he gets undressed. Having undressed down to his shirt, he thinks he can feel a boil on his bottom. I at once inspect the place and assure him it's nothing but a flea-bite, whereupon he goes to bed. He had to laugh, particularly when I told him how Muncker was embarrassed when I confessed to him that I was concerned with the drama. As for the Kaulas, Muncker was as good as engaged to the daughter. Muncker wasn't as bad as I thought he was, by the way. He was even capable of quite unselfish acts. I wish him good night, and can't help laughing at the hydrochloric acid treatment when I get back to my room. I sleep extremely badly.

27 AUGUST 1889

Welti comes over about nine. As all yesterday's beer is still sloshing around in my belly, I stay in bed and sleep until nearly one o'clock, once Welti has made himself some cocoa and gone away again. Then I get up laboriously and go to lunch in as gingerly a manner as I can, then to the barber, then to a café, and finally back home to get changed. It's been pouring with rain all day long. Late in the afternoon the sky clears a little. I go to Schwabing at five, anxiously worried that I may arrive too early, and, on the other hand, worried that this worry may make me late. I am received by Frl. Herzog II, who is pleased to see me, regrets she didn't see me last time, and apologizes for not having asked me to tea before now. In the drawing-room I find Matthäi and Welti sitting side by side. I apologize at once to Matthäi in case my note yesterday had turned out somewhat muddled, as I put it. Matthäi has no more than a moment to spare, as a lady is expecting him at the theatre at six o'clock. Frl. Herzog hasn't arrived yet, she's been invited to coffee by Frau Blank. Phylax is lying under the table, and has the merit of serving from time to time as a life-raft for the conversation. Matthäi and Welti are already deeply engrossed in a literary discussion. They are long since out of sight of any normal eye. I therefore confine my attention to Frl. Herzog II, thus making sure that I don't mar the conversation of the others.

Frl. Herzog II speaks as if she had her mouth full of porridge. She talks a good deal all the same, and gives me the impression of being a very silly person. What she thought she was doing on the stage in her time becomes more and more of a mystery to me. I mention *The Power of Darkness*,[52] and she asks me if that's the story where the hero commits suicide right at the beginning. She's thinking of Raskolnikoff,[53] in fact. As Frl. Herzog still shows no sign of turning up, Matthäi finally gets to his feet. He can't keep the lady waiting any longer. Welti urges him to return straight away, which he promises to do. I have spoken to him only once, to ask him whether he is perhaps familiar with *The Power of Darkness*. He assures me he knows it very well, but was it perhaps a drama or something of the sort? After his departure the conversation turns to the art exhibition, to a large painting by Jokisch in fact,[54] in which a female martyr lies naked on the sea-shore, with her hands bound and her head and feet extended into the foreground, so that her posterior, relegated to the background, appears to be raised up. Welti had taken offence at this posterior. He now goes to great lengths to explain the reasons for this fact to Frl. Herzog II, who, for her part, advances the most trite

86

phrases. The point is that she's in love with Jokisch. Years ago he had had the room next to her and her sister. He's in love with her sister, of course, but as he has been turned down by her, she, the other sister, had fallen for him, but he, for his part, is not in love with her. Frl. Herzog, incidentally, has had two pictures painted by him, 500 marks apiece, which are still hanging in her drawing-room. Welti is beginning to complain loudly that he's hungry, when the bell at the garden gate rings.

Two voices become audible. One belongs to Frl. Weckerlin, who has seen Frl. Herzog home. In spite of the pouring rain, Herzog accompanies her a few hundred paces back again. Then Weckerlin accompanies Herzog back once more to the garden gate. The bell rings a second time. Then come the goodbyes, with both of them talking non-stop at the same time, of course. Shortly afterwards Frl. Herzog comes into the small drawing-room in a very tasteful black lace dress with gold trimmings. The gossip round the coffee table has induced a euphoric mood. She makes a subdued sort of entrance, gazing straight ahead, as though still under the spell of some inner inspiration, and allows Welti and her two sisters to remove her hat and shawl. Finally she flings herself down on the sofa in a state of perfect bliss. No, how Weckerlin had bitched, how she'd abused Dressler![55] And the language she'd used! Last week Dressler had turned up for the piano rehearsal dead drunk. Levi had said he wasn't there to be made a fool of.[56] Oh, she drank all right! She drank to keep her courage up. And not just champagne, she was long past that. She was on to spirits. Welti, who had managed to get himself a welcome kiss by dint of considerable efforts when she first entered, claims that he had raised his hat to Dressler that very day. 'You never did!' interjects Frl. Herzog. He had met her, had been on the point of speaking to her, but had in the end walked past, after greeting her politely. Herzog recounts the story of the schnaps with the sort of rapture with which a young wife might announce to her husband that she feels she is pregnant. First of all she had settled down comfortably, then leaned forward towards Welti's ear, made several false starts, clearly feeling a shade embarrassed after all, then finally burst out with it.

We proceed to tea as rapidly as possible. Welti claims he's extraordinarily hungry after seeing all that flesh in the annual exhibition and yet not being able to eat it. Amongst other topics,

Phylax is the subject of conversation: this morning he had been measured for a muzzle, in preparation for his sojourn in Berlin. He had pulled a very odd face at the sight of it. Now he is to get a handsome collar with bells on it as well. Welti objects to this, because of the incessant tinkling. I ask her if she's not afraid it will make the dog nervous. She thinks there is nothing to fear on those grounds. Matthäi arrives. He has had a shave, and had very nearly fallen full length in the mud as he was getting off the tram. In connection with the vanity of Matkovsky,[57] who throws every female a glance, as if to say: My profoundest sympathy!, Matthäi tells a story about an officer in Danzig. He doesn't tell the story badly, but he's long-winded. After the opening sentences Welti's interest is captured by Phylax, who is alleged to have fouled Herzog's dress. Herzog reckons it's because he hasn't been outside today. Matthäi carries on doggedly with his story. I've noticed on a number of occasions that Welti is incapable of listening in company. He has no powers of observation, either. The one thing may very well follow from the other. If someone else starts talking at some length, then he gets restive and begins looking desperately round for some cause that will excuse his restlessness, i.e. assume the responsibility for it.

After taking tea we go back into the drawing-room, where Herzog sings. Matthäi suggests the little room is liable to be burst open by her voice, whereupon Welti opens the door to the adjoining room, and the window there. Matthäi asks for Mozart's 'Cradle Song', to which Welti plays the accompaniment, not without being soundly scolded, of course, for his pains. I find the blaring quality of Herzog's voice – 'blaring' is not the right expression, because her voice has nothing disagreeable about it, scarcely a trace of tremolo, in spite of its power – I find its resonance very appealing. It seems to me like the jet of a shower-bath, compared to an ordinary, refreshing bath. In conclusion she sings a poem by Stieler,[58] and requests the gentlemen to compose a second verse to it, since she couldn't sing it in public in its present form. Both the others scornfully reject the suggestion. I promise to do my best. As he's leaving Matthäi calls out some mocking remark to me, but in doing so neglects to say goodbye to Frl. Herzog II.

After he has gone, I tease Welti about various remarks he made to me concerning Heine and Byron. Herzog indicates to me by an encouraging smile that she is pleased at this skirmish. About nine o'clock, each of us lights a cigarillo, and I accompany Welti to the theatre. We are one heart and one soul. He describes how he felt when he saw Munich again, how the various houses where he'd lived had acquired a historical interest, and how, when he saw it all again, he was reminded of his arrival in Munich as a totally innocent fresher (he doesn't use this expression), with his little school cap, having seen absolutely nothing of the world, and how the theatre had become a decisive element in his development. He's going to the theatre to listen to Frl. Pewni as the Woodland Bird. He has to give a report to Frl. Herzog. In the meantime I go to the Franziskaner and meet Matthäi there, together with Dr Buchholz, the secretary and literary manager of the Munich Court Theatre. The conversation revolves around Dr Wörner in America, and other topics I'm not familiar with. Then Welti turns up and tells us that the drama is better in Berlin, the orchestra, on the other hand, worse, and then various artists are put through the mill. Matthäi turns to me now and again, and draws my attention to a little girl sitting opposite who keeps staring at us solemnly. As soon as she notices we are watching her, however, she very quickly shows initial signs of gauche affectation and posing. I am positively delighted with Matthäi's friendliness and his interest in facial expressions. I restrain my enthusiasm, so as not to put him off. Meanwhile, Welti and Buchholz are knocking the stuffing out of a new Goethe edition by Erich Schmidt.[59] Welti has to be back at the theatre by eleven o'clock.

We separate, and Welti and I make our way to the Kletzengarten, where the musicians welcome us with every conceivable sign of cordiality – in the first place, Kutschenreuter and Scherzer, then Ölgärtner, Lehner, Rauftler and Brummer.[60] The people Welti's looking for, i.e. Bennat and Sander, don't put in an appearance, it's true, but the atmosphere is very lively all the same. Kutschenreuter even takes the liberty of proposing a toast to Welti's fiancée, but he takes no notice. In spite of all Kutschenreuter's joviality, Welti still doesn't deem him worthy of that privilege. On the other hand, he tells us once again that the theatre is better in Berlin, but the orchestra is worse, and that's because the musicians had to play so much ballet under the old Emperor,[61] and because there was opera, evening after evening. Then the local conductors, absent colleagues, März, Bayreuth, Cosima and Siegfried are roundly abused,[62] and about midnight we part with best wishes for the future and many a hearty handshake. Welti doesn't seem to feel as let down by Bennat's failure to turn up as I had supposed. In front of the street-door he asks me for bicarbonate, and when I reply that I've got a whole packet upstairs, he makes some remark about being considerate, which I take to refer to a cab which has just stopped across the street. In my room I make him some cocoa, and someone hammers on the ceiling below. I instantly grab my stick and bang back. Welti goes off to bed. I'm very worked up, and so I pace backwards and forwards for some time still.

28 AUGUST 1889

Since Welti finds me still in bed, he goes to the Café Minerva, in order not to waste time. I sleep until half past eleven, and when I get back from the café, I find him in front of the street-door with all his bags and baggage. Herzog has insisted after all that he should travel with her, for the sake of Phylax, if for no other reason. This or that might happen, and there she would be, all alone with the dog. But he wanted to down a glass of good Munich beer before leaving, so off we go to the Deutsches Haus. I've always noticed that, when you're parting from someone for some length of time, and hence presumably have a great deal to say to each other, then you generally don't know what to say. You're lucky if at least you're not obliged to say something befitting the occasion, but can pass over the parting in silence, as if it were more or less taken for granted. That is in fact what happens in the Deutsches Haus. We talk about Baste and her companion, until at last Welti assures me after all that a letter from me would always be welcome, that I should let him hear from me now and then, since I had more free time than him: he had, firstly, to earn his daily bread, and, apart from that, he had to fetch and carry – I would know what he meant – actually had to fetch and carry. He says 'apporten', but what he really means is 'apportieren', and has in fact picked the only accurate expression, but he speaks with an utter lack of resentment, such as I wouldn't have believed the most infatuated lover capable of. It appears to be part of his function, not only to be his wife's husband, but also actually to be her errand boy. He obviously feels happy in this role. It affords him the same satisfaction as other idealists find in rescuing the object of their affections from some danger or other at the risk of their own lives. Who would have suspected that an altruist of this kind would emerge from such a boastful subjectivist. At the station we meet Herzog I, II and III, II holding Phylax in her arms. Welti and I carry the luggage into a compartment where a gentleman is sitting together with his mother. He has barely set eyes on the dog before he starts to growl, but then says that we should ask his mother. But this remark is ignored by all concerned. The three Frl. Herzogs are in floods of tears. It doesn't occur to Welti either to put in a conciliatory word on behalf of Phylax. Frl. Herzog I and II and I say goodbye to each other, and, as they are being conducted back to their compartment by friends who arrived later on, I say my final farewells. I stroll slowly off in the direction of my apartment. On the Maximiliansplatz, in front of the Goethe monument, it occurs to me that I saw Goethe as large as life last night. He was dressed in a light-coloured costume of his own period. His figure he had taken from the actor Matkowsky in Berlin. A strange glow emanated from this apparition, as from the body of Christ in Rembrandt's *Burial of Christ*. All of a sudden I recall that today is Goethe's birthday.

29 AUGUST 1889

First half of Act I revised.[63]

30 AUGUST 1889

Finished revising. Lazed around.

31 AUGUST 1889

Lazed around.

1 SEPTEMBER 1889

I decided yesterday to go and visit Dr Elias. The purpose I mainly have in mind is concerned with Matthäi. I haven't the faintest notion of an idea for the opening of the second act. I could well do with some sort of stimulus, then. So I put on my top-hat and go to lunch in the Kletzengarten. To my joyful surprise I am joined there by Matthäi. The subject of conversation is Jungdeutschland,[64] for which he expresses his scorn in the plainest terms.

After we have left the restaurant, I ask him if he's going to a café. Certainly, would I perhaps join him in a game of chess? – I say I'm no hero on the chess-board. – He had forgotten to put on a tie. Otherwise he looks extremely smart and respectable. On our way to the Café Karlstor, near the synagogue, we are accosted by an old woman. She'd been running around here for the last three hours, her children were on the Promenade. Did we know where she could get something to eat, but with Jews, of course, and not too expensive. Matthäi asks me if I'll come along, and we escort the woman to a Jewish retaurant near the Löwengrube, where, as Matthäi tells me later, probably the best food in Munich is to be had. The woman is from Cracow and has just arrived this morning from Vienna with a letter to the local rabbi. He'll then give her further directions for her journey. She's on her way to America, in fact, together with her children.

Matthäi is probably even more shortsighted than Tomarkin, although he only uses no. 5 lenses. That's why he fails to see all sorts of things, as, for example, Frl. Herzog II, when he was saying goodbye out there at their apartment. The chess-board seems incredibly unfamiliar to me. I simply can't get my bearings. Matthäi is clearly bored to tears. But since Dr Bernheim, with whom he'd have liked to play another game, has already departed, he suggests we play again, on condition that he doesn't take any of my pieces. But it soon turns out that this is not feasible. So then he makes me a present of his queen, whereupon I am lucky enough to beat him. We play another game of the same kind, and I beat him again. I then accompany him home. Fortunately, it is by now too late to call on Dr Elias. Matthäi questions me about the state of affairs in Zürich, whether Switzerland didn't have a standing army, just in case the Socialists took it into their heads to set fire to the city. I ask him what sort of ideas he has about the Socialists. In connection with the Rambergstrasse,[65] I tell him how a friend of mine had thrown himself off the Mythen because he was in love with his landlady.[66] He found it incomprehensible, says Matthäi, how anyone could take his own life for love. Shortage of cash, yes. But for love?

He goes off to call on a director's wife whom he hasn't seen for three weeks, while I dart into a confectioner's to calm my nerves, and then enjoy the twilight in the Englischer Garten before taking supper at home. I feel utterly worn out and instantly fall asleep on the sofa.

When I wake up I'm in such a solemnly exalted frame of mind that I have no desire to go out for a beer. So I go to bed, although it has only just turned ten. The first time for as long as I can remember that I've gone to bed before midnight.

2 SEPTEMBER 1889

After lunch I take a walk out as far as Menterschwaige.[67] As I'm sitting there with my beer, a whole gaggle of geese come up to me and start to beg most importunately. It seems to me that the main feature of the goose's character is 'godfearing impertinence'. The bare-faced insistence with which they accost you demonstrates this, as does their garrulousness, their mild demeanour. Whether the goose is more stupid than other birds, I wouldn't care to say. It's true that their fondness for noise, their own noisy behaviour give grounds for this assumption. Their facial features suggest it as well, the way the eye is set so high up, with a correspondingly low brow and an incredibly flat skull. If you place the eye equally high up on a human profile, you will observe the same effect. The goose's profile, incidentally, is Greek. Caricatures of a Greek profile will always bear a striking resemblance to that of the goose. The swan's profile is marked by the way the beak begins low down, with a correspondingly rounded brow and a deep-set eye. These features give the swan that gravely pensive expression which stands in the same relation to the Greek profile as the heads of Andrea del Sarto's Madonnas to those of Raphael. The conversation of geese as they sit round in a circle suggests more sense than the conversation at a ladies' coffee party. In the case of geese, only one cackles at a time, whereas, with a coffee party, at least half of those present are talking at the same time. The geese's cackling also manifests the most diverse and extremely expressive variations and appears to have a particularly insistent character because the speaker usually addresses a particular member of the assembled company, who thrusts her head towards the speaker with equal eagerness. Hence, we may well conclude that the cackling is not simply an expression of the speaker's own feeling, but is also intended to convey this feeling to someone else. If you look closely, you will find it is distinctly inflammatory in character. It's only when their excitement is stirred up to an even higher pitch by some intrusive incident or other that the geese gabble in chorus.

Suddenly the loud cry of a goose is heard from behind the house, whereupon all those present put their heads together and start to cackle. All at once they rise together as if at a given signal, burst out into a heart-rending cry, beat their wings, line up in single file, and rush as fast as they can towards the spot the cry came from. But however strident the screaming of a gaggle of geese may be, it stops instantly at the sound of the sibilant: Pst! This 'Pst!' seems to have a physiological effect on the organs: its efficacy is not derived merely from convention. I was reminded of the medical student Gehring in hospital: he lay night and day in a lethargic coma and kept on groaning every time he drew a breath. While he totally failed to respond in any way to argument and to pleas not to disturb the other patients, his groaning would cease the moment someone called out: Pst! The waitress gives the geese scraps of bread, remarking as she does so that the female member of the company picks them delicately from her hand, while the males simply snatch them from her. She's just a real lady, she says. This lady bears the fitting and characteristic name of Gretchen. The waitress addresses the others as 'louts', just as the keeper in the Berlin Tiergarten addressed the royal tiger. I walk to Grosshesselohe through the glorious evening, take the tram back to Munich, stroll down the Neuhauserstrasse and finally drop into the Münchner Kindl. The restaurant is fairly empty and the guests a dull crew. I take a seat right in front of the stage and am able to appreciate Frl. Scholz's handsome legs at my leisure. At home I wash from head to foot, and the water turns the colour of Salvator beer.

3 SEPTEMBER 1889

I'm tormented by bugs all night, and when the little beasts retreat to their lairs towards morning, the carpenter starts laying a new floor in the adjoining room. So I get up in something of an ill temper, especially as it's unbearably hot. After I've lunched in the sweat of my brow, I go to the Schack Gallery,[68] where I'm particularly intrigued by Genelli's ingenious compositions. There's a bold Naturalism in these unabashed nymphs, in these faintly demonic, hunchbacked *amoretti*. It is all nevertheless very relaxed and suggestive of complete intellectual freedom. Over a period of years I had imagined Tintoretto's *Venezia* to be a good deal more attractive than she actually is. Her physique, it's true, does in fact correspond to my memory of it.

On the other hand, I find that her facial features have aged, as if the years had been *lustra*. I spend a long time in front of Andrea del Sarto's *Madonna*. This is indeed a girl on whose brow the Holy Spirit shone. She would be to my taste. The intelligent gravity in these features appeals a thousand times more strongly to me than the love in those of the Sistine Madonna. I imagine Anna Launhardt in the image of this Holy Virgin. If I'd been Andrea del Sarto, I'd have got the girl to study medicine. Faced by Titian's *Lavinia*,[69] I feel faintly embarrassed. At first I can only look at her furtively, from the side, but I do like her. I'm only afraid she might step out of the picture. As I'm leaving the Gallery I see an elderly lady, accompanied by an even more elderly gentleman, descending the stairs from the Schwind room.[70] Pointing to Michelangelo's *Creation of Man* on her right, she says, 'Is that Adam? – He's far too young for Adam, Adam looks older than that.' The gentleman, who is already a picture ahead of her, replies, 'Look, that's Alarich, they're lowering him into the cesspit.' In the meantime the lady has seen the Visitors' Book lying on the table, and says in a rather offhand manner, 'Aren't you going to sign the book?'

In the garden of the Glyptothek I find an opening for the second and third act at last. I spin out the thread a bit further sitting on a bench in the Maximilianstrasse. Go home for supper, and the return to the Café Roth, where I take up the thread once again.

4 SEPTEMBER 1889

After lunch I go down into the meadows by the Isar under an overcast sky, eagerly occupied with E.,[71] but am suddenly overtaken about six by a violent thunderstorm, dash into a confectioner's, and go on about seven to the Gärtnertheater. They're doing *The Bells of Corneville*.[72] This is an operetta that treats a pleasantly romantic theme in charming and sprightly tunes. I still remember as if it were yesterday, how delighted Schaffner was ten years ago when he saw it performed in some flea-pit in Aarau. Frl. Meininger, with her dark eyes and Greek profile, is a fairly passable soubrette, especially when viewed from the front. In profile the tip of her nose droops and is drawn in when she laughs. Then there's no mistaking the Jewess. What I particularly like about Frl. Meininger is the graceful way she has of placing those small feet of hers. As Germaine she's dressed in a

95

close-fitting bodice and a blue skirt of medium length that reaches halfway down her calf. This calf, however, is slender rather than plump, perhaps because it is covered with a black stocking. Black or red tights make the legs seem slimmer than they really are, while blue, white, or flesh-coloured tights have the opposite effect. It would certainly produce an unpleasant effect if two stout calves were to emerge beneath the slender bodice. Meininger can't sing, she's no nightingale. But she is a lark, she twitters quite prettily, and her voice is not unpleasant in any register. Until twelve o'clock in the Franziskaner.

5 SEPTEMBER 1889

The number five seems to me to bear some resemblance to the actor Davideit.[73] I don't really know why: does Davideit bear any sort of resemblance to a five? That doesn't appear to be the case. For, if I want to compare this five with something else, it reminds me of an ancient Pharaoh. And this one reminds me of Hammi. I dreamt of Papa again last night. He was so meek. He didn't say a single word about all the things that have happened since he died. He only wished he'd been allowed to live out his few years in peace. There was indeed something spectral about him, especially in the timidly furtive way he whispered his request. He seemed to be afraid that, if other people joined us, they would drive him away. He was standing among his antiques in the central room of the far wing, where during his lifetime the large table had been set up with the armour, and the antlers, and the cabinet with the Turkish muskets. And now I can remember quite distinctly how it all happened. I was standing at the table opposite the window and fumbling with the curtains. He entered quickly through the door on the right with his customary springy walk, wearing a black jacket of thin material and altogether somewhat casual in his attire. He took no more than a couple of steps into the room and looked nervously at both doors. From there he threw me such a beseeching look that I felt a lump rise in my throat. And yet I didn't even move towards him.

It's a strange sort of hermit's life I lead now. Once again I haven't spoken a word to a living soul since Sunday, and I probably won't have a chance to do so before next Sunday. But I've got used to that. I'm not dying for human companionship in the way I was during my first few weeks here. In fact I'm mostly engaged in very lively conversation with some acquaintance or other. On my way back from the theatre last night I had a talk with Schaffner. I did everything I could to revive the old intimacy between us. I spoke Swiss German. And so we sat for something like half an hour in the same booth in the Ratskeller where I had a farewell drink with Welti four years ago. I spend a few hours with Thomar almost every day: but we never quarrel as we so often used to. We are always one heart and soul, and laugh at our own jokes with a certain sentimentality. A few days ago I recited Henckell's 'Emergency Law' to him in Henckell's manner.[74] He roared with delight, clapped, corrected me here and there in his baroque manner, and his large eyes were inflamed and filled with tears. When we met again after my triumphs, I asked him straight away to do me a favour. Otherwise he wouldn't have found it in his heart to associate with me on our former footing. He would have searched and searched until he detected some sign that I wasn't the same man I had been before my success. Then he would have turned his back on me, with regret, but with an insurmountable feeling of disgust, even supposing he had been totally dependent on my company. Whereas my relationship with Thomar is tranquil and cordial, my relationship with Matthäi is assuming a critical aspect. Every time I've met him since last Sunday the same subject has cropped up, and on each occasion I've grown excited and been carried away, in spite of myself. I kept citing Welti as an example when I talked to him. Generally speaking, Welti has to serve in this way pretty often. As far as he's concerned, I'm very near to conceiving what Thomar calls a speechless fury. Matthäi still remains the same, cool, grave individual. At noon today I came across him sitting on a bench under the trees by the Alte Pinakothek. During our conversation I ventured to crack a joke, but it slid off him like water off a bronze statue, leaving not a trace behind. The reason for this fiasco may, it's true, lie in a certain servile diffidence with which I conducted the experiment. About three o'clock yesterday morning I was sitting with Pariser and someone else in the H B K and I suggested to Pariser he should make a bet with me that I would, or, as the case might be, wouldn't become Matthäi's closest friend within six weeks. On condition only that he shouldn't give me away to Matthäi before the expiry of that period. Afterwards he could say whatever he liked, since, assuming I'd won the bet, I would be able to parry that stroke as well.

In the meantime I'm still most diligently occupied with the question of my daughter's education. One thing is certain now, as far as I'm concerned: much as I have appreciated city life during the last few years, if ever I settle down somewhere for good, either with a family, or as a recluse, or as Ali Baba Pasha of Janina, then it will be in the country, preferably in Switzerland, preferably in the lovely Aargau, and preferably, above all, in Lenzburg, but since that probably won't be feasible, then opposite the Lenzburg, in Wildenstein.[75] Wildegg I find a dreary hole.[76] On the other hand, I would like to live and die in Wildenstein, specifically to die on the broad, gravelled terrace facing west, opposite the setting sun, the misty blue range of the Jura, and the silvery gleam of the Aare down in the valley below. There I would find everything that makes life comfortable and, above all, space, plenty of space, and an Elysian calm. There my children would romp to their heart's content, as we once did in the Feldheim and the Kastler valleys, down on the broad meadow where we once played football with the Drummonds,[77] where they would fly their kites. And in winter I would have a stage erected for them in one of the spacious halls of the castle, where they could put into practice whatever their imagination gave birth to. To be precise, however, I wouldn't want more than a single daughter. I've been thinking about a name for her, but still haven't found one. For my part, I would probably call her Mali. It goes without saying that she's clever. Above all, she must be beautiful like her model, her aunt. When her aunt comes to visit now and again, she won't notice the resemblance, but the child will take her fancy, so I will be doubly proud. Mali is not to grow up like a wild rose. Mali is to learn as early as possible that life is a serious business, but without having to forfeit thereby the freshness of youth. She is to become, not poorer, but richer than other girls. I'll send her to the poor of Feldheim,[78] she'll have to report to me on their plight, and I'll hand over what I have, for her to share out. I'll train her to read to me as soon as possible, whether she understands what she's reading, or not. She must feel that she is no more than a means to an end. Her own interest will be responsibly stimulated in this way. I won't have her learn to play the piano, but the mandolin, on which she will accompany her mother's or her own singing in the long winter evenings. In short, I'll urge her as far as possible to live for the enjoyment of her fellow-creatures, so that she'll be endowed with the happiest childhood any person can possibly have, a childhood particularly rich and happy in memory, and that is, after all, the main thing. And from the first dawning of consciousness her very own spiritual life will unfold within her, independent of us all, untrammelled as a god, autonomous, childishly fanciful combinations of elements of reality, an innocent and innocuous patrimony which will not vanish without trace, like some trivial trumpery concocted from fairy-tales and tinsel, for once the body has developed to its harmonious maturity, once aspirations have assumed a more positive character, then an integrated sphere of ideas, at least equally harmonious, will be born from that womb, a sphere of ideas which embraces the nocturnal side of life, as well as its bright side, without being thereby dimmed, or even sullied.

In the recesses of my soul I still cherish one secret, heartfelt wish; but the atmosphere seems to me to be too hallowed for this wish to be spoken aloud. And yet it is as innocent as this entire figment of my imagination, and it also has the merit of having served as the point of departure for this digression. It is simply the perpetual repetition of the same old theme, but nevertheless: honour to him, to whom honour is due. On that terrace facing west, on the battlements of the turret, in the corridors, in the staircase to the tower, in the courtyard and garden I would have Mali walk in the black costume of a pageboy. Possibly the only consequence would be that she would have more occasion to have regard to physical grace than girls by and large do these days, seeing that they wear long skirts. You only have to look at their legs when they're sitting down, especially. If the eye, thirsting for beauty, glides down from a pretty face to an even prettier bodice, and finally arrives enraptured at the legs, then it might well be nauseated, were that possible, by the sight of legs awkwardly sprawled every which way, that evoke the same sense of revulsion as an old pair of shoes that some drunkard has flung into a corner of an evening.

Subject for a drama: In spite of his poverty, an artist supports a model who comes to borrow from him every now and then. (Painter, sculptor) lives in extreme penury. His friend explains to him the axiom that there is no such thing as an unrecognized genius. To the girl with whom he's lived together for years, he states that he can carry on for years as things are at the moment. But if the good fortune he has longed for should now arrive – he won't guarantee not to go off his head. At the close of the first act his luck does in fact turn. By sheer chance he wins a competition, and the critics declare him to be immortal. Ladies of the highest rank fight for the privilege of sitting for him. In the second act he gives full rein to his love of luxury. The girl proposes to leave him, she will be nothing but a handicap for him now. He makes her the very centre of his happiness. But signs of megalomania begin to appear. In the last act this megalomania bursts out on the occasion of the wedding. His last words are: If only I don't go mad.

After lunch I go to the Alte Pinakothek, where I actually devote my attention mainly to the visitors. In the last gallery on the right I see a girl with a slender figure and clean-cut features pressed into a corner with a sketchbook in which she is making a sketch of the picture opposite. She seems to find my gaze irksome and is on the point of closing her sketchbook. I move away with a certain feeling of admiration and wonder whether I, too, might not perhaps be able to compile a collection of reminiscences of this kind. I'm sure it would give me enormous pleasure, and, after all, there would be more to be learned in that way than through the perpetual repetition of the same airy phantoms I commit to paper day by day. When I see how the girl shields her attempts from prying eyes with an almost chaste gesture, it inspires me with the confidence to do the same in a similar embarrassing position. She must have excellent eyesight, incidentally, to be able to take up her stance so far away from her model. An Englishwoman, I imagine.

Making my way through the Dutch collections, I encounter another pair of Englishwomen. In their company is a lad of about fifteen with a very poor posture and not a trace of youthful freshness in his features. He has a strongly marked profile, but there is no particular intelligence in his look, for all that; he is unusually pallid and has a weary, lack-lustre, expressionless eye. His legs, on the other hand, are distinctly handsome, being clad in grey shorts, black stockings and sensible laced shoes with patent leather uppers. His legs are not affected by his slovenly posture. His gait is not at all ungainly, he keeps his knees taut, and from time to time swivels round on his toes. As for the pictures, he doesn't subscribe to the same taste as his female companions. In front of certain pictures which they pass by as if they simply weren't hung there, he pauses for a relatively long time, keeping his left hand constantly in his pocket. I

Wedekind's sister Erika as Susanna in Mozart's *Marriage of Figaro*.

follow him through the Dutch collections and through all the other rooms, as far as the exit.

I turn back then to find my girl with the sketchbook. I find her sitting on a divan gazing fixedly at a character study of a man's head. I sit down back to back with her, exchange a wordless greeting with Angelika Kauffmann,[79] turn round and watch my fair one over my shoulder. An elegant little white hat with a sharply turned up brim trimmed in pale blue velvet is perched on her thick, darkish blonde hair. I devote my rapt attention to the expressive line of her half-profile, which reveals no more of the eye than the eyelashes. But the grave sagacity of those projecting lashes! While I'm still marvelling at this sight and seeking to grasp it, she raises her left hand, bends her fingers inwards and puts them to her lips in a gesture that is not exactly elegant. The large window that lights the room is on the right. The light floods through the hollow of her hand, illuminating its entire inner surface and casting a hundred little shadows. A sight for the gods. Her hand is not unduly small, nor is it large, but in this position, under this lighting, it has a vitality such as I have never before observed in youthful hands. The folds that cast stark shadows and reflections here are not those of age, nor yet those of manual labour. They are the unadulterated, untrammelled expression of a transcendental spirituality. The little finger is not extended, the ring finger is not elegantly crooked, there is no grace, much less any concession to custom. This hand is, in the most literal sense of the word, spiritualized. Hence its beauty. The experience, incidentally, lasts for no more than a couple of seconds.

6 SEPTEMBER 1889

I buy a sketchbook, a no. 1 pencil and an eraser – and find both the galleries closed. During the course of the morning a wedding was to have taken place in the Ludwigskirche. As the couple belong to the highest ranks of society, a crowd gathers. The priest is already standing at the altar, when the ceremony is cancelled. In the meantime, however, a little pinscher, a positively delightful little beast, has fallen mortally in love with Frau Mühlberger's Bella, and follows her into the kitchen. Not only does Bella show total indifference to his advances, she turns out to be hypocritical and wicked. Her handsome suitor prances round her with helplessly imploring looks, and she permits him to approach her time after time, only to snap at him then without warning. This doesn't have the slightest effect on the pinscher, only his gaze grows a shade more forlorn. Frau Mühlberger, who genuinely feels sorry for him, finally shuts Bella up in the adjoining closet. The pinscher lies down on the threshold. Soon, however, he jumps up, runs to Frau Mühlberger, who is busy in the front room, and throws her beseeching glances. For two whole hours he does all he can to touch Frau Mühlberger's heart – fawning, standing on his hind legs and barking indignantly. Every so often he runs back to Bella's prison for a moment or two, so as to piddle briefly against the doorpost, but then resumes his efforts again. Finally Frau Mühlberger can stand it no longer and decides to risk another attempt at conciliation. The good woman is close to tears. But Bella shows herself to be not a whit less vicious. She sticks close by her mistress, allows the hapless philanderer to come up to her, and then snaps at him. In the street, says Frau Mühlberger, they get on quite well. They had played together right up to the street-door. Apparently it was only within her own four walls that Bella grew jealous of the interloper, just as cute Jeannette was jealous of her Théophile after she had been discovered with him by her mistress, the celebrated Miss Oceana. Frau Mühlberger even carries her humane sympathy to the point of holding Bella's head. But the pinscher is no Gianettino Doria;[80] he cannot bring himself to ravish the object of his love. He lets his ears droop disconsolately. Oh, these idealists!

After lunch Frau Mühlberger is told that the pinscher probably belongs in the Georgenstrasse. She takes him at once to the house in question, where he receives a rapturous welcome, and she is allowed to depart without a word of thanks. If a dog without a collar follows her home again, she'll take it to the police station, and its owners will have to pay a 30-mark fine.

Late in the afternoon a sentimental longing for my lute overcomes me. If it still exists, perhaps I'll have it sent here after all for the winter.

7 SEPTEMBER 1889

First sign of a gumboil. I treat it at once with figs. At eleven o'clock in the evening I meet Pariser in the Hoftheater, and he takes me to Denk's. The procuress[81] has been replaced by another waitress who cuts a stylish figure silhouetted against the bull's eye window panes by the bar in an apron that reaches all the way down to the ground. True, she's rather tall and skinny, but of a classical loveliness. The conversation is very animated. Pariser tells me about Bayreuth and the Holy Grail, to which Kapellmeister Levy was not admitted,[82] adding with a cautiously sly and furtive glance in my direction that only individuals of German stock were allowed in. After I have accompanied him back to his front door, I go on to the Café Central. I gossip a good deal about Frl. Herzog's sisters.

8 SEPTEMBER 1889

Since I didn't sleep all night, I stay in bed until half past one. My swollen cheek prevents me from retaining a single idea.

I stroll through the streets, buy some figs and a pocket mirror, and land up in the Herzogspitalstrasse, in front of a church,[83] from which comes the sound of singing. The closing phrases are just being sung in the gallery. The solo voices are not particularly fine, but the sumptuous gravity of the music does not call for fine voices. As the performers don't actually sing out of key, the harshness and artlessness of their voices do not impair the effect. The congregation is kneeling round the side-altar, filling every corner of the church. The Host is displayed on the side-altar. One of the choirboys with a stolid sheep's face keeps his eyes cast down and every so often raises his hand to his mouth and yawns. The other, with clean-cut, highly intelligent features, has his fine eyes steadfastly turned on the Host. After the Mass is over, there are prayers, where again one of the choristers keeps his eyes riveted on the ground with a totally impassive expression, while the other gazes up at the childish image of the Madonna with manifest devotion, bowing his head ever so slightly from time to time. The priest has the face of a cobbler, suffused with an expression of sentimental suffering. Not suffering for the sake of the crucified Christ, but self-pity. I don't blame him. The beads of the rosary slip through his fingers like centuries in the hour-glass of eternity. I'd like very much to know what he's dreaming about to kill time while his lips babble the Ave. When the sister in hospital knelt down for vespers,[84] I generally had some fascinating subject prepared, with which I could occupy my thoughts for as long as was necessary. If I was caught napping before taking this precaution, then there was no escape. Such devotional practices have the power to dissipate thought. In this event I had no choice but to be a devout Christian, since this at least made the time pass more quickly than the mental standstill one would otherwise have suffered during prayers. In the case of morning prayers such precautions were unnecessary, as one generally carried on sleeping with clasped hands and a thermometer under one arm until the coffee was ready on the bedside table.

I stroll up and down the Maximilianstrasse a few times before going home for supper. I have a pretty fair toothache and feel generally off-colour. I go to the Café Roth and down beer after beer until the pain abates. After midnight I drop into the Café Central. In the Amalienstrasse I take a sheer delight in watching a brawl. About a score of men are squaring up to each other outside a café, each of them intent on delivering a speech in his own defence. One window after another is flung open in the neighbouring houses. White-clad figures make their appearance, complaining about this commotion in the middle of the night. Some of them call for the police. But since not one of the orators takes the slightest notice, the figures withdraw. A cyclist rides up. While he's still some distance away he hands his machine to a girl dressed in blue, and comes over to join in the row. I go up to the girl, who cuts quite an attractive figure, bare-headed and wearing a simple cotton dress. But she draws back, the cyclist returns, still in an excited state, takes his bicycle and leads the girl by the hand down the street. The girl tries to calm him down and asks him to let her get on his bicycle with him. Or else she could sit up in front. He says, that's not on, and they walk pretty quickly, side by side, down the Schellingstrasse, and turn into the Türkenstrasse. I follow. In the middle of the street he hands her his bicycle again, and goes over to a doorway. A drunk is lying on the pavement, propped up against the door. The young man tries to rouse him, in vain. I light a match, and his face is revealed, covered in blood, likewise his shirt and tie. A deep cut on his head. Now three young men approach from the opposite direction, they say he can't just be left to lie there. I ask where the nearest police station is. They have just come from there.

They'd been ringing doorbells for the last quarter of an hour. Not a mouse had stirred. Everyone present now offers his comment on the police force. In the meantime the girl in the blue cotton dress has approached, showing keen concern for the victim and eager to inspect him by the light of a match. Her companion asks her what she hopes to see. I strike a match, and the girl is horrified, feeling his blood-encrusted wounds with slim white fingers. But the cyclist urges her to come away, it will be daybreak any moment now, and she follows him, albeit with some reluctance. I set off for the police station, however, and two of the gentlemen who have just been there join me so as to show me the way. One of them, a little journeyman baker, tells me in somewhat muddled fashion what had happened.

The drunk had sworn at a passing cyclist from the pavement, and five or six of the cyclist's mates had then set about him with cudgels until he collapsed. He and his friend had then dragged the drunk into the Türkenstrasse, but he couldn't just be left lying there.

I spend a good ten minutes ringing the doorbell, without a sign of life appearing. Finally, a window is opened on the second floor, a constable appears and says, yes, all right. A profound silence once more ensues. But then two policemen come down the road, and we lead them to the spot, describing the man's injuries in the most lurid terms. The victim is asked very insistently for his name, whereupon he states that he's called Georg Scheffler, lives at no. 28 Türkengraben, belongs here, and has been at work all day, although it's Sunday. Ten men had assaulted him. True, he'd already been drunk at the time. The constable questions him in a mild and disarming tone, like a mother talking to her child who is to blame for his own misfortune. After the helpless victim has been assisted to his feet and supported on both sides, a record of his injuries is made. If the wound is deep, he'll have to be taken to hospital, but it turns out to be superficial, although he has massive, bloodstained bruises on his brow and on the back of his head. One of the policemen makes notes of the whole business, particularly the baker's statement, together with his particulars, residence, age, antecedents, marital status, and so on and so forth, with the baker providing the necessary illumination at the expense of his own matches. And then it's off to the Türkengraben! The constables hold the shipwrecked hero between them, while the rest of us follow behind. At the first street corner, however, the procession disperses.

Arriving back at my front door, I watch the long façade of the Academy emerging clearly from the surrounding darkness in the first light of dawn. After a couple of hours' peaceful sleep I wake up in unholy agony. After writhing around for an hour, I get up and light the lamp, although it's already broad daylight, lay Heine's *Winter's Tale* on the brass ring,[85] and set up my newly acquired pocket mirror on it with the aid of a packet of Pulvis pectoralis. Then comes the operation. The mountain is rent asunder, and the spring flows so copiously you could have used it for pudding sauce. While I was writhing in agony all day yesterday, I read the entire chapter in Niemeyer on syphilis. I commonly regain my good humour when I read this sort of thing. It's not only fascinating, but also inspiring and

The Café Luitpold in Munich about 1900.

goes some way to alleviating an irksome mental lethargy.

Today, at lunch in the Kletzengarten, I meet Bennat, who is also wrestling with toothache. There is a young lady sitting opposite us who has just had an abscess on a tooth lanced, and hence cannot eat anything. Such encounters also offer a modicum of relief, because you take a pride in offering sympathy, rather than having it offered to you. I found truly keen, sincere and hence gratifying sympathy among the waitresses in the Café Luitpold. Lina Höpfl[86] recommended scalding hot poultices. They wouldn't do a lot of good, though.

9 SEPTEMBER 1889

As I enter the Café after lunch, Lina Höpfl is sitting by her customary pillar with a shabby little poetry album in her hand, making pencil notes. She says she's writing down here everything she means to say to him, so that she won't be at a loss for words. Who knows whether she'll even get the chance. This 'he' is in fact a Japanese doctor by the name of Koîkzi Shibato. She says if he asked her to go to Japan with him this very day, she wouldn't have a moment's hesitation. But it seems to me that he's been unfaithful to her. At any rate she is furiously angry with him. As it is, she's already had to put up with a great deal on his account. I had no idea what a state of affairs she had left behind at home. Nobody could understand how she had landed up with this Japanese. She was already generally known as the

Japanese Princess. Apparently she's ashamed of her lover. She can't bring herself to be proud of the exotic. She subscribes to the *Medizinisches Wochenblatt* for the benefit of him and his friends, and gives me each issue to read as soon as it comes out. I ask her to let me have her poetry album for a moment. She tears out the dressing-down she has started to compose and hands it to me, saying there are a number of very fine poems in it, the first of them from *Der Trompeter von Säckingen*.[87]

The Café Luitpold has in fact become my home from home, as I anticipated when I was still in Berlin. It's true, you're liable to have the very buttons stolen from your trousers, and anyone who brings a new overcoat with him does well to sit on it, otherwise he might not have the chance to do so afterwards. The illustrated papers generally vanish from their folders the very first day: the empty folders evoke a certain embarrassment in the reader, when he has taken the trouble to pick them out, taken them to his seat, and then opened one after the other with dwindling assurance. On the other hand, the place offers so many advantages that one is prepared to overlook a good deal. What I particularly like is the lighting: a soft overhead light by day that reaches into every corner without dazzling you, and at night the illumination of the brightly decorated domes from concealed sources, so that the peristyle and the side colonnades assume a delightful fairylike appearance. And for a hermit like myself, the crowds of people who continually throng the rooms mean a great deal. Now and then you find an acquaintance among them, or at least imagine you have found one. I saw Schwiglin there several days running, with her Greek profile and her revolutionary stride, but by the time I'd made up my mind to approach her, she had long since left Munich.

From Lina Höpfl's Poetry Album

If only I had but the freedom to go
With thee to far regions where oranges glow,
With blue skies above, where soft breezes blow,
Where myrtle and laurel entangled do grow.
It's there, oh, how gladly I'd wander with thee,
If thou art not here, what's left then for me?
Where paths traverse the cloud-capped ridge,

Where o'er the wooded torrent there sways a dizzy bridge,
Where dragons lurk to spawn their evil brood,
Where crags go plunging down and over them the flood.
It's there, oh, how gladly I'd wander with thee,
If thou are not here, what's left then for me?

I go to the garden gate
To breathe the scented air,
For him I mean to wait,
Who'll surely seek me there.

The Teacher of Mezodur[88]

In Mezodur a teacher lived,
Sigmund Zus by name,
A worthy fellow he,
Of modest local fame.
A husband, and a father, too,
Three children, still quite small.
And yet unhappy was his life –
A grievous doubt assailed his mind:
Unfaithful was his wife.
Another man than he himself
Had given those children life.
So, tortured by this jealousy
And sure he'd been deceived,
In dread delusion fixed,
A lethal plan was soon conceived.
One night he forced his hapless spouse
To make a full confession out
That he himself had framed,
A sentence of her death, no doubt,
And when the father there she named
Of her dear children – oh, dear God –
He shot the wretched babes forthwith
And slew them in their bed.
And when he'd done this ghastly deed
She signed the paper, too,
Courageous in her mortal need.
So thereupon he made her lie

Upon that fatal bed
And spurning all her tearful pleas
He shot her also dead.
His hand he turned against himself – God forfend –
And thus did meet his dreadful end.
The serving-maid was forced to hold
The candlestick to light his final fate
And, horror-stricken, told the tale
Before the magistrate.

The first page of the album contains a number of verses from 'It Was Just Too Beautiful'. On the second last page there is a whole series of barons and knights pencilled in, presumably Lina's visitors. The last page boasts a list of all the Munich student fraternities: Swabians, the Palatinate, Bavarians, the Isar fraternity, Franconians, Makari, Brunswickers.

10 NOVEMBER 1889

I've been working on the second act since 9 September, and still haven't finished it.[89] There are still three scenes missing, and my creative powers are impaired. Towards the end of last month my landlady acquired two new lodgers, both painters, one a Viennese, the other from Hanover. The Hanoverian, Herr Frische . . .[90]

31 JANUARY 1890

Today is, if I'm not mistaken, the last day of January 1890. I've started writing again from sheer necessity. I had meant to do so already while I was in Lenzburg, but Lenzburg and here are two different things. Here I have my work, my *Eppur si Muove*, which in fact moves so little that I positively feel like Penelope, unravelling each night what she has woven the whole day long. It's true, the day is not all that long in my case. As a rule I spend ten hours sleeping, and don't get up before twelve. Should I write down everything that has happened to me since work on this volume was discontinued? Why not? After all, I'm writing merely for the sake of writing. I could pass my time just as easily with needlework, like any well-bred damsel.

On 9 November '89 I had resolved to compose a graphic account of my life and the manner in which it revolves more and more round the Café Luitpold. At that time I had no company other than the Kletzengarten and the Professor of German,[91] and couldn't decide which I found the more repulsive. I was leading a dream life that generally petered out on the woodland trail of sex. I detested my solitude, and yet didn't have the heart to escape from it. It was in the Café Luitpold that I felt most at ease. The crowds of people, the elfin overhead lighting, the regiment of waitresses, on whom I had mostly conferred my own private names, for instance: the Spectre, the Elephant, Astarte, the Frog, etc. *En masse*, with their black skirts and white aprons, they seemed to me like a flock of magpies. I personally was served by the Elephant. This Elephant was distinctly consumptive and had a rather stupid, sensuous expression which drew me to her.

This was, by the way, Lina Höpfl, from whose diary I copied the above poems. At that time Lina had two sweethearts, a fellow from Regensburg and a Japanese by the name of Koîkzi Shibato, for whose benefit, as she told me, she took the *Medizinisches Wochenblatt*, which, incidentally, was not true. Lina Höpfl was, as I said, anything but a feast for the eyes, but pretty choosy all the same. I remained faithful to her nevertheless, partly from sheer idleness, partly because I could watch the others that much better, without the risk of either having to flirt with them or else be neglected.

Lina Höpfl gave up the Café Luitpold and took a job with the newly opened Café Dengler. She was replaced by Marie, the girl who used to serve the water for her, the Frog, a nice child of an extremely nondescript kind, towards whom I never felt anything but a painful sense of delicacy. At that time the adjacent tables were being served by another Lina, the counterpart to Lina Höpfl, for whom I tried in vain to find a nickname. She seemed to have crawled straight out of the pages of the *Journal amusant*, snub nose, stony eyes, full lips and a finely turned figure and all. She could have taken Klara Ziegler's place on the stage of the Court Theatre.[92] Her temperament was indomitable, her gift of the gab irrepressible, and she was on the game from morning to night with the stamina of a stallion. The sixty-year old opera singer Nachbauer sought her favours with the greatest assiduity,[93] while his son, a flashy youth of twenty, finally rented a room for her and taught her all manner of things, as her colleagues put it. These colleagues, amongst them one who was the very image of Max's *Astarte*,[94] ran her down, said she was crazy and would end up in Giesing.[95] Once, when they were all going to bed, one of them had said to her: I'll bet Lina's not a virgin any more. People generally took that sort of thing in their stride, and simply denied it, but Lina had sat bolt upright in bed in nothing but her shift, wringing her hands and screaming: As true as I'm sitting here on this mattress, as true as there's a God in Heaven, on my honour and my salvation, I'm a virgin – and she hadn't calmed down all night. Whenever things quietened down, she started proclaiming her virginity all over again.

After she had quite indubitably forfeited the same, Herr Nachbauer junior let her go back to being a waitress. I met her no more than four weeks later, also in the Café Dengler. She had grown paler and was less excitable. It had been pleasanter in the Café Luitpold, but she'd rather starve than go back there. She couldn't go on the stage, because she was too poor, and she wasn't inclined to try it on the off-chance. She would never believe, incidentally, that Daddy Nachbauer was in the habit of dyeing his hair. I, for my part, mean to persevere with these notes, since they exercise such a beneficial influence on my state of mind. Others have recourse to a girl, I stick to my diary, Joseph that I am! Paragon of virtue! And to think that I'm proud of it. Oh, irony, strange are thy ways.

1 FEBRUARY 1890

The alarm begins to clatter at nine o'clock. I have decided to pay Mauer a visit. His mother is ill, and he is currently working with a model who is said to be well worth seeing. When she lies there in front of him she's just asking to be kissed, but she doesn't rouse his lust, possibly because she's a bit stupid. Otherwise, if sexual desire for a model arises, he deals with the matter straight away, so as to have an asexual attitude to her while he's working. I lie in until my landlady brings me my monthly bill, which I can't pay, together with a letter from Donald.

Donald has tried unsuccessfully to get a place in a Zürich high school, and it was then agreed that he should take the matriculation examination for foreigners. Next morning, mother sends him a telegram withdrawing her consent, turns up in person in the afternoon, and faces him with the choice of either becoming a printer, or else going back to the grammar school in Aarau. With a show of friendship she manages to coax his watch from him and takes him back to Lenzburg, from where he writes to me the same evening, asking me to send him some money so that he can join me here. I write to him as well as to Mama that I'll enter him for the matriculation for foreigners at my own expense, and go on basking in my own magnanimity until twelve o'clock at night, without doing a stroke of work. Then I go out to the Luitpold in the bitter cold, in the hope of seeing some masked revellers.

Mauer, who is sitting alone at a table, informs me straight away that there are no dances today, since tomorrow is a holiday, Candlemas. We discuss Makart and agree that he cannot have been a sensuous hedonist, he is nothing but a sensuous theoretician, a sensualistic idealist.[96] We talk about Frische, of whose career I'm beginning virtually to despair up to a point. He invited me to his studio today to view the new gilded frame. Standing in front of his picture, he can barely find words to explain for my benefit how much the picture gains thereby. He asks me whether I don't agree that the angel's robe really flutters, it does flutter, he reckons, there's no other word for it. He has painted a muddy yellow petticoat on his angel, who is virtually floating in three different sorts of aureole. He says he's not going to add another stroke, it's finished now, he'll just make the hand a shade lighter, make the outline of the head a bit sharper, change the tone of the sky and alter the chalice, then he would invite the director round, and possibly get a scholarship. The frame cost him 58 marks. Without some of the shiny bits that were gilded with real gold it would have cost 10 marks less, but it was those shiny bits which so strongly enhanced the effect. The worse his picture grows, the more optimistic Frische becomes, but he's an unfortunate soul. He has now started on a life-size Dutch fishwife who already looks as much like Eugen Blaas's life-size Italian fishwife as it is possible for a Dutchwoman to look like an Italian.[97] Of course, he has no idea of this. He'll be spared this revelation until his picture is three-quarters finished. His model, a girl of eighteen whose mother came from South Tyrol, has a pretty, brutally sensuous little face, eyelashes as long as your finger, a splendid white bust with over-developed breasts, and has had a child of her own for the last two years. When I went to see him the time before last I caught sight of Frische through the door, which was ajar: Frische was sitting beside her and both of them were plunged in profound silence. After she's gone, however, he indignantly and insistently repudiates my comments on the situation. He must be pretty mixed up inside. Another model, a handsome, slender figure, knocks at the door and asks if Theres has already gone. When she's left, Frische tells me she's pregnant and doesn't know who's responsible. She got herself this 'sportsman's farewell' at the gymnastic festival. There are a number of other models also carting the same sort of sportsman's greeting around with them. Up till now she's been living with Theres in the house of Theres's parents, but now she's pregnant the parents won't let her into the house, and not long ago she spent the whole night in an empty apartment next door, lying on the threshold of the communicating door. She's now just seventeen.

Since there's nothing left to drink in the Luitpold by 2 a.m., we set off in the hope of finding a hide-out somewhere else. There's music in the Goldener Hirsch in the Türkenstrasse. We go in and find a party of officers, each of whom has brought his girl with him. There's no more beer, and in any case it's closing time for civilians. We wander on. The little Luitpold is crowded out, but there's nothing to be had, other than a schnaps, then everyone is turned out. With very little confidence we set course for the Blüte, our last resort. We're still a long way down the Blütenstrasse when Mauer grunts in a tone of resignation: Nothing doing. I think to myself, superstitious beggar! But I hope all the same that he hasn't been mistaken. Then I hear quite distinctly the throbbing of a double bass and say so frankly, whereupon Mauer rebukes me, only to let out a joyful shout next minute, when he catches sight of the brightly lit windows of the hall, with the dancing couples flitting past them. In the kitchen we are directed into a corner, the cook presses a button, and off we go. Mauer is speechless with delight. Eiffel Tower! Eiffel Tower! he whispers ecstatically. He tries to plant a final kiss on the cook, but the lift drags him from her arms. We have to be very careful not to bang our heads. All of a sudden, there we are, at the entrance to the hall. I point out to Mauer that there's a table for the academic gentry, and we're just making our way towards it when he suddenly disappears from my side. Next minute I catch sight of him waltzing furiously past with a stout brunette. When the dance is over he leads her across to our table. She's the sweetheart of one of the academic gentlemen there by the name of Petin, an Austrian, who takes me under his wing with the greatest solicitude. He gives the impression of being a quiet, reticent person, a child of nature, whose power is lodged deep in the recesses of his being. His sweetheart is obviously a servant-girl, broad in the beam and tall, common, without being actually vulgar, but in possession of exceptionally tender flesh. Herr Petin's brother is sitting next to him, also with a buxom wench in his arms. She has pitch-black eyes, a generous mouth, and is got up in Oriental costume. The gentleman had told her that, if she went to the ball, she would have to go as an Orientalist, and so she had come as an Orientalist. Mauer asks her who this gentleman was. The gentleman was Herr Pigelhain, so she is dubbed Frau Pigelhain by the assembled company. Behind me is a slim model in a light-coloured girlish dress, and two tables further on is a girl in Swabian costume with a very refined profile. Herr Petin senior has taken rather a fancy to her, but is no end annoyed to find she is dim-witted. Indeed, seen full face she gives the impression of the very dullest respectability, without a trace of youthful zest about her, in spite of her ample figure and her freshness. Apart from these few there is nothing remarkable in the crowd that consists of Messrs Tailor and Glovemaker, complete with wife and child. A fat, boozy old Lizzie in a skimpy jacket and Lederhose is shouting out the numbers for a lottery that's been set up by the wall, screeching fiendishly and getting gradually more and more stoned as she moves from table to table. The whole carry-on is supposed to be the ball given by some choral society or other, which actually assembles from time to time in the middle of the hall to squawk out a four-part yodel. There is, alas, no more dancing. So we go on tippling until we're the last survivors, and the caretaker comes in with his long pole to turn out the last of the gaslights. He pleads with us to leave. But there are still three full bottles on the table, and we swear we won't withdraw until we've drunk the lot at our leisure. He should turn out the lights, for God's sake, and bring us a candle. This he does, in fact, when he sees there is nothing else for it, brings us the candle, turns out all the lights, and says no one will be able to leave the building before half-past seven. I reassure our ladies, you can always get out, that's no problem, and then there is singing and speeches, the ladies smoke their cigarettes, and the Petin brothers turn out to be as generous lovers as any gatecrasher could possibly wish. About seven the ladies urge us to leave. Mauer is somewhat taken aback when he's asked to pay for another six bottles, but he's been putting them on the slate all evening. In the street I observe that he's pretty far gone. He falls on the neck of every female and kisses them passionately. The majority are aged crones on their way to fetch milk or bread. Then the Petin brothers break away and go on ahead with their womenfolk. At the corner of the Theresienstrasse I offer Mauer my hand in farewell. He is just on the point of steering a diagonal course across the street in the direction of an elderly charwoman.

2 FEBRUARY 1890

I sleep until one o'clock. On getting up I meet Mauer, who claims he can't recall any details. Frische, on the other hand had already lied to Frau Mühlberger early in the morning, saying that he had been with us. During the evening in the Kletzengarten the painter Renzing had been elbowed out of our company.

3 FEBRUARY 1890

In the evening to the Luitpold, where I feel incredibly alone among a hundred females in costume. I go to bed at four in this glum mood and read the whole of the 1848 Berlin revolution in order to revive my spirits. I then sleep like a log from seven until one.

4 FEBRUARY 1890

Herr Bachmann and his conversation drive me out of the Café Luitpold. I go into the Café Maximilian, from there to a confectioner's, and finally, in the bitter cold, to the Gärtnertheater to see Sudermann's *Honour*.[98] I'm so much taken by the play that I still cannot bring myself to write a word about it. I fetch Bennat from *Götterdämmerung* and go with him to the Kletzengarten, where I make the acquaintance of the African explorer Dr Schwarz.

PARIS

I MAY 1892–23 JANUARY 1894

I MAY 1892

A letter from Mama to say the castle has been sold. Weinhöppel is present at my *levée*, singing and playing the guitar for my benefit. Afterwards we fetch Katja for lunch. After lunch the three of us withdraw to my room and drink tea. Suddenly Amsel turns up and proceeds to make himself very much at home. By way of farewell he sings us two Italian arias. To dinner with Katja, then to the Café Divans de la Madeleine.

2 MAY 1892

I get to the Swiss Consulate too late, fetch Katja for dinner and show her the Nouveau Cirque: *Le Roi Dagobert*. Until two o'clock in the Pont Neuf.

3 MAY 1892

Sign my power of attorney at the Swiss Consulate, where Dr Stumm stamps me as a Swiss. Write to Mama.[1] Dine with Katja and Weinhöppel, and discuss the Ballet Roquanedin at the Eden Theatre with him. Until two in the Pont Neuf, where we drink Baron Habermann's health in Américain.[2] Then I take the pair of them to an all-night café in the Halles, where Katja gets totally drunk. She refuses to take my arm, and I leave her to Weinhöppel, who trots out triumphantly with her into the Rue Montmartre. I keep out of sight and follow them about a hundred paces to the rear. Weinhöppel at

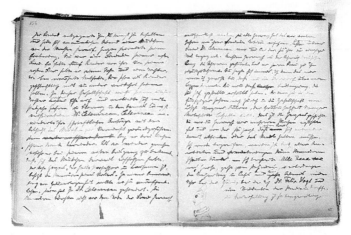

The manuscript of the Paris diary.

last asks a passer-by, who directs him in the opposite direction. So they contrive to make their way over the Pont Neuf, which is just beginning to emerge in the first light of dawn, and get into the Boulevard St Germain, where they once more lose the track. They set out towards the Bastille. On the Boulevard St Michel they ask their way again and turn back the way they came. As they pass me, Katja asks me for her key. At the Eglise St Germain-des-Prés they lose their bearings once more and wait for me. I cross to the opposite pavement, they pursue me. I take refuge in a urinal and make them wait ages for me. Katja leans against a tree and starts crying. Finally they start walking round and round the urinal, come to the conclusion that I'm no longer inside, and set off again in search of the Rue Bonaparte. After wandering round for ages they return to my urinal, where I stick my umbrella out under the screen. They've finally found the right way. I once again follow them at a distance of a hundred yards, until Katja disappears in the entrance to the Hotel St Georges. Weinhöppel then comes up to my room. I go to bed about six.

4 MAY 1892

Go to Katja's, but don't find her in. Thinking it may be Frl. Hüny's 'at home' day, I go there, but am turned away.[3] After I've gone to bed Leontine turns up; I'm pretty ill-tempered, don't kiss her even once.

The title-page of Wedekind's Paris diary, 1892.

5 MAY 1892

Give Leontine a louis d'or, with which she at once buys a skirt and a pair of shoes. She comes back to ask for more. Weinhöppel comes in and asks if I have Frl. —'s address. In the afternoon I go to Katja and take her to the Eldorado.

6 MAY 1892

Farewell letter to Leontine, which I deliver in person. She has made me a present of crabs again. I'm sick to death of her filthy habits. I promised to take Katja to the *vernissage*[4] in the Champs de Mars, but arrive three hours too soon. She's in a foul temper, having just had a letter from Rosa Krüger to say she can't come, because Elisabeth has had one of her attacks. I dictate a letter for her to send in reply, promising her that both of them will come on the strength of it. Katja curses Paris, she feels anything but well and talks of leaving next day. After we've spent the evening in the Café [?], she accompanies me back to my room, but won't agree to do anything, claiming she's having her period. She tries to get affectionate, which I won't allow.

7 MAY 1892

Get tickets for *La Vie de Bohème* and go to the Odéon with Katja in the evening. Afterwards in my room the same scene as yesterday.

Katja asks me not to flirt with Elisabeth, if the Krügers come. We arrange a trip to Versailles for tomorrow, Sunday. I'm to fetch her at eleven.

8 MAY 1892

About one Weinhöppel turns up, I'm still in bed. I get up slowly and send him on ahead to Katja. She's had a telegram from the Krügers to say they'll be here on Wednesday. While we're having coffee in her room Miss Marx comes in and says all sorts of nice things about the *vernissage*. We go to the Restaurant Marguerite for dinner, drink four bottles of champagne, and when it's getting on for morning drive to the Café du Chien qui Fume, near the Halles. We return in broad daylight. Weinhöppel can barely stand. Once he's made it to my room, he reads me a number of letters from mistresses in Munich. He says he expects them to follow him here from Munich.

9 MAY 1892

After dinner in the Folies Bergères with Katja, afterwards to the Brasserie Pont Neuf, then in Le Chien qui Fume until two in the morning, then a cab back to my place. After a show of coyness she gets into bed. We stay in bed until twelve. Then I take her to lunch. In the afternoon she drags me off to the Champs de Mars, where I get a fearful toothache. In the evening in the Pont Neuf until twelve. Then back to my room in a cab. I take her home about three in the morning.

11 MAY 1892

Get up about two in the afternoon, treat my toothache, go for a walk, have dinner and lie down on the bed at home. Leontine comes at eleven, tells me a pack of lies, I give her 20 francs. She goes away, I wrestle with the bed-bugs for a while, and fall asleep very late.

12 MAY 1892

As I go into Duval's at midday and see Katja sitting there with the two Krügers, I get such a chilly reception that I sit down at the adjoining table. I hope I might be able to work again, but get nothing done. Letter to Bierbaum.[5] Go to bed at eleven.

13 MAY 1892

Longing for Katja. Wander round the streets without finding her. Evening at home.

14 MAY 1892

Evening in the Brasserie Pont Neuf in the hope that Katja might come. Then Leontine comes in with a very pretty girl, Jeanne, who also lives in the Hotel Voltaire, the living image of Anastasia. I find Leontine extremely repugnant. She robs me blind at her front door – the last time, I hope to God.

15 MAY 1892

Write five poems and send them to Bierbaum. Afternoon in the Salon Champs Elysées, evening at home.

16 MAY 1892

I walk past the Hotel St Georges every evening, to make sure my ladies are at home and behaving themselves. In fact, their light is always on. Otherwise, I am very virtuous, and feel my creative powers recuperating gradually.

17 MAY 1892

The letter to T. Plümacher written at last. After lunch I go and fetch Prell for a beer, having given Marthe Barbot a miss, in spite of her sparkling eyes. At the Ribot exhibition in the afternoon.[6] My longing for Katja and my anger are both abating. I write poems and play a good deal on my guitar in order to speed my recovery.

18 MAY 1892

Worked during the day. In the evening I decide to visit the ladies. Elisabeth Krüger is truly an exceptionally pretty creature. If anything, she has changed for the better. In the course of conversation I learn that Emilie and Isidore Lengnick arrived the same day. After a while Emilie Lengnick comes in to greet the ladies. Isidore is tired from the journey. After taking leave of the ladies, I go to the Brasserie Pont Neuf.

19 MAY 1892

In the evening together with Prell, Geffken, Knopp and a Berlin painter, with whom I stay until two o'clock in the Café d'Harcourt after the session in the Pont Neuf is over. I find Leontine in my room. She has written me a long letter, which I'm to read in her presence. She's in a wretched state and proposes to go into hospital tomorrow. She spends the night with me.

20 MAY 1892

A short, quite desperate letter from Mama to say that the sale of the castle has fallen through because of the Felsen business.

21 MAY 1892

I don't sleep all night, get up at seven, and start work. Weinhöppel turns up at twelve and reads me letters from two of his pupils who intend to follow him here. At one o'clock I go to the Musée du Luxembourg and gossip for an hour with Katja in front of her picture. She maintains she wasn't to blame for the scene in Duval's. I reply, she should prove it by the way she behaves. After we have left the museum, the two Krügers emerge, much to my astonishment. They go off home. I fetch Katja theatre tickets for *Kean* at the Odéon.[7] As I'm taking her home, she says she'd rather I picked her up at the Luxembourg, since there's always a row at home. And she also asks me to spend tomorrow afternoon alone with her; if only she knew how to get away. Evening in the Hippodrome.

22 MAY 1892

I wait for Katja in a café. We take a cab to St Cloud, sit down in front of the restaurant, and drink until it's time to go back. We dine together at Marguerite's and then drive back to my room at one

The text of Wedekind's hitherto unpublished song, 'The new Communion' (cont. pp. 125–7).

o'clock, where I invite her to get into bed. She's wearing a brand new silk dress from the Louvre that's too short for her and hence fastened up with a hundred pins. The opening is even sewn askew. I demolish the entire contraption and dump her into bed. In spite of the good supper with champagne, I can't manage more than a couple of tributes: her confounded practice of refusing to take off her underclothes may be to blame for that. I don't care in the least for her caresses. Her lips are flabby and she slobbers all over my face. I keep on pouring cognac into her, and the powerful aroma comes back at me. Elle me veut tailler une . . ., mais elle me mord les testicules que je crie par douleur.[8] At the same time she keeps on making such clumsy attempts to address me in the familiar form that I simply can't bring myself to reply in the same terms. Between four and five, in broad daylight, I take her home, and go to bed about seven.

23 MAY 1892

Evening in the Cirque d'Eté.

24 MAY 1892

I go to the Hotel St Georges in the afternoon, find Katja on her own, and ask her to explain her behaviour. The outcome is that we go to the Moulin Rouge. I see Isidore Lengnick for a moment before we leave. Katja carries on all evening in the most fatuously offensive manner possible.

25 MAY 1892

After I've called on Frl. Hüny, I go in search of Isidore Lengnick, don't find her at home, but meet Prell instead, with whom I dine in the Golden Pheasant. I give him a card to pass on to Lengnick, and go to bed early, without, however, being able to fall asleep before daybreak. I'm furious with Katja, and resolve to get my hands on Elisabeth Krüger via Lengnick.

26 MAY 1892

I find no one at home in the Hotel St Georges. Lengnick has left a card asking me to come to the Louvre tomorrow. Evening in the Concert Ambassadeur on the Champs Elysées. Find Leontine in my room.

27 MAY 1892

Meet Lengnick in the Louvre, but find her so lacking in understanding that I can't bring myself to ask her to go out with me. I go to the Luxembourg, where Elisabeth Krüger tells me that she, her sister and Lengnick were at the exhibition on the Champs de Mars, together with Prell, yesterday. They'd like to go to the Hippodrome tomorrow evening. I ask Katja what on earth she thought she was doing on Saturday.

28 MAY 1892

In the evening I go to the Hotel St Georges to fetch the girls and take them to the Hippodrome. Elisabeth Krüger tells me the others don't want to go. Fed up with the part I'm playing, I decide to give up the struggle, but to make the situation as impossible for Katja as she made it for me. A sixteen-page letter to Elisabeth Krüger. I feel much relieved, and in the evening I go once again to see the *Femme de Narcisse* at the Théâtre Renaissance.

29 MAY 1892

At lunch I meet Mme Geinsinger and Mme Neumann. I tell Mme Neumann about Amsel. She would like to make his acquaintance. I call on Weinhöppel so as to be able to write and tell her his address. He tells me the story of his attempted suicide. We dine together and go to the Jardin de Paris. Very sophisticated variety show. Brilliant danseuse. Extremely elegant audience. Weinhöppel is in a constant state of ecstasy. We sit in a café behind the Opera until three o'clock. In the end, a superbly handsome creature in dressing-gown and overcoat appears and I procure her for Weinhöppel at the cost of a few kisses. Weinhöppel takes the bait somewhat reluctantly, since he's invited to lunch with three ladies tomorrow.

30 MAY 1892

After I've recovered from a thoroughgoing hangover, I go looking for Schuppi, meaning to drag her off to the Jardin de Paris. But she's only just got up for the first time in three weeks and she's suffering from neuralgia. What's more, a thunderstorm breaks while I'm with her. After we've chatted for a couple of hours I go to lunch, and subsequently in search of a twelve-year old child. After wandering around for ages I find one on the Boulevard Rochechouart, but unfortunately she is eighteen. I take her to a hotel and do her barely satisfactory justice for 10 francs, although I quite fancy her, and she is very nice to me. I'm utterly shattered, however. After the first feeble attempt I'm bathed in perspiration. I'm not too worried, however, and pump as much beer into myself as I can before staggering off home.

31 MAY 1892

I begin to suspect that Katja has suppressed my letter.

1 JUNE 1892

I go to the Luxembourg and find out in devious ways that Katja has read out my letter. I feel as if I'd been poisoned. I write her a letter accusing her of misappropriation. I feel capable of any sort of mean behaviour towards her.

2 JUNE 1892

Katja sends me a postcard asking me to call on her. I find a virtual tribunal awaiting me. She herself, the shameless hussy, is in the middle, flanked by the two sisters. She has shown them the letter. I say as much as can be said in the presence of the ladies, and after the letters have been burned and we have shaken hands to seal the bargain, I depart highly satisfied. I find Prell, Schlichting, Langhammer, Höninger, Geffken and Knapp in the Maison Fara. The whole company, except for Prell, goes to Bullier's, a lively dance-hall with a garden for the summer season. Langhammer, Schlichting and I drop into the Café d'Harcourt afterwards. I have barely got home before Leontine arrives – also an unparalleled piece of cheek after she has stolen her photograph from me. I have only once spent a pleasanter evening with her. She climbs on to my shoulders and rides round the room, we dance together. Finally she gets into evening dress, black trousers, tails, white tie and opera-hat, and gives impressions of Yvette Gilbert, Bruant, Paulus, etc. As day is breaking we go to bed. She falls asleep instantly. After we have had breakfast in bed together, she departs. I decide not to let her in any more. Hardly has she gone, before Weinhöppel makes his appearance. He sings to me for three hours on end. I'm enraptured. We go to a café and I hope I may be able to work after dinner, but I'm so weary that I fall asleep. I wake up at two, get into bed and read Nietzsche until seven in the morning.

4 JUNE 1892

I get up at seven and buy myself the makings of breakfast, work until eleven, then drive to Chois and back. Afternoon in the exhibition on the Champs de Mars. In the evening at Bullier's, where I treat two charming tarts, Madame Fernande, etc. I promise to call on her. Come home at midnight and write until three.

5 JUNE 1892

In the evening after dinner I go to a café and then to Bullier's. The place is packed with Whitsun visitors, soldiers, factory girls dancing their clumsy cancan. I haven't got to the far end before the friend of my fair lady from yesterday comes up to me. Glad to get out of the crush, I offer her some refreshment. We find seats in the garden and chat. She has a Gabriel Max head, and a perfectly lovely figure, is very poised and doesn't care for cafés, but prefers the Opéra Comique, Théâtre Français et la peinture. Elle monte aussi à cheval,[9] not astride like the others, however, but like a lady. I feel very much at my ease in her company and take her to the Café d'Harcourt. After a few brandies we have supper. We empty two bottles of wine, while I make tactful enquiries about her profession in an attempt to enliven the conversation. She proposes to pursue it for another two years at most before entering a convent. She is a native of the French Jura and came to Paris with her first lover. Her parents think she is working in a fashion house. It's no wonder, incidentally, if the girls get vicious in the course of time, having been let down so often before. I like her very much indeed, mainly because of her tragic apathy.

We set off home in a rather tipsy state. At her front door I tell her, firstly, that I've only got 10 francs, secondly, that I've had too much to drink. She shows me into a large, charmingly furnished room with a view on to a spacious garden with lofty trees. By the open window stands a broad-leafed palm, with another by the mirror. Somewhat ironically bemused by my situation, I drop into an armchair and frankly express my astonishment. My fair lady then begins to cry, tears pouring down her face. I was making fun of her, she couldn't help it if she wasn't as pretty and as chic as other women. In order to prolong this delightful scene, I put my 10 francs on the mantelpiece and say, unfortunately that's all I have. She assures me between sobs that that isn't the point. When, at last, I try to comfort her, she falls at my feet, flings her arms round my knees, and declares that this is where she belongs. Then I stroke her hair and ask her to get into bed. She's wearing a tight-fitting black dress buttoned up to the neck, of an elegance I have not observed in the case of other respectable ladies. I fling off my clothes and get into bed with her. She is as wholesome as a peeled apple and artlessly ardent to a degree I have never experienced with any other woman. It goes without saying that I take the liberty of indulging in my customary predilections, which seem nevertheless to give her great pleasure. At last dawn breaks, the sparrows twitter in the tall trees, I get dressed quickly and go on my way. Rachel.

6 JUNE 1892

At twelve o'clock Weinhöppel comes to borrow money from me. We lunch together, go to a café, and then through the Tuileries Gardens. In the evening I take a stroll along the boulevards and go to bed early.

7 JUNE 1892

In the evening, by myself in the Jardin de Paris. At midnight I meet M. Brehant and M. Moutreuil in the Brasserie Pont Neuf. We talk about Leontine. The gentlemen have just come from a brothel where Brehant is the local favourite. We agree that I should go there with him some time next week.

8 JUNE 1892

After lunch I meet the pastel painter Burger in the courtyard of the Louvre.[10] I accompany him to his photographer, and then to the Brasserie Pont Neuf. We talk a great deal about the ladies of Paris. He had taken a mistress, lived with her for six weeks, and then had the greatest difficulty in getting rid of her. Now he is revelling in his golden liberty and detests everything that goes by the name of woman. We part about twelve, after he has asked me to visit him in his studio tomorrow. On the way home, Leontine comes to meet me on the Boulevard St Michel. She had wanted to see whether I was in the Brasserie PN [Pont Neuf], and then perhaps to visit me at home. I buy her a large bunch of roses, give her 10 francs, and send her about her business. Until two o'clock in the Café d'Harcourt.

9 JUNE 1892

After working until five, I call on Burger. He has a marvellous studio in Montmartre. He has a number of Parisiennes done in pastel set up on his easels, besides the King of Württemberg on his death-bed, painted at the request of the Queen. I go to the Maison Fara at seven o'clock. Knopp comes in with two friends, then Prell and Geffken. Geffken says Schlichting probably won't be coming, whereupon I decide privately to abandon the party immediately after dinner. In

Frank and Tilly Wedekind in *Earth Spirit*.

the end, Schlichting does come after all, along with Langhammer. The three of us beat a retreat, on the pretext that we're going to a brothel. We go to Bullier's, find my lovely Rachel there, and go to supper with her in the Café d'Harcourt. Schlichting and Langhammer are delighted with her, particularly her Max Gabriel head. We go on drinking in high spirits until two. Then I see Rachel home and stay in her arms until daybreak.

10 JUNE 1892

Worked all day long.

11 JUNE 1892

Weinhöppel shows up early in the morning, i.e. at one o'clock. Seeing I have to work, he goes away again. I promise I may call for him tomorrow, Sunday.

12 JUNE 1892

Work all day long. In the evening I hope to meet Schlichting and Langhammer at Yvette Gilbert's; go into the Champs Elysées, where I get an idea for a gruesome tragedy.[11] I work all day on a draft of the first act, go to the Café d'Harcourt, meet Rachel, take her home and stay with her until four. She tells me she has a baby by her first lover, now two years old. It's with a nursemaid in the country. She had deliberately had the child, so as to have something to remember her lover by. It had been born at seven months as a result of a fall downstairs, and hence had hardly affected her figure. It had to be kept under glass to ensure an even temperature and had been fed with a medicine dropper. Her lover had met all the expenses. She meant to take the child back now, so that she could go for walks with it in the afternoons.

13 JUNE 1892

Weinhöppel arrives at one o'clock. We stroll through the city, visit a café, go to dinner together, and then to the Casino de Paris. Strolling among the tarts of the Casino, he reads me a letter from his last mistress, a seventeen-year-old Munich seamstress. The girl's afraid she's going off her head. We stay in the Café Wetzel behind the Opera until three o'clock. His two pupils are due to arrive tomorrow. He accompanies me all the way back to my front door, it's broad daylight. I invite him to come up to my room for a brandy, but as we go in, I notice that Leontine has taken my key. Since I intend to throw her out, I ask him to leave. I find Leontine in bed in my room. She has brought me up a card from Langhammer inviting me to the Moulin Rouge tomorrow. I tell her we have to part company. The candle has burned down and is guttering dimly. That's our love, I say, it's on the point of expiring. Since she makes no move to get up, I offer to act as her personal maid. She then gets up and dresses as I gaze out of the window. After she has dressed she sits down by the window and bursts into tears. I tell her I've seen any number of people crying, both men and women, in heartbreaking fashion. Her weeping wasn't a patch on theirs. She asks for a handkerchief. Why must you cry, if you haven't even got a handkerchief? She says she hasn't a sou in her pocket, I should give her 10 francs. If I wasn't prepared to make her a present of the 10 francs, then I should make her a loan. She swears she'll give it back, as true as she's sitting there, as true as there's a God in Heaven. She swears she'll bring it back. I tell her, instead of lending her 10 francs which she can give back to me, I'll make her a present of 5 francs. She doesn't care for this suggestion. Now you just have the choice of leaving with 5 francs, or leaving without 5 francs. – Je préfère avec![12] She'll say hallo to me in the street, that is, if I permit it, but she will never set foot in my room again. After she's gone, I get into bed.

14 JUNE 1892

Evening with Schlichting and Langhammer in the Moulin Rouge. A very fine day. Afterwards in the Café Wetzel, where Langhammer reads me his sketch – a poor imitation of Hermann Bahr.[13] I give him a few practical tips. After I have accompanied the gentlemen to Brie's, we part company and I go to bed.

15 JUNE 1892

Worked during the day. In the evening I draft the second act of my gruesome tragedy in the Café de l'Opéra, go to bed early, don't sleep all night and get up at seven in the morning.

16 JUNE 1892

After working until twelve I go to the Luxembourg, where I meet Frl. Rosa Krüger. When she catches sight of me, she blushes bright red, greets me with exquisite cordiality, we talk about the salon for a few minutes, Elisabeth Krüger joins us, I take my leave. I go to the Maison

Fara for dinner, expecting to meet Langhammer, but find myself totally alone. On my way home the landlord seizes me by the arm in front of the Brasserie Pont Neuf: Voici les dames![14] Frl. Juncker is sitting on the terrace, together with Frl. Krüger. I make a sketchy bow and continue on my way. I'm dying for little Marie from the Ancienne Comédie. I can't find her, and about one o'clock I go into the Café d'Harcourt, where Rachel makes her appearance in a brand new dress. I see her home and she shows me her photographs. I stay with her until four o'clock. Au ciel on mange des gâteaux, on boit du vin blanc.[15]

17 JUNE 1892

Work until three in a very good mood. Find a letter from Aunt Plümacher and a review from the *Milwaukee Freethinker* in my letter-box.[16] Send off copies to Maximilian Harden, Dr F. Lange, Otto Brahm, Fritz Mauthner.[17] In the evening carried on working until one, then in the Café d'Harcourt until two.

18 JUNE 1892

Letter to Dr Paetow in Berlin.[18] Go to the Café d'Harcourt at one o'clock. Fernande sits down beside me. We talk about Rachel. I toy with the idea of sleeping with Fernande tonight, but in the meantime she has vanished. Having worked myself up in this way, I hunt around in the brasseries of the Rue Soufflot and find a shabbily dressed girl with great, mysterious eyes. After fairly protracted negotiations I go back with her to her room, which has a pleasantly domestic atmosphere. After she has got undressed, she sits on my lap: 'Faites-moi un petit cadeau!'[19] I run my hand over a scar on her thigh, which somewhat takes me aback. She tells me that her needle had once broken off, she is a morphine addict, in fact. She couldn't very well afford to be ill, since she had a number of friends among the housemen at the hospital. I can see, indeed, that her thigh is completely covered with minute punctures. I ask her if she still has any need to faire la noce.[20] Oh, yes, it made you all the more excited. Was she menstruating, then? I get into bed, very relaxed and not at all lusting for sex. She gives herself two injections, washes, and gets into bed with me. Then she begins abusing her girlfriend in an endless

Saharet, a celebrated dancer and courtesan at the turn of the century.

torrent of words, at the same time coaxing my unmentionable member. At last we get to the point, mais il faut le monter. Je suis très étroite.[21] She's not wrong, and seems in fact to be stimulated, elle grince des dents,[22] if it's not all play-acting. After she has washed herself, and also washed me most conscientiously, and we're lying in bed again, she gives me a newspaper, picks up one herself and begins to read, working me over once more, but in a purely mechanical fashion. In the meantime we agree that we might well go to Bovy's. It has just got light, we get dressed. After combing out her dog's curls, she picks him up, and we go to Bovy's, where there is still a fairly large crowd of customers. After we have restored our strength with apple pie and some glasses of milk, we part company. Her name is Marie Louise, 25 Rue Monge. I go to bed, read Nietzsche for an hour, and fall asleep around six.

19 JUNE 1892

It would seem that I've fallen in love with the fat little blonde dancer at the Moulin Rouge. I've been dreaming of her all week. At the very thought of her I can't help sticking out my tongue.

I get up about three, take a walk for about an hour, and return home to work. I make no progress. After dinner I go to the Café du Congrès, and make no progress there either. I trot off to the Moulin Rouge. The audience is of the repulsively Sunday-best kind. I'm just on the point of leaving the hall when I spot the fat little dancer rehearsing her *pas*. But I'm not shaved, I'm wearing trousers with frayed turn-ups, and – as far as I'm concerned, the most ominous factor – I'm still somewhat weary from last night, it seems. Mind you, it wouldn't be my fault if I didn't make it with her. I watch her dance a couple of times, but then, all at once, she's vanished. She won't get away from me next time. In any case, it's past twelve [midnight]. I go home to work, but make no progress. – As I was dining at Duval's [on the Boulevard Malesherbes] at eight in the evening, Rachel came past in her new dress. She rapped on the window and greeted me with that sweet, dreamy grace she has.

20 JUNE 1892

Late in the afternoon I get a shave and go to the Moulin Rouge. I wait in vain until almost twelve o'clock for the fat little blonde dancer. Shortly before closing time a nice young creature in a kind of seaside resort costume whom I've watched dancing all evening with tolerable enjoyment comes up and asks me for a small favour. Blue eyes in a little blonde head, seventeen years old at the most, with very voluptuous lips. She reminds me of someone, but I can't think who. She still has on her neck the bruises that testify to yesterday's love-making. After the hall has closed, I go to the Café de la Paix for a moment, take supper in the Chien qui Fume, and go home about four.

21 JUNE 1892

After working all day, I go to Weinhöppel's about six. I can hear his pupils singing while I'm still in the corridor. He comes out of their room to welcome me in his own room. He says, in the first place, he's totally worn out, and, secondly —. If only she were pretty, at least. And she's jealous, into the bargain. He had succeeded in teaching her cunnilingus, so that at least he didn't have to look at her face. While he's telling me this, two ladies appear alternately at the window opposite. They make anything but a ravishing impression on me. He joyfully accepts my suggestion that we should go to the Moulin Rouge. It was to be hoped that his ladies wouldn't come with us. My assurance that he will be able to watch Jeanne la Folle sends him into transports of delight.[23] The ladies come to dinner with us, and I can well understand his problem. The more agreeable of the two, Frl. — is long past that certain age, without ever having actually experienced it. The other, Frl. —, with a pendulous nose and slanting eyes, is positively common. During the meal they entertain me entirely at the expense of Weinhöppel. After we have contrived to dump the ladies, we climb up to the Moulin Rouge: Weinhöppel is already with Jeanne la Folle in spirit, I'm preoccupied with my plump little blonde piglet. Scarcely have we entered before Weinhöppel's attention is captured by a tall, good-looking girl with a charming head and an Eastern cast of countenance whom we used to see dancing at one time in the Jardin de Paris. She dances in fact very indifferently. Jeanne la Folle fails to appear on the scene, so we concentrate on my heart-throb, the plump little blonde piglet, who doesn't, however, do anything out of the ordinary today. I'm on the point of inviting her to join us, when the girl with the Eastern features comes down from the stage arm in arm with one of the dancers and asks us to stand them a beer. Weinhöppel is wildly enthusiastic, but since I was the one she spoke to, I stake my claim to the Eastern lady. She was born in Alexandria, performed on the trapeze for years, then had a fall during her acrobatic turn, had been upset before every salto since then, and had hence taken up belly-dancing. She travelled all over Germany and Russia as a belly-dancer with the Baya company. She had been in Moscow, Petersburg, Novgorod, Berlin, Munich and Hanover, speaks English, Russian, German, a smattering of each language. She starts teasing me in the most endearing fashion, to the delight of those around us. She straight away begins making fun of my imperial beard. To Weinhöppel, who has turned his back on his own lady in speechless admiration, she addresses a few words in charming German with an Arabic accent that reminds me of Ikonomopulos. If we go up to her room with her, she'll do a belly-dance for us. I say I can't afford it. She wants a louis d'or for herself and her friend together. Weinhöppel declares he is willing to pay his share. We leave the hall: he tries to make his escape at the exit, but when he hears that the ladies live together, he joins us. And so we land up in a room that's decorated with oriental draperies, weapons, bird-cages, cushions and other junk of that sort. Here, the ladies at once undress, on account of the overpowering heat. The cancan dancer, a very pretty girl incidentally, is somewhat offended by Weinhöppel's neglect. By dint of a certain amount of polite attention I manage to soothe her ruffled feelings, so that she's ready to make the most of the part she has to play. Kadudja[24] has barely got undressed before Weinhöppel leaps on her. I grab him by the collar and heave him into the far corner of the room. I give Kadudja 30 francs for the pair of us. She informs her friend, who has followed our negotiations with some suspicion, and the ladies acknowledge our generosity. Kadudja disappears into the adjoining room and I make to follow her. Her friend holds me back, however: there's a surprise to come. Kadudja returns in a diaphanous black lace gown that reaches down to her feet. I seize a mandolin that's hanging on the wall, Weinhöppel a tambourine, and we strike up the belly-dance. Kadudja dances for a good half hour with great verve, perfect control and a delightful variety of facial expression. Weinhöppel is fascinated merely by the passionate rolling of her dark eyes, I'm captivated by the evolutions of her body. After she has finished, her friend begins a cancan, to which I play the solo part from the quadrille. She dances with great agility, but as frigidly as any doll. Kadudja says the two of us can occupy the bed in the next room, the others could stay on the divan. I follow her into a wretched little closet with a very comfortable wide bed and have my pleasure of her in two different ways. When we come back into the room, Weinhöppel is already getting dressed. We say goodbye and go to supper in the Café Wetzel. Weinhöppel is delighted with Kadudja. She is indeed so endearing, so unaffected and so good-humoured in everything she does and says that I can well understand his enthusiasm. While she was dancing, he burst out with the exclamation, 'these marvellous legs', which she repeated in such a comic fashion with an Arabic accent, that my own heart turned over. 'Qu'est-ce que ça signifie?'[25] her friend asked. 'Des jambes magnifiques',[26] I explained to her. Kadudja said she had already heard the words quite often in Germany. Her friend replied that she herself had only once been in Monaco. That was the sum total of her travels. Did he know Monaco, she asks Weinhöppel. Weinhöppel, rapt in contemplation of Kadudja, brushes the question aside irritably without bothering to reply. He claims to have enjoyed himself very adequately with his lady, incidentally, and admires his own potency, having been obliged — to have intercourse three times during the past week. All the same, she turned out not to be susceptible to his beloved Mimi.

We part about four. I drag myself off home, dog-tired, read for an hour, and then fall asleep.

22 JUNE 1892

After working all day, I meet Rachel in the Café d'Harcourt about one o'clock in the morning. She says she hasn't even had lunch yet, so we have supper together. When I offer to take her home, she excuses herself, saying she has a headache. That's because I told her I hadn't a sou in my pocket. I point out what a curious coincidence this is, whereupon she bursts into tears and promises she'll convince me of the opposite tomorrow. She starts talking about her feelings. I reply that it's most unwise to have feelings, you invariably come off worst.

23 JUNE 1892

To pass the time between dinner and midnight, I propose to go to the Elysée Montmartre, but find the place closed. I go to the Moulin Rouge. On my first circuit round the hall I meet Kadudja and her friend. I tell Kadudja I left my eyeglasses in her room, I'd come and fetch them tomorrow or the day after. She says she'll expect me the day after tomorrow, and will keep her afternoon free. During the next quadrille I see Jeanne la Folle dancing surrounded by a small circle of spectators. She dances in a heavy, black velvet gown with a crimson lining, but barefoot. She is said to be heavily addicted to morphine, as might be guessed from the perpetually dazed look in her great eyes. I'm sorry Weinhöppel isn't present. Her audience shows every sign of appreciation, and she does everything she can to earn their applause. When the quadrille is over I get on an omnibus and ride to the Café d'Harcourt. I see Rachel home after we've had supper together. As we enter her room, her guinea-pig hops towards her. She smothers it with her caresses: 'Mon tout petit, petit, petit Rickicki!'[27] I stay with her until daybreak. When I get home I notice I have left my cigarette holder in her apartment.

24 JUNE 1892

Meet Rachel in the evening in the Café d'Harcourt, take her home in order to fetch my cigarette holder, but, of course, remain in her arms. We've drunk a good deal of wine, and she's a little tipsy. During our initial embrace a violent thunderstorm breaks out. She has a fit of hysterics, talks about God and the Devil, and says the whole horizon is engulfed in flames every time I kiss her.

25 JUNE 1892

Get up about three, then work throughout the night and the following day until five in the evening. To Bullier's in the evening.

27 JUNE 1892

Decorate my room with a tapestry. Buy photographs, etc.

28/29 JUNE 1892

Worked.

30 JUNE 1892

Had supper with Rachel in the Café d'Harcourt. I stay with her until twelve o'clock next day. Sleeping with her is a very wholesome experience. I'd thank heaven if only I could get rid of her, all the same. As we part, she promises to visit me in the next day or two, early in the morning, as early as possible.

1 JULY 1892

In the evening after dinner I go to a bar near the Gare St Lazare, in the hope of meeting Weinhöppel. I don't find him, however, and go to a concert in the Hotel Terminus featuring two fiddles, a double-bass and a piano. The piano is played by a girl in black, not at all bad-looking, who restores her strength during the intervals with liberal measures of absinthe. The audience is not distinguished, but rather out of the way, a motley crew. I feel so weak that I drive straight home after the concert.

2 JULY 1892

In the evening after dinner I go and listen to a gipsy band on the Boulevard des Capucines. Afterwards in the Café d'Harcourt until two o'clock.

3 JULY 1892

After failing to fall asleep until it's nearly morning, I get up at three in the afternoon and only just manage to drag myself to the Madeleine. I'm dying for company, for a sensible word or two. I decide to call on Weinhöppel and to spend the evening with him, if with anyone, even if his ladies join the party. I find him in his room, busily writing letters. He tells me that his lady is fortunately in bed, since, fortunately, she is not well, as, fortunately, she's having her period. The other lady is being entertained by Herr Wormser, who fortunately has fallen in love with her, and hence relieved Weinhöppel of half his burden. Herr Wormser's voice can in fact be heard from the half-curtained window opposite, interspersed with Frl. von S.'s lascivious bleating giggle. Weinhöppel suggests going to the Jardin de Paris. We have a sumptuous dinner at Duval's and stroll down the Champs Elysées in glorious evening sunshine. We watch the first half of the variety show, and since there is no dance and the audience is distinctly plebeian, we take a cab to the Moulin Rouge at ten o'clock. We've scarcely entered the hall when I spot Kadudja and give her a wide berth. Since Jeanne la Folle is nowhere to be seen, much to Weinhöppel's disappointment, we make do with the plump little blonde piglet, who does in fact excel herself today. Weinhöppel is consequently able to appreciate my enthusiasm to the full. Finally, Kadudja also comes on and dances. Weinhöppel watches her for a few minutes, but I lead him back to our blonde lady. In the end we do after all meet Kadudja in the middle of the hall. She asks me why I didn't come for my spectacles on the day we'd arranged. I say I've been unwell, I'd fallen off a bus. She says, as she reties my tie, I should fetch them this evening. I say I'll come during the next day or two. She says, she's heard that tale before. I should come up there and then, I could leave straight away afterwards. I say, I've heard that tale before, but I had no money on me. She says, it's free today. Finally she asks me to dance with her. I decline, but when I notice that Weinhöppel's brow is urging me to agree, I hand him my umbrella. I dance as if inspired by some superior power, I get into the swing of it so smoothly, and don't stop until she's exhausted. I'm on the point of collapse as well. Kadudja thinks we ought to have something to eat in her room. My strength being totally spent, I agree, and the three of us leave the hall. By this time I have an absolutely splitting headache. At her door I make another feeble attempt to say goodbye. In vain, Kadudja says she doesn't love me any more.

While she's away fetching wine from the bar next door, I tell Weinhöppel I'd give up a kingdom if only I didn't have to make love to her. Weinhöppel says, if that's the only trouble, he'll do the job in a jiffy. That restores my energy up to a point. Once we've got upstairs, Kadudja gets us to sit down on cushions, hands us each a fan, fetches glasses and gets undressed. When she notices that Weinhöppel seems somewhat dejected, she asks if she should fetch her friend. But Weinhöppel says her friend is too frigid for his taste. After she has undressed, she drops into an armchair and lifts up her shift, so that Weinhöppel can fan her belly. She has excellent Turkish cigarettes, and I get her to puff the smoke into my mouth. She performs the same experiment with the wine, incidentally, which I drink from her lips. Then she shows us what progress she has made in the cancan. Over the head of her bed she has fixed a pulley with a rope running over it. She hauls her leg up on this rope every night. I put my arm under the back of her knee so as to perform Jeanne la Folle's *tour de force* with her. Finally we retreat into the closet, while Weinhöppel has recourse to her mandolin. She gets up again, however, to whisper in Weinhöppel's ear that he should help himself, making her meaning clear by means of an unmistakable gesture. I find myself to be after all in rather better fettle than I had imagined, especially considering that my splitting headache continues unabated.

When we return, Weinhöppel has already learned to play the belly-dance. I get dressed and, of course, can't find my cuffs at the last moment. Kadudja says she has pawned all her jewellery, and then pawned the pawn tickets. I should just see what she has bought. She leads me into the kitchen, where stands a large bicycle. I say that one of her friends has left it there as a pledge of his love, because I can see it's not a lady's model. But Kadudja says she's going to have the cross-bar removed and replaced by a curved bar. Then she shows me her three-year subscription to a bicycle school. We take our leave, sit in the Café Wetzel until one, when I have myself driven home, dead tired. Weinhöppel says he's going to call on Kadudja during the next day or two.

4 JULY 1892

Get up at nine and work until twelve. But I'm absolutely fagged out in the afternoon and evening.

5 JULY 1892

Try to work but it's no good.

6 JULY 1892

I feel a great deal better, but I'm in such an unprecedented state of nervous tension after breakfast that I simply have to find some outlet for it. In sheer desperation I plunge into the Printemps department store and get myself measured for a suit. That helps to calm me down, but not to the point where I would be capable of retaining an idea in my head. Summoning up all my moral courage, I resolve to take a cold bath. I have to conjure up memories of my Munich escapades before I can get myself into the water, but I feel so invigorated afterwards that I work until twelve o'clock. It's after midnight when I go to the Café d'Harcourt. I haven't the slightest desire to meet Rachel. I haven't even entered, however, before our eyes meet. I turn round discreetly and set off down the Boulevard. At once I hear footsteps behind me. A tap on my shoulder. Wasn't I on my way to the Café d'Harcourt? Of course, I had looked for her, but hadn't found her. – I should go to my usual seat, she'd come and join me in a moment. We say au revoir for the moment.

I walk round the upstairs terrace and round the back of the Café to the Rue Soufflot and sit down in a bar there. I've barely been sitting there for a quarter of an hour when a very pretty child, simply dressed, comes up to me and enquires after Leontine. She spoke to me in the street three days ago. Didn't I know where Leontine was, she'd disappeared for the last three weeks, nobody had set eyes on her, and it was a pity, because she was a good girl. She doesn't call her Leontine, by the way, but Sarah. After I've told her I've had no word from Leontine, she asks me whether I'm going on to the Brasserie Pont Neuf. – Where had she heard that I was in the habit of going there? – She'd met me there with Sarah. – Was her name Jeanne, then, and did she live in the Hôtel Voltaire? – But of course.

It is impossible, however, to detect any resemblance between her and Anastasia in Munich. I look in vain for that softness of feature, the full lips, the Madonna eyes which had so impressed me when I saw her in the Brasserie Pont Neuf. I offer her a beer, but she is here with her lover. While I'm still talking to her, Rachel walks past, glowering, with a reptilian glare and slovenly reptilian movements. I fail to see her, of course. The ladies say goodbye. Rachel at once sits down beside me. This is fine by me – for my own sake. It will hasten the break. After a while, however, I begin to find this squalid, stuffy bar disagreeable, so I let her tow me back to the Café d'Harcourt. The more awkward the situation, the more I take comfort in the thought: It's the last time! Accordingly, I see her back to her apartment. Another incident in the corridor, involving the concierge: Someone has taken her key. I imagine, of course, it's a customer and hope I can make good my escape at this point. But it is in fact a girl-friend who has been discharged from hospital that day. Someone had kicked her in the belly. Rachel insists on sleeping at my place. And so she comes back with me to my room, where she finds everything is very sweet. She asks me to play for her, and dresses up in my clothes, which suit her much better than Leontine. She really does look charming in them, a twelve-year-old urchin one would love to kiss – but that's all, really. She has no notion of all the comic tricks Leontine used to play in her role as gamin. We drink a lot of spirits, and my love is flat and stale.

7 JULY 1892

Rachel gets up about twelve, dresses and leaves. In her brightly coloured dress, with her leisurely movements, her elegant posture she is such a formidably handsome figure that I ask myself with intense satisfaction what kind of figure the best of the Lenzburg girls would cut alongside her. I get up about three, go for a bath, and work on until it's broad daylight next day.

8 JULY 1892

Rachel arrives before nine o'clock. We drink tea together, then she takes her clothes off and lies down beside me. We get up about two. She takes offence at some remark I've made, begins to cry and leaves – a move which absolves me from the temptation to pay her for her visit. After I've taken a bath, Weinhöppel comes round about six, plays to me for a bit, then we go out for a meal and come back to my place, where I read him my comedy.[28] His comments are very cordial, but I'm bound to say I felt much more at my ease while I was reading. We go to Bullier, which we find closed, then to the Source, then to the Café d'Harcourt, where we wait in vain until two o'clock for Rachel to turn up. I accompany him to the Chien qui Fume, we take supper together, and at five each of us gets a cab to go home.

9 JULY 1892
Worked.

10 JULY 1892

Buy *Rose et Ninette* by Daudet.

II JULY 1892

Finished Schwigerling. Meet Rachel in the Café d'Harcourt late in the evening. She comes back home with me. I make her a present of my photograph.

12 JULY 1892 .

A knock at the door early in the morning. I think it's the waiter with my tea and open the door. But it wasn't my door, it was my neighbour's. Not long afterwards there's another knock at the door. Assuming it's the waiter, I go to the door. But it's the laundry-maid. Since Rachel is lying on the bed stark naked, I ask her to come back later. In bed Rachel receives me with reproaches and suspicions, it wasn't the laundry-maid, but another woman coming to visit me. She knows all about that sort of laundry-maid. After a while there's another knock, and the waiter brings in my tea. We have breakfast in bed together. A little later there's a fourth knock. Supposing it's the laundry-maid, I leap up, rummage in the cupboard for the dirty linen, and, since I'm dressed in nothing but a shirt, I push it through the doorway with my foot. In front of the door little Jeanne is standing and, a few paces behind her by the window, Leontine. Without even waiting to gather up my dirty linen, I slam the door shut and go back to Rachel, who overwhelms me with a torrent of abuse. About two we get up, and after she has taken her leave I work until six, then go round to Weinhöppel's, to fetch him as arranged so that we can go to Neuilly to see *America Rediscovered*. But it's raining and it's an open-air performance. He tells me a long tale about Frl. von S. Last night she had Herr W. come up to her room with her and had then thrown him out in the most disgraceful manner after he had sat in an armchair for two hours waiting for the happy consummation. The following day he had written her a very decent farewell letter in the noblest terms. After he has played me some of his songs, which I listen to with the profoundest pleasure in spite of my hunger, we go to dinner at Duval's and then drive to the Moulin Rouge. I've barely entered when I spot Kadudja standing in the office, and grab Weinhöppel's sleeve to drag him past as rapidly as possible. Since the place is packed full, we take a box, but before we can get up to it Kadudja is already at our side. So I invite her in and sit with her by the stage, with Weinhöppel behind us. The *variété* has nothing interesting to offer. After the quadrille Kadudja's friend joins us. I let her have my seat and pay her a couple of compliments on her dancing. In the meantime Weinhöppel is arranging to meet Kadudja. After the show Kadudja asks me to explain to him in German that he should expect her after midnight and not book another lady, as she's keeping her evening for him. The ladies take their leave, because they're performing in the first polka. We take a turn or two round the ballroom and unexpectedly run into Weinhöppel's love, Fernande, 15 Rue Naples, from the Café Wetzel, with another quite pretty little creature. The ladies beg us for a few donkey's tears,[29] and are as insatiable as can be. Jeanne la Folle is nowhere to be seen: I depart shortly before twelve, leaving Weinhöppel to his fate, and move on to the Café Wetzel. He gives me his last louis d'or, just in case – 'but don't go and buy yourself a pussy with it.' After I've sat by myself in the café for about an hour, Weinhöppel comes in, followed by Fernande and her friend. The pair of them at once join us. I ask him about Kadudja. He is delighted – still pretty drunk. I ask him where he picked up these women, then. He doesn't know. The ladies tell me they've spent an hour riding the roundabout on the Boulevard Rochechouart. Weinhöppel tells me Kadudja went with him as far as the Boulevard. It looks as if the women had followed him from there. When we ask for the bill about three o'clock, Weinhöppel's last louis d'or goes down the drain after all, except for a negligible amount. I leap into a cab and drive home.

13 JULY 1892

I put on my new suit, get myself shaved, and go to call on Frl. Jung. As far as a copyist for my play is concerned, she turns to her secretary, Herr St., who promises to send me someone on Sunday. I tell her about Weinhöppel. She shows me a very flattering portrait of the Conrad-Ramlo family. She maintains that *Rose et Ninette* was merely sketched out by Daudet. The subtle details of the characterization came from his wife, who revises all his work. *Sappho* was the last thing he wrote on his own.[30] She'd been sorry to see how he'd started drifting around since then and had taken less and less part in the creation of his works. The descriptions of social life are said to be exaggerated – French society is a good deal better than its reputation, as opposed to German society. The fact that two of Weinhöppel's pupils followed him here strikes her as very German.

14 JULY 1892

National holiday. At midnight I go to the Source for an hour.

15 JULY 1892

Worked.

16 JULY 1892

Find Rachel in the Café d'Harcourt at midnight. She's a bit tipsy, very excited and ready to sleep with me at any price. After offering objections for some time, I take her with me. We drink a lot of spirits.

17 JULY 1892

I get up at nine o'clock and have just got dressed when there's a knock. I draw the curtains in front of the alcove and ask Herr Weintraub to come in. He asks for 45 francs for copying the manuscript and spends an hour telling me how badly off he is. We read Hebrew together, and I serve him a schnaps. After he's gone, I get back into bed with Rachel. We get up about four and go to lunch. She would simply love to go bathing with me in Chernetre, but I'm too lazy. We part after coffee.

18 JULY 1892

I'm very upset because Rachel has kept my ring. As soon as I've got up I buy a box of sweets for her child and call on her. The child is with its nurse. She gives me my ring, along with her photograph. After lunch I go to the Cirque d'Eté, where the Lee clowns are still performing,[31] and where I'm especially impressed by a clairvoyante. She sees everything in fact, the date on every coin in your purse.

19 JULY 1892

As I enter the Café d'Harcourt tonight, I notice a figure who is the very image of Kadudja. But she's not as tall and has a different hairdo. How would Kadudja turn up in the Café d'Harcourt? She smiles at me, of course, but I take no notice. Soon Rachel comes in, well and truly stewed, and sits down at my table, saying she's very excited, I'm to take her home with me. I give her something to eat and drink, buy her a large spider,[32] but tell her I can't take her home. As I'm talking to her, I can see in a mirror how Kadudja gets up and leaves the café on the arm of a gentleman. Just before she gets to the door, she turns round again; it's definitely not her. On the way home Rachel loses her spider. We call in at Bovy's to get sandwiches and a cake and then go up to my room. She keeps on moaning about her spider. In bed she talks about past ecstasies, but I can't make up my mind to encourage her.

20 JULY 1892

Mr Lewis left his card here yesterday.[33] After Rachel has patched my last shirt, I call on him. He's been here for the past three days. I find him in the company of his French tutor, whom he had carted all the way to Germany with him. Miss Marx left a few days ago. Fred Bulard has set up as a private tutor in Boston. He himself has the prospect of a job as a sports instructor. He goes to the Comédie Française every evening, and is as highly strung as a race-horse in other respects as well. Sometime next week he wants to go with me and call on Weinhöppel. In Munich the Americans have fallen out with Pottkifer because of Feller. We go to lunch, when I tell him about a few of my escapades, which, however, achieve no more than a *succès d'estime*.

Yesterday in the Café d'Harcourt somebody sat on my top hat. As a result I've been wearing my *chapeau* ... which gave me a violent toothache in the evening.

21 JULY 1892

In the evening, as I'm dining at Duval's on the Boulevard des Capucines, there's a gentleman sitting opposite who keeps cursing the insufferable heat to himself in German. He looks like a commercial traveller. I respond to his monologue all the same. He's just come from Egypt, and is shocked by the cancan pictures on display here, especially as they are interspersed with portraits of the saints. I advise him to see the phenomenon *in natura*, so we go to the Moulin Rouge together. He's already beginning to seem to me a cut above a commercial traveller, perhaps someone from the embassy in Cairo. He finds the cancan very interesting indeed. If his wife was here, he would definitely bring her along. In the meantime I'm accosted by Estella, and then by her friend Andrée, with whom we drink a beer. He takes a great fancy to her and finds it hard to tear himself away. When we have sat down to another beer, he picks up two antique tarts, who soon leave us, however. They've only just gone when Kadudja turns up, scolding me because I didn't say hallo to her in the Café d'Harcourt: she'd been there with a friend who used to live in the *quartier* and wanted to show her the café. My companion talks to her, first in Arabic, then in Russian. Then I dance a brilliant mazurka with her. During her final quadrille, however, we beat a hasty retreat, take a cab and drive to the Café d'Harcourt, my companion having been told about it by a Romanian he had met on the train. To my great disgust, Rachel is wearing a somewhat shabby dress. I introduce my companion as an old friend I haven't seen for ten years. He pats her legs enthusiastically, which she objects to, however, as an inexcusable liberty. He is utterly petrified at this rebuke. To keep her occupied while we talk politics, I order supper for her. At two o'clock I walk as far as the bridge with my anonymous acquaintance, and as we part he admits that a Parisian *cocotte* is quite a different proposition from a Berlin scrubber.

22 JULY 1892

A card announcing the engagement of Professor Dr Carl Schmidt[34] to Charlotte Herdtwalker of Hamburg.

I meet Rachel in the Café d'Harcourt. I have no desire to go along with her, but she says she has bought something I must see. We fetch a bottle of wine and a cake from Bovy's and go up to her apartment. I'm pretty well fagged out and instantly fall into one of her high-backed armchairs. She gets undressed, flings on a black nightdress with red stripes, and while we talk for a couple of hours about all manner of things, she clambers around on her other extremely rickety high-backed armchair. She's going on holiday in a fortnight, she says. She's taking her *bébé* and is going to pretend to her parents that it's her employer's child. She could do that quite easily, because it still doesn't speak a word. She shows me the vests she's sewing, clothes for *bébé*, a little blue jacket with lace trimmings. Last of all, she shows me a savings bank book with a balance of 500 francs. I'm surprised, as I've never seen her with a man. It's true, she says, she has very few friends, *bébé*'s father and two or three others. She very rarely picked up anyone in a café. She tells me about how she dreams of moonlight, sylvan solitude, an indissoluble bond of love outside wedlock. She tells me about her youth, lonely walks across flowery meadows in the twilight, or about the autumn, when she sat all by herself up on a mountain. Everything had been so serene and sad. Her youngest brother, the one with his hat pulled down over his brow in her family photograph, was just like her. She loved him more than anyone else. She would like to have a son who was similar to her brother, he would have to belong entirely to her, he mustn't talk to anyone else, only walk alone with her in the woods and dream – she didn't know herself what they would dream. When she opens the curtains, the morning sun is shining in the garden of the Louvre. We quickly get into bed. I wake up after I've slept for little more than an hour, tormented by fearful toothache and bitten all over by bed-bugs. I fling on my clothes, go home, make myself as strong a brew as possible, go to bed and sleep until three in the afternoon.

23 JULY 1892

I go to the Luxembourg, where I grow fonder and fonder of Manet's Venus, the only picture in a truly noble style. Then I go bathing in the Seine on account of my toothache.

A letter of congratulation from Mali. She is boarding in Geneva. Mieze is celebrating one triumph after another in Lenzburg. Willy, they say, is ten times better off being unhappy in Africa than he would be if he were happy in Europe. She asks me to send her *Spring Awakening*.

24 JULY 1892

My birthday. I don't suffer from the fit of the blues that I usually experience on this occasion. It leaves me absolutely cold. In the Café Larue during the evening I draft the third act of my gruesome

Frank and Tilly Wedekind in *Earth Spirit*.

tragedy,[35] call on Weinhöppel, but don't find him in, get on the train and go to Neuilly to see the *America Rediscovered* show.

25 JULY 1892

Get the review from the *Vossische Zeitung*, along with a letter from Dr Paetow. Write straight away to H. . . . After I've taken a bath in the evening, I go to see Weinhöppel. After he has played me a couple of pieces and said goodbye to his ladies, we have dinner together and drive to the Moulin Rouge. All the tables are taken, so we take a box. The quadrille is brilliantly danced, especially by our friend, who honours us by throwing us a glance now and then from the stage. On our first tour of the hall she meets us, together with Kadudja. Kadudja would like to run away with me. I tell her I have no money. She says she's rich, she doesn't need any money, and shows me a number of louis d'or that she keeps beneath a garter on the back of her leg, so that they gleam through the black silk mesh of her stocking above the brocade slippers that have her name embroidered on them. I put her off until later.

Weinhöppel tells me he saw the plump blonde piglet, my long adored ideal, a few days ago. That very moment she brushes past us after rehearsing her *pas* in front of a mirror. Alas, she is no longer wearing her dress with the *décolleté*. After the next quadrille I offer her a drink, which she accepts with a passionately tender glance at Weinhöppel. I can see that I've lost the game, but put up with my defeat without too much distress. She speaks Parisian French so rapidly that I find it hard to follow her. Weinhöppel tries to compliment her on her ears, but the attempt somehow goes adrift, and I have to intervene. I point out Weinhöppel's good features to her – she's called Jeanne – his imposing physique, while behind her back he's busy putting his last louis d'or into an envelope and stuffing it into a hidden pocket. I point out to her what a dismal part I'm playing. Weinhöppel takes this seriously, and while she goes off to her quadrille, he assures me by way of consolation that I am after all much more handsome than he is. She comes back and Weinhöppel, abandoning any further attempt at conversation, adopts a pose that is simultaneously heroic and languishing. His eyes get smaller, his jaw juts out, and a portentous thundercloud descends on his low brow. At the same time he digs her in the ribs every so often, so as to convince her of the fervour of his feelings. He dances the next dance with her and returns, pallid and in distress: in the middle of the dance he had had violent palpitations and an attack of diarrhoea. Jeanne has brought back with her the Danish girl, Siphon, alias Morpion, with whom she shares her apartment. I do my best to look after the girls properly. Meanwhile, Jeanne informs the Danish girl Siphon that she's had an attack of diarrhoea. I communicate this information to Weinhöppel, who falls into a renewed reverie at this evidence of natural sympathy. The Danish girl, Siphon, tells me she's really a singer and is going back to America this coming winter. She had sung in Peru and Chile, in Lima, Valparaiso, Acapulco, etc. She'd very much like to go to Germany some time, especially to Munich. She asks me if you get there by ship. After the dancing is over, I leave Weinhöppel alone with the ladies, go to the Café Wetzel, where Adèle joins me, and drive home dog-tired at two o'clock.

26 JULY 1892

After dining at Duval's I meet my Egyptologist on the boulevard. We stroll along the Champs Elysées and sit down in a bar by the Madeleine. He's an Egyptologist and is on his way to London on business and also means to give a lecture there. He tells me about the death of the late Viceroy,[36] who is alleged to have died of the clap. Life in Cairo during the winter, it seems, is very extravagant and lavish because of the many foreigners who brought in large amounts of cash. Up till now roulette had been played everywhere quite openly. International action had now curbed the gambling up to a point, but those who held the banks, mostly Greeks, took it all in their stride. The tarts strolling past constantly arouse his admiration. He keeps thinking about his wife lying in hospital in Bremen. He's been married for six years, in fact, and they would like to have a little boy. After all, it just wasn't the thing, if you kept thinking time and time again that there's nothing doing. He only had to let slip a word, and his wife's eyes filled with tears. And so she had had the operation now. He hadn't thought her sterility mattered all that much. But it had turned out that she had three malformations of the uterus. Now she'd been operated on, it would be much better. I give him my sincerest good wishes. We go on to talk a great deal about Biblical mythology, Asherah, etc.[37]

He describes his journey from St Jean d'Arcon to Jerusalem for my benefit. He'd been warmly welcomed in Samaria, because he's translating the Bible into Samarian. He had spent a night with Bedouins on Mount Tabor and it had almost cost him his life. Jerusalem is the world's worst haunt of hypocrites. Englishmen came to have heavy crosses made by local carpenters which they then dragged through the city and up to Golgotha. One of them had had to get the carpenter to saw a chunk off his, because it was too heavy.

Each of them was determined to act some part from the Gospels. At the same time, the local population was currently turning out vast numbers of foundlings so as to populate a foundling hospital that had been endowed by some German countess or other. The city was already so over-provided with foundations of one sort and another that she'd found it impossible to establish any other sort of institution. The Jews in Jerusalem all draw a pension on which they can live quite comfortably. Ragged Turkish soldiers stand guard outside the Church of the Holy Sepulchre in order to settle disputes between the various Christian nations. France has precedence, then comes Russia. The influence of Russia in Palestine is enormous, he says. He has no doubt that the country will fall to Russia sooner or later. So we get round to the Crimean War, the Tunisian and the East African question. He knows Wissmann personally.[38] Whenever Wissmann was in Cairo he drank and whored fearfully, but he had the constitution to stand it. Emin Pasha,[39] intimidated by German bureaucracy, is once more conducting affairs entirely on his own initiative.

I see my friend home and then go to bed.

27 JULY 1892

Fetch Rachel from the Café d'Harcourt. She gets completely undressed in my room, apart from her vest, a diaphanous pink petticoat and her black stockings. In this outfit, with her hair let down and holding her black fan, she wallows around on my sofa between my guitar, my various fat lexicons and a couple of shapeless hessian cushions. She takes up one delicious pose after another, at the same time sucking down to the last drop a lemon which happened to be lying on the table. The lemon inspires her – and me as well – with lascivious ideas. After we've got into bed she sucks me off, which I can't stand for long, as I find it drives me to utter distraction. The next morning she tells me she had dreamt about her mother all night. She had desperately wanted to suck her mother's cunt. At first her mother wouldn't let her, but then she had consented, and it had been so sweet, so sweet.

28 JULY 1892

Stay at home and do a bit of work.

29 JULY 1892

After dinner I call on Weinhöppel and find him in the company of his ladies. He plays me a few pieces. Then I ask Frl. Sch— to sing. Her singing makes up in full for her unprepossessing appearance. After a while, Herr Wormser makes his appearance. He claims to have heard of me from his sister, who does a bit of writing, but this is probably a mistake. We go to the Brasserie Molard, and then Wormser invites us back to his place for a glass of genuine Black Forest Kirschwasser. We've barely got upstairs before he starts to hypnotize us, beginning with Frl. v. S—, who succumbs to his influence with voluptuous sobs. I ask him to try me. He instantly detects a sympathetic warmth in me. After he has put me to sleep a couple of times, he can't get me to wake up again. Although he rouses me a number of times, I relapse each time into a hypnotic trance. At last he manages to get me to stand up. But when Weinhöppel suddenly gazes intently into my eyes, I fall backwards flat on my back. The company are then seized by a speechless panic, the ladies start having fits, Wormser rushes from the room. Weinhöppel is the only person to keep his head, putting his mouth to my ear and telling me we're going to the Café Wetzel to drink another Américain. My senses are thereupon restored. We see the ladies home. In the Café Wetzel, Weinhöppel tells us about his escapade with the blonde piglet: she had come back home with him, she had spent the entire night there, he'd given her no more than 7 francs, she was a woman the like of whom he'd never kissed before, etc., etc. I leap into a cab and drive home.

30 JULY 1892

At home.

31 JULY 1892

Weintraub arrives at ten o'clock with the transcript he's made. We drink a glass of beer together, while he tells me about the battles fought by beggars amongst themselves in the vicinity of the Hôtel de Ville. I'm suffering from an acute gastric infection, and after lunch I go off to the Salvation Army. A few rows in front of me the Countess Kessler is sitting in deep mourning. We exchange glances from time to time, but I don't manage to catch her after the service. After dinner I go back. Field Marshal Borth, the daughter of the late lady General, is giving a sermon. She gave birth only a week ago and is consequently endowed with all the fey fervour of the childbed. Nevertheless, her unwomanly harshness grates on me.

Sitting next to me is a young man with an immense bushy wig that's streaked with grey. He tells me that he's a poet of the Décadence, had founded a Chat-Noir in Bordeaux,[40] but had now given all that up to become a lieutenant in the Salvation Army. He carries his books and his poems about in a valise, leaving his apartment with them in the morning, then sitting down on some bench or other, where he reads and writes all day long. He lives on bread and water. That weakens his constitution, of course, and often he can barely drag himself upstairs, but his soul grows ever more radiant and free. His ultimate aim is madness, and it seems to me he's well on the way there. About a month ago, a sculptor did in fact starve to death in the Rue Monge, at no. 37. In his death-throes he banged on the wall, the door was broken down, but he was already beyond human aid. My companion had no sooner read this than he set out for Paris. He went to 37 Rue Monge, and asked the landlady to give him the room where the sculptor had died. – Didn't a young sculptor starve to death here? – Yes, he did. – Give me his room.

The landlady, they say, very nearly fainted, which I can well believe, given my companion's appearance. The hapless sculptor is said to have already paid him at least one visit. He himself is twenty-two years old and, in contrast to his farouche appearance, has a positively girlish charm and a sort of inner happiness. When he speaks he places his fingers on his lower lip. He claims to be half Spanish and half French and to come from a prosperous family. He had been a commercial traveller, then an editor, had become addicted to absinthe in this capacity, had often kept company with women, but was still a virgin. Chastity, he says, affords a state of mind that is incomparably more gratifying that the satisfaction of natural appetites. I argue fiercely with him, trying to persuade him to desert from the Salvation Army and to set up in Paris as a sort of Dieffenbach.[41] As we're parting at the corner of the Boulevard St Germain, he rummages around in his valise and finally digs out a sonnet which he gives me to remember him by. Leon Escalus, publiciste.

A Parisian *cocotte* from the Moulin Rouge.

1 AUGUST 1892

Go to the Moulin Rouge in the evening and unexpectedly come across Weinhöppel with his pupil. That evening when he had come home with Jeanne, Frl. Sch. had had a vision. She suddenly wakes up with a start about eleven and can't get the idea out of her head that her Richard is in the arms of another woman. She looks at the clock and tells herself it's nonsense, it's much too early. In fact he must actually have been there in the house with her about eleven. Her palpitations still don't abate. She keeps thinking of Kadudja, whom he has pointed out to her, but her vision persistently leads her away

158

from Kadudja. And so, improbable as it may seem, she finally lights on the little blonde. But Weinhöppel has trained her well in his barbaric fashion. She swallows her jealousy with some difficulty, and a week later goes to the Moulin Rouge with him, to give him a chance to revive his feelings. Weinhöppel tells me that one hot afternoon, a couple of days after his infidelity, she had spent half an hour sucking him off with the greatest composure. Immediately after they had had sexual intercourse, while his penis was still dripping, she had remarked with a deep sigh of relief, now it was over, overcome – her anger with him, that is. It had been the first sexual intercourse since his —.

While I sit with her over a beer, Weinhöppel goes off in search of his Jeanne. He returns in a foul temper, having failed to find her, and has the effrontery to vent his fury on his wretched pupil. He has bullied his pupil to the point where she daren't move a muscle in his presence. She has to put up with every sort of humiliation. When I'm present, he tries to cover up by pretending it's all in fun. The poor girl sits there as if she were on the rack, suspecting some fresh humiliation behind every word he utters. Shortly before closing time we make another tour of the hall. Jeanne is dancing in the middle of a large circle of spectators. The moment she sets eyes on Weinhöppel, she breaks off in the middle of the quadrille and rushes out of the room. This adds fresh fuel to his passion. Shortly afterwards we watch Jeanne la Folle in very reduced — attempting a few leaps. Her features are distorted, her hair is bedraggled. You could tell she's a morphine addict from a hundred yards away. We then move on together to the Café Wetzel, where Weinhöppel's — reaches its climax. I feel so shattered, however, that I let him do as he pleases.

2 AUGUST 1892

At home.

3 AUGUST 1892

Drive over to Frl. Hüny, who, they tell me, has gone off to the country, which I find hard to believe, send *Schwigerling* to Entsch.[42] Write to Thomar. Fetch Rachel from the café. She is delighted with the frame I've bought for her picture. After we've chatted for a couple of hours, we lie down together. But I'm in a very odd frame of mind after that business with Hüny, so that I spurn her caresses after our first skirmish. I'm afflicted by a strange sort of sadness. All of a sudden Rachel's mood changes, she quickly gets dressed and is on the point of leaving, in fact. I lock the door and put the key under my pillow. After she's found it nevertheless, I pull off one of her shoes and lock it in my wardrobe. At the same time I keep wondering whether I shouldn't let her go after all. But since she seems to mean it in earnest, I can't make up my mind to do so. Finally, about five o'clock, I pretend to fall asleep, hoping to tire her out. But she still stays sitting on the sofa. At first light she extinguishes the candles and sits looking out of the window. Then she creeps up to the bed, looking for the key. Having tried force to no avail, I have recourse to reason as my final ploy, undress her with her assistance, and fling her into bed. With no more than brief interruptions by a couple of passages of arms, and by the waiter bringing in my chocolate, we sleep right through until the afternoon. Then I drive to the Gare St Lazare and sit down in front of the Brasserie Molard. Shortly afterwards little Andrée de Villiers walks past. I ask her to take a seat, hoping that her company will restore me somewhat after my encounter with Rachel. She had a client last night who didn't give her a sou, etc., etc. I can understand practically nothing of her chatter. She keeps me company as far as the Rue Provence.

After that I call on Weinhöppel, whom I find in the company of his ladies. Not long after, Mr Derval's aunt arrives. Derval was a singer at Covent Garden in London. Weinhöppel made his acquaintance through Amsel. Since then he's been coaching him in Wagner. The aunt has taken a particular fancy to him. She was a great singer in her time. Now she's a shrivelled-up little old lady, but still very agile. She sang together with Dalli at La Scala, comes from some Australian island originally, and speaks French with a strong English accent. It was she who introduced Weinhöppel to Elena Sang, to whom he dedicated one of his songs. Incidentally, he expects to get an appointment as conductor in one of the cafés chantants here in October. A gipsy, first violin at Lamonreux, has pretty well promised him for certain. After the ladies have gone off to dine with the old lady, we go to dinner at Duval's, and then on to the Moulin Rouge. The first person we notice in the audience is Jeanne la Folle. Once our eyes have met, she gets up from her seat and disappears. I pursue her all the way through the hall, but can't find her in the end. In the meantime, Weinhöppel has picked up little Andrée. In his pocket he's got a gold-embroidered belt that cost him three francs which he means to give to his beloved Jeanne, the plump one. He does present her with it in fact, she puts it on at once and dances in it. When we sit down for a beer she naturally brings along a friend for me, to whom I can hardly devote a decent amount of attention because I'm so very weary. As he wants to take his Jeanne home with him, I leave him alone with the ladies at twelve o'clock, drink another half bottle in the Brasserie Pont Neuf, and then go to bed.

3 DECEMBER 1892

I've only just got up when Herr Muth calls on me. It's almost four o'clock. We walk through the Luxembourg Gardens, with him drawing my attention to the subtle tints of the autumn landscape. He has met Munkácsy at the Hungarian Club.[43] Munkácsy has invited him to visit him in his studio. He means to write an article about Munkácsy, although he knows practically nothing about his pictures. I tell him about the most important of them. He asks me if I'd be interested in seeing Munkácsy's studio. He'll ask Munkácsy, and we might go together some time. This gives Herr Muth new status in my eyes, especially as they say some very pretty girls go to the meetings of the Hungarian Club. I do my best not to make my eagerness too obvious, so that Herr Muth doesn't get an inflated idea of his own affability, and consequently grow weary in well-doing. Going down Montparnasse towards the Invalides he raves enthusiastically about Pierre Loti.[44] It soon transpires that he hasn't read a line of Loti, but merely one or two reviews in various magazines. Seized by a reverential thrill, we make our way across the Place de la Concorde, and as we come to the first of the club houses bought by Baron Hirsch, Muth starts reviling the Jews once again. I let him drivel on, but as he shows no sign of stopping, I point out to him that Munkácsy is a Jew. He had no idea, but he'll make enquiries. On the Boulevard des Italiens he tells me such a filthy anti-Semitic story about smelling Jews, involving himself, his friend Lienhard[45] and a Jewish playwright, that I lose my temper. He so disgusts me that I'm tempted to send him packing. The prospect of meeting Munkácsy restrains me. I tell him no decent man is an anti-

Semite, and no anti-Semite can be considered a decent man, and he then starts qualifying his anti-Semitism, claiming it's an emotional issue, for which the proper expression is lacking, he would be inclined to term it nationalism. I retort that the Jews aren't a nation, and the Christians had no right to exclude them from their national communities, and, excited as I am, I ask him to have dinner with me. He accepts, provided I foot the bill, but he wouldn't go on anywhere afterwards.

We dine together in Duval's, where he finds the beefsteak too tough, and we more or less sink our differences in a discussion on this topic. So he does in fact accompany me to the Folies Bergères, on condition that he may refund me the admission charge. I assure him he can be my debtor for as long as he likes. The Folies Bergères is pretty well sold out. We get a pair of folding seats near the stage. Muth commandeers my opera glasses and then complains that he can see the make-up too distinctly. Every time he has to get up to let people pass he utters an indignant grunt. In the box to our right sits a marvellously handsome woman in black satin with a massive diamond brooch where her bosom ought to be. She has a snow-white complexion, short, dark arched eyebrows, hair dyed a reddish tint, a hefty snub nose, and overall an expression reminiscent of John Henry Mackay,[46] manifested especially in her world-weary smile and the world-weary droop of her mouth – which suggests that under her plump cheeks she has lost her canine teeth. When I whisper to Muth that she reminds me of Lord Byron, he replies that he was on the point of saying the very same thing to me.

Behind us in the pit attention is clearly divided. The audience's gaze keeps straying from the stage to the bewitchingly beautiful mistress above us. A rather pretty tart sitting in the same row as me can't take her eyes off her. The show has nothing much of interest to offer me. I've already seen the ballet three times. Mlle Campana doesn't manage to display her artistic talents to the full.[47] The most attractive feature is the dancers' backs, which can be seen as far down as the waist in every case, some of them strikingly lovely, not excessively padded but yet not skeletal. During the interval we visit the garden, where, wedged into the fearful crush, we watch the beautiful Fatma. Muth, who hadn't the faintest notion of the belly-dance until half an hour ago, and who watches it goggle-eyed, claims to have seen it performed in Algiers in a much more natural fashion.

As we're leaving the place we find ourselves behind the handsome mistress: she is being escorted by a bent old greybeard, who is fending off a pack of young dandies. Muth tells me she's the very image of a girl he knew in Berlin, and he would prove it by showing me his album, only it happened to be in Berlin, the resemblance had struck him the moment he had set eyes on her, only he couldn't think straight away who she reminded him of.

We walk along the Rue Montmartre in the pouring rain. Muth, who hasn't brought an umbrella, shares mine. It's got holes in it, true, but that doesn't worry him, he says. He offers to foot the bill in the Palette d'Or. I ask him not to, he can take me to see Munkácsy instead. He says this is an offensive remark, and puts his money back in his pocket. He shows me his army service record, from which I gather that he's a Catholic and has an unblemished military record. He tells me about his journey from Spain to Algiers, but gets no further than the fearful bout of seasickness he had suffered. In Algiers he went for a walk and ate some cactus figs. On his way back he had contrived the downfall of a waiter who had overcharged him for his berth. He's been in the Netherlands, in Spain, in Italy and Africa, without noticing anything particularly remarkable. In Berlin he had once spent all night in bed with a prostitute who hadn't let him turn her over on her back. His literary acquaintances are Lienhard and, especially, Wilhelm Walloth.[48] As far as the lyric goes, his needs are met by Droste-Hülshoff.[49] The only two poems he cares for in Henckell's *Diorama* are those to which I happen to have drawn his attention.[50] Girls with snub noses he can't stand. I tell him no other kind of girl is capable of arousing me. He replies that that's the very reason he can't stand them, they would excite him too much. He is of slender build and walks like a youthful Lutheran zealot, his legs are thin and sinewy, his knees are firmly locked, his back bowed, neck thrust forward, a stereotyped frown on his face, every step marked by a curt nod of the head. Whenever we turn round, he skips round behind me in order to get back on my left side. In spite of this energetic walk, there's something creepily reptilian about him, he frequently complains that he's on edge, he's obviously anaemic, suffers from imagined ailments, inclines to vegetarianism, mastur-bates and raves in and out of season in the most bombastic terms about the authentic, down-to-earth Teutonic nature. 'Utterly Ger-man' is his favourite expression, Luther his ideal; in a drawer at home

The dancer Cléo de Merode. A photograph taken about 1900.

he keeps a Westphalian ham, and makes himself a watery brew of cocoa to go with it every evening. He sports a short, silky black beard, has frightfully sweet lips, a strongly hooked nose, twinkling eyes and a hand of which he is very proud, and on which he wears a lady's ring in the style of the forties. He thinks the French girls take him for an Englishman, on account of his somewhat shabby light-coloured check suit. Ever since I've known him he's been talking about a top-hat he intends to buy himself. What binds me to him is the fact that, since Weinhöppel's departure, I often spend a fortnight without meeting a soul. I'm suddenly afflicted by a splitting head-ache, and we go home about three.

4 DECEMBER 1892

Get up about two, go out for breakfast and meet Rachel right outside the restaurant. She's about to pass me with a petulant glance, but I stop her. She's wearing a new coat, pale purple with a double collar and a white veil: she looks fresh and healthy. I scrutinize her in vain for symptoms of syphilis. She's on her way back from the Châtelet,[51] where she had picked up two tickets for the *Damnation of Faust*.[52] She asks me if I still have her 'Symphonie d'Amour'. Yes, I'll bring it to her in the Café d'Harcourt. – She'll come and fetch it herself, will I be at home about eleven? – Yes, it will be a great pleasure for me. – But I'm not to be unfaithful to her before tomorrow. Am I still living with that consumptive little creature? – Who did she mean? No. I'd never lived with her. I didn't even know her.

I accompany her a few paces, then go to lunch and back home late in the afternoon, so as to finish off the first act of my *Astarte*.[53] As I'm sitting in front of the fire about eleven, there's a gentle knock at the door. I don't stir. It's Henriette. She has crept soundlessly upstairs, taking care not to cough on the staircase, and has got as far as the door, afraid that if I hear her, I may turn the key in the lock. The key is in fact already turned. For the last week I've been at home behind locked doors. She knocks one more, tries the handle, then there's not another sound. I sit motionless, staring into the coals. I think she's waiting for me to open the door after a while, to see whether she's gone away. I go on waiting until I hear the street door downstairs bang shut. Then I go back to my desk and continue working. I finish about four, get into bed and read the last hundred pages of *Bel Ami*.[54] Then it occurs to me that Henry in Canossa, facing Gregory VII,[55] with Beatrix and Mathilde in the background, might be a suitable subject for Munkácsy. I read through the relevant articles in the encyclopedia. In the meantime day dawns, and the waiter brings in the coffee.

5 DECEMBER 1892

Rachel had announced her intention of coming at eleven. So I get up at ten, get dressed as quickly as I can, and just manage to make my escape a few minutes before eleven. I go straight to Herr Muth, who's still lying in bed. He reads me a series of poems by Walloth. They are on about the same aesthetic level as Mackay's, without being based on the same sort of powerful personality. He draws my attention to the revolution that his friend Lienhard has effected in literature. I read a number of obscene diatribes against Heine couched in a juvenile style, and tell Muth that this kind of ineptitude, combined with the audacity to find fault with his betters, deserves nothing better than a resounding box on the ears.

On this note we go to lunch. Muth has read my *Spring Awakening* the previous evening. He had simply failed to notice the act of sexual intercourse that figures in the play. He's thinking of writing a book in which he would characterize the most recent French writers with the help of extracts from their major works. He would concoct some biographical notes from Lemaître's reviews.[56] But it would have to be the extracts that gave the book the necessary thickness. In this way you could pocket a fairly respectable fee without working yourself to death. Unfortunately, too few books were published in Germany. In France, a book of that sort would run through hundreds of reprints. We stroll down the Boulevard St Germain as far as the German Embassy in the most glorious sunshine. Count Arco from Munich had given a speech at a meeting in Paris. Muth reported the speech for the *Wiener Tageblatt* and is just on his way to show his article to Count Arco. He personally could see nothing shameful in doing this. I say we all have to prostitute ourselves in one way or another. Muth replies that, unfortunately, he has no talent in that respect. I stroll across the Place de la Concorde to the Madeleine in the evening sunshine and settle down in the Café Larue. Muth soon reappears. Count Arco had tried to press 20 francs into his hand, but he had refused to take it. He'd probably go there fairly frequently, it would mount up then, and he might well do better in the end. After we've talked about Goethe and Schiller until seven, I drive him to the Maison Fara, and from there to the Cirque d'Hiver. Muth wonders in fact whether we shouldn't go instead to one of the little theatres I had spoken to him about with such enthusiasm. I ask him to go to the theatre by himself, however; you could move around in the circus, that was quite a different matter. Muth says he doesn't like going to places by himself anyway. Right at the beginning I notice that the Lee brothers aren't there any longer. Their place has been taken by a pair of Italian clowns who put on an act that is lacking in wit but makes up for it in effrontery. The Necrophiles are not on the bill either, nor the Seven-Hundredweight Men. I am captivated by a slim twelve-year-old lad who performs all sorts of acrobatics with great agility and daring on a barebacked horse, a spirited steeplechaser with narrow withers and nervously trembling limbs. The jockey is so execrable that I'm overcome by weariness and fall asleep at Muth's side. I've only just wakened up when the cloakroom attendant brings me the following note:

Cordial greetings from Willi Morgenstern, alias Rudinoff.[57] As I come on in the second half of the programme, I cannot, alas, join you at your seat. Would you be so kind as to wait for me at the entrance to the stables during the interval.

W. MORGENSTERN

I barely have to read the name Morgenstern before I'm at the entrance. As we fall into each other's arms, I'm on the verge of tears. The horizon all round me was so dismally dark, when all of a sudden a whole world opens up before me. Morgenstern keeps stammering over and over again: You can't think what a joy it is! Oh no, this joy! We move into the roomy, deserted stables, since he daren't speak German so loudly among his colleagues. He is booked at a salary of 1,000 francs a month. He sees me sitting there and wonders: That gentleman looks mighty like Wedekind! No, the very image of Wedekind! Who would have thought such a likeness possible! When I address a few words to Muth, he cries: It's him! It's him!, rushes up into a box and writes me the note. The stage-hands round him, he says, must have thought he'd gone mad. Since he's just about to get changed, we part until the interval. I'm utterly rejuvenated. Returning to Muth, I outline Morgenstern's character and his enormous versatility in a few words. In the interval we meet at the entrance to the stables and stroll round with the other spectators. Morgenstern has been in Brussels, in Antwerp, in Amsterdam, in Cologne, Colmar etc. In Düsseldorf he had seen Shereshefsky's picture on display,[58] he had met Linde in the Eldorado in Antwerp as Linde was on his way to

India. Pohl is said to be still in Egypt. He's had no news from Munich for a year. I ask him if Gerard is still performing, and he points her out on the programme, the third act from the end. Morgenstern is the second last. After the show we wait for him at the stage-door. His silhouettes, unpretentious as they are, were received with most applause. In his capacity as an imitator of bird-calls he elaborates a kiss which features in one of his silhouettes. After we've waited for a while in the rain, Gerard appears, one arm leaning on her lover, the other supported on a short crutch. She's limping, but seems able to suppress the limp for the ten minutes that her act lasts. She is no less pretty than she appears on the hoarding, but looks pitifully ill. At last Morgenstern appears in his cape and ample velvet beret, which, together with his pointed beard, give him the appearance of a Rembrandt. We go into the Café de la Terrasse. Muth repeats every one of my remarks in different words, laughs only when I laugh, and keeps on trying to stay on my left side. Before Morgenstern joined us, he had beseeched me to see that it didn't get too late. In the Café de la Terrasse Morgenstern shows us his album of press-cuttings, various acts by the performer he works for, with startling advertisements, such as 'a practical fat paunch for sale, gigantic ears with electrical heating device, lions, a tiger-cat with the tip of its tail missing', etc. etc.

We talk a great deal about Munich, about the Dichtelei and Dr Flörke,[59] the Café Luitpold, finally Morgenstern gets round to talking about anti-Semites, and I introduce Muth to him as such. When Morgenstern calmly asks him for his reasons, Muth instantly puts his tail between his legs. On our way home Muth has the phenomenal cheek to quote in his own defence all the arguments I had advanced against his anti-Semitism a couple of days ago. The three of us agree to meet for cocoa at my place on Wednesday. After Morgenstern has said goodbye, I say to Muth: Now you're in the shit. Muth then abandons his own point of view and goes over totally to mine as I had defined it for his benefit, accusing me of tactlessness. I point this out to him, telling him as we part that I expect him on Wednesday. He accepts on condition that we don't talk about anti-Semitism, since that was for him an emotional issue he wouldn't let anyone meddle with. I go home, read for a bit and then fall asleep.

An engraving of the Rue Caulaincourt, Montmartre by Willi Rudinoff
(Wilhelm Morgenstern). Wedekind had been friends with Rudinoff since 1887,
and met him again in Paris.

6 DECEMBER 1892

In a café I write to Donald that I'll send him *Zarathustra* along with
the proofs of his articles at the weekend.[60] When I get home, I find his
'Living in New York' so feeble that I decide to re-write it from
beginning to end, but don't get very far.

7 DECEMBER 1892

Get up at twelve, buy crockery, cocoa and biscuits, and wait for my
guests. Morgenstern turns up at four o'clock. We make music
together. He reads me his memoirs, which he is reconstructing from
memory. I advise him to make notes every day and give him a day
from my time in Paris as an example.

It's our first visit to Kadudja. As we sit in front of the fire,
Morgenstern tells me about Durow.[61] Durow trains dogs, goats, pigs
and rats. He gets 4,000 francs a month, goes around smothered in
diamonds, keeps a couple of servants, and a carriage with a pair of
Russian ponies, gets drunk on champagne, and has his sexual
services paid for in cash by the Parisian prostitutes. Morgenstern

went to tea with him. He decorates his rooms with lace, and in his spare time paints large pictures, which he copies with considerable skill from small photographs. Since he doesn't know how to paint flesh, he paints lace veils over it. In Russia he is a popular favourite. In Petersburg he have row with police chief. Police chief is called Gresser. In circus ring is placing gold rouble. Pig is fetching gold rouble. Is placing silver rouble. Pig is fetching silver rouble. Is placing paper rouble. Pig is not fetching paper rouble. He says: Paper rouble is so bad that pig is not fetching paper rouble. Is fined 50 roubles. He pays fine and is making same again next day. Is getting fined and threatened to deport. Day after is Saturday, all Jews is coming to circus, so can speak to them German. Also comes police chief, Gresser, to see if he again make pig to fetch gold rouble. He has this time three pigs, says to public: This is little pig. This pig bigger pig ('gresser Schwein'), this pig is all bigger ('ganz gresser'). Is getting exiled. Is friend of Emperor's adjutant. Is coming to Emperor. Emperor is tearing up deportation order. Says: Stupid nonsense!

Durow was once a schoolmaster. You can tell at a glance what a common fellow he is. But there's no doubt that, in himself, he's an artist. We go to dinner in the Restaurant de la Bourse, and from there to the Café de la Terrasse. After we've parted, I run through all the bookshops on the Boulevard in search of Maupassant's *Mont Oriol*,[62] without finding it. I drive home and spend the rest of the night reading the whole story of my flirtation with Minna in my '89 diary. In Berlin I felt very much inclined to burn this episode, but now I'm glad that I didn't.

8 DECEMBER 1892

Get up very late and am still in my shirt and underpants when there's a knock at the door. I call out: 'Qui est là?'[63] No reply. I open the door, and there stands Henriette. She says she's just come to talk to me for a minute. Why hadn't I come to visit her last week? I had promised to come on Wednesday or Thursday, she claims. It wasn't nice of me to keep her waiting. The day before yesterday she'd climbed four flights of stairs to my room about eleven o'clock, but my door had been locked. I say, yes, unfortunately I'd been out. And my light that she'd seen from the street below? – I'd forgotten to put it out. – And my key, which hadn't been hanging in the office? – I'd taken it with me by mistake. – Yes, yes, she knew all that. It wasn't nice of me to let her climb four flights of stairs and then not even open the door. She had thought, perhaps Rachel was with me, and that's why she'd gone away again. I tell her Rachel had called on me the following morning, but I hadn't been at home then either. She says I'd always been so sweet to her, why was I different all of a sudden. If I didn't want to have any more to do with her, then I only had to say so. I tell her I'm still sweet to her when she's there, I couldn't be anything but sweet to her. That's why I'd prefer her not to come. As I say this, I slip a louis into her hand. I tell her I'd been writing a ballet for the Folies Bergères but I couldn't get on with it.[64] I'd been writing a comedy for Berlin, but that wasn't going well either.[65] When I came to Paris three months ago, I'd had money. Now it was different. She says, very well, now I'd told her that, she wouldn't come any more. I tell her she shouldn't feel offended, since she knew very well that I didn't go with other women. She reckons she's not so sure about that. After all, I was on the other side of the river almost every evening. Then she lists for my benefit all the evenings I haven't been at home during the past fortnight. It seems she walks past every evening to see whether I'm at home or not. Her cough had got better since the cold had turned dry. In her long overcoat, with a dress laced up to the neck, her broad-brimmed hat with the feather, she does indeed look like a little lady, or, rather, like a child dressed up as a lady, what with her great eyes, her delicate snub nose, her generous mouth and her abundance of dark chestnut hair, which possibly contribute most of all to this effect. She intended to go to the masked ball once more before she died. She would go dressed up as a black cat. She'd buy rabbit fur and drape the lower part of her body in that, with bare arms, and somewhat *décolletée*. She says she'll look charming. She accompanies me as far as the Seine, and says as she takes her leave that she won't come any more. I walk down the Boulevard Sebastopol as far as the Gare de l'Est and buy a pair of galoshes at the corner of the Boulevard Magenta, as Morgenstern advised me to do yesterday. I've just finished doing this, when I meet Morgenstern, who introduces me to his companion, a Herr Lewis. – Do you know what happened to me last night? – No. – A girl stole 200 francs from me. – You don't say! – Stolen out of my pocket! – Poor devil! – And put the empty purse back again. He's deeply dejected. There were two of them. He met them in a restaurant after the show, they gave him a language lesson: he was to repeat after them: Oh, ne voulez vous prendre.[66] Then he'd gone to the Hotel So-and-so with them, had about 20 centimes' worth of fun, and when he opened his purse at home, it was empty. He reported the theft to the police today, the gentleman should excuse his bad French, he happened to be a foreigner. The inspector replied that his French wasn't so bad: after all, he was enough of a Parisian to go to a hotel with a couple of ladies. Morgenstern says, he'd not meant to tell a soul about the incident at first, but now he'd told half of Paris, first Herr Lewis, then Herr Lewis's sister, then her husband, and finally even her children. Now here he was, telling me, and just on his way to the circus to tell his director and ask him for an advance. We both advise him not to do that, he should simply say that he'd squandered the cash on his own account. Morgenstern keeps on working out how often he could have afforded a holiday for that sum, how far he could have travelled on it, what size of room he could have rented, and how many pairs of boots he could have worn out. We advise him to imagine rather that he'd spent the night in the arms of a sexy dancer from the grand opera, there were people who paid four times as much for the privilege and had no more to show for it in the end than he had. But he still insists that he'd not had more than 20 centimes' worth of fun. We go to Georges for a meal and afterwards to the Café de la Terrasse, where Morgenstern seeks comfort in the newspapers, while Lewis tells me a great deal about his sister. She writes for German papers, is associated with Pollini in Hamburg,[67] translates French plays and writes novels on her own account. After we have arranged to meet on Sunday, I go off home, after buying *Mont Oriol* and a thick quarto notebook near the Odéon; in this I resume the notes I interrupted at the beginning of August, starting with 3 December. I go on writing until three, read until seven, and then fall asleep until two o'clock in the afternoon.

9 DECEMBER 1892

I had meant to be at M. Leblanc's by eleven,[68] but don't get up until four, stroll about for an hour, buying a chunk of chicken which I gnaw off the bone when I get home, then work until twelve, catch the last omnibus to the Café de la Terrasse, read through the *Fliegende Blätter* there, and am back home just after one o'clock.

10 DECEMBER 1892

Once more I don't get up until late in the afternoon, go to the Restaurant de la Bourse for dinner and then to the Casino de Paris. At the door I realize that the first grand ball of the season is being held, and that there is an entry charge of 5 francs. Not having eaten lunch, I permit myself this luxury. The show has nothing entertaining to offer. Just behind me my neighbour from Munich, M. Horley is sitting, together with his nephew. I'm sorry I've not been introduced to him. I once dined together with one of his daughters at the Sussners,[69] but without making her acquaintance. Only a few aged prostitutes turn up at the ball in costume, there's nothing smart or attractive, so I decide to leave the hall about twelve and go to the Café de la Terrasse in the hope of meeting Morgenstern. He's just that minute left. I stroll home through the Faubourg St Denis, being jostled by some old whores. One of them recites her attractions as if she were saying a paternoster. Tu ne payes pas cher, je serais très gentille, je ferais un bon feu, je sais de petites cochonneries etc.[70]

11 DECEMBER 1892

I meet Morgenstern in the Café de la Terrasse at half past five in the afternoon, and he introduces me to his friend Frau Gotthelf. Frau Gotthelf is a Hamburg Jewess who has lived in Paris with her husband and children for the last eight years – a plump little person with a nice, almost pretty face which lacks any typical Jewish features, while her children, who are sitting round her, all represent distinct Jewish types. She is an astute translator, adapts Parisian drawing-room dramas for Pollini in Hamburg, writes novels that are serialized in the *Hamburger Fremdenblatt* and is personally acquainted with a number of Parisian writers, Coppée etc.[71] She tells me the plot of *Les Paroles restent* in a way that could hardly be bettered.[72] After she's finished, I explain to her the trouble I've had with the flea ballet. She says I should be careful that my idea isn't pinched in the editorial offices and advises me to go straight to Auderan. I tell her about my play *Schwigerling*. She asks if I'll read it to her, and I agree to do so; I'll send her my *Spring Awakening* beforehand, however. She's deeply concerned about the 200 francs that were stolen from Morgenstern. When Morgenstern was at my place he read me two letters from his best friend, an advertising agent and great idealist by whose friendship Morgenstern placed great store. And now this man has blackened him in his sister's eyes: he, Morgenstern, was greedy for the thunderous applause of his audience, he was well on the way to becoming nothing but a strolling conjurer, he had been dazzled by Mammon and had forfeited all his idealistic aspirations. Morgenstern's sister is a creature of warm and profound sentiments. During puberty she suffered from periodic convulsions, had fits of rage from time to time, during which she talked in the most obscene terms and accused herself in public of being pregnant with an illegitimate child. In response to his friend's slanders she writes Morgenstern a letter full of bitter reproaches, and Morgenstern fears that this upset may drive her back into a depression or a state of insanity. He writes back to her in the most affectionate terms, quoting his friendship with Frau Gotthelf and with me and beseeching her to come to Paris so that she can witness his superior ambitions with her own eyes, and asks Frau Gotthelf to confirm all he says by means of an accompanying note. He has disposed of the friend of his youth in an indignant six-page letter. This latter, together with his letter to his sister, his sister's letter to Morgenstern, along with his friend's last two letters to him are passed round among all those present, including the children, and as far as Morgenstern's attitude in the business is concerned, he is accorded unanimous and enthusiastic approval. After Frau Gotthelf, together with her children, has taken her leave, Morgenstern, Herr Lewis and I go to Restaurant de la Bourse for dinner, during which Herr Lewis shows himself by his remarks in the course of the conversation to be a perfect ass. After dinner we go our separate ways, I go home and go to bed early.

12 DECEMBER 1892

Get up at nine and go to the editorial offices [of] Camille Selden. We talk about Maupassant, who used to cruise around in the Mediterranean on his yacht whenever he sensed the onset of his madness. He had always gone in for rowing, as well as gymnastics and fencing. We talk about Baudelaire. He's too strong meat for Frl. Hüny, but Frl. Breslau raves about him, she was especially delighted with his 'Charogne'.[73] Frl. Breslau writes to Frl. Hüny about my *Spring*

Frank Wedekind as the Masked Man in *Spring Awakening*. The play was first performed on 20 November 1906 at the Berlin Kammerspiele.

Awakening that it's full of talent, in spite of its incredible crudities. We talk about Dr Conrad. Hüny is upset because he told Muth that he had been divorced from his first wife . . . go home in a very excited frame of mind, work until four in the morning and then read until seven.

13 DECEMBER 1892

When I return from dinner at eight o'clock in the evening I find the enclosed letter in my mail-box.[74]

13 décembre

Mon cher ami,

Je me trouve dans un grand embarras et je t'assure que je ne m'attendais pas à cela. Je dois 35 frs à ma propriétaire, elle m'a fermé la porte et mon manteau était resté dans la chambre.

Je t'avais bien promis de ne plus rien te demander, mais tu sais comme je suis malade. Surtout depuis deux ou trois jours je crache le sang.

J'espère que j'en aurais bientôt fini avec la vie. Si tu pouvais me rendre encore ce dernier service, je t'assure que je te serais bien reconnaissante.

Le médecin m'a dit que quand je cracherais le sang je n'en aurais plus pour longtemps.

Alors je t'en supplie, rends-moi ce dernier service, je serais bien heureuse.

Ta pauvre Henriette qui t'embrasse et qui compte sur toi.

Henriette

Si cela ne t'ennuie pas apporte-le-moi au café ou au 12, rue des Carmes, chez la blanchisseuse, pour le moment c'est chez elle que je suis. Merci mille fois d'avance.

I feel very sorry that I'm unable to help her, not having much more myself. What I regret most is that she left her overcoat behind, because it's only three weeks since I bought it for her. I light a fire and with a great effort manage to compose the epistle to M. Leblanc. At midnight I go to La Source to get something to eat, and perhaps to finish off the letter there. There's a grand students' ball at Bullier's. I'm just on the point of going home, when a masked figure looks in through the half-open door. One of the men present goes towards her, comes back to his seat, flings on his overcoat and escorts the girl out. This has the same effect on me as when a chaste youth observes an arm being disrobed. I pay and go to the Café d'Harcourt. It's half past one, and Henriette will have in any case gone home by now. As a rule Rachel doesn't go out at all on Tuesdays.

I sit down at my usual place and order an Américain. Three elderly whores are sitting at the next table, engrossed in lively conversation. The crowd surges past, some pretty girls in masks among them. I'm greatly reassured to find not a single known face in the whole café. As they don't close at two o'clock, I order another Américain, and immediately afterwards Clarisse rushes up to me, arm in arm with a girl-friend. Clarisse is a rather small, markedly brunette girl with pretty features, dazzling teeth, full, dark lips and great pitch-black eyes. I've known her since the third day of my second stay in Paris. With her talkative, shallow, perpetually hilarious manner, she reminds me inevitably of Mieze, while her appearance irresistibly recalls someone else: I've been trying off and on for the past three months to think who it is, but in vain. And now I try once again to get on the track, but without success. What keeps me safe from her is her uncomprehending and distracted behaviour in bed. Once, when I'd not been able to sleep for four nights running, I went to her, simply to sleep, and I did in fact sleep the whole night through after being lulled into slumber by her ceaseless chatter, and didn't wake until four o'clock the following day, it was some holiday or other. She had got up at eight in the morning, had arranged her wardrobe, had gone out for lunch and had returned. Every time I awoke for a moment, I heard her chattering to herself and singing. At the same time she was busy with her hats, of which she possessed a score or so. She dresses tastefully and with discrimination, but doesn't strike me as exactly a paragon of hygiene. When I asked her if she had syphilis, she replied, not so far. She was bound to get it sooner or later, everybody did. Had I had it yet? – Yes. – So much the better, then I was safe from it. – She asks me if I'll sleep with her. I say no, but if she'd like a drink, she should take a seat. She sits down beside me, together with her girl-friend. The talk turns to Henriette, who lives across the street from her in the Rue des Carmes. Clarisse claims that she keeps pimps. Why wouldn't I come with her tonight? I say I'm waiting for Henriette. She says Henriette has already been and gone home again. At any rate, she wouldn't be back. I should go with her. I say no. She retorts: You're madly in love with her. I say, yes. After a while I go for a piss. All at once Clarisse rushes into the toilet, wouldn't I come with her tonight? – I say I'll think about it. She urges me to give her a definite answer. I'm just on the point of giving in, when a man comes in and chucks her out of the door.

When I go back into the restaurant, Henriette is sitting at our table, her huge eyes brimming with fat tears. I ask her to sit next to me. Clarisse is abusing her at the top of her voice. The three elderly whores sitting at the adjoining table suddenly take Henriette's side, however, and after squabbling for a bit longer Clarisse clears off, along with her girl-friend. I ask Henriette what she's crying for. Because she hasn't the strength to fight back, otherwise she'd have given Clarisse a piece of her mind. I tell her straight away that I can't give her the 35 francs. After drinking a few Américains, we go to the Gambrinus and have supper there with a few bottles of wine. The restaurant is full of masked revellers. We are the last to leave, around five o'clock. Back in my room I make grog and tea. We sit down in front of the open fire and chat. Henriette gets very lively. She puts on my overcoat and my opera-hat and enacts for my benefit a scene involving a young Parisian and a high-class prostitute: the initial encounter, the supper at Silvain's, the scene before going to bed, and the parting the following afternoon. She maintains that 100-franc notes are not all that common. She had been given one on five occasions – twice during the Exhibition, twice, later on, by her pimp, and once by a foreigner in a wide-brimmed desperado's hat and cloak. She had trembled in fear of her life all night, he had had a terrifying pair of eyes. He had told her she wasn't cut out for this trade, she wouldn't make good in it, she would have cause to remember him. She kept thinking, if only he'd go, he won't give me anything anyway. But that didn't matter, if only he didn't kill her. I ask, he was a virgin, I expect? – Oh, no, he knew about love, all right. Next morning he had got up without taking her again. She was thinking, he certainly won't pay. She had followed his every move- ment as she lay in bed, still fearing some sudden fit of fury. He was bound to beat her up, at the very least. He had repeated what he had said the previous evening. She should turn back, she wasn't born to be a sinner. When he'd flung on his cloak and pulled his hat down over his face, he had pulled out his wallet and placed a banknote on the table. She was so astonished that she didn't know what to say, but thought to herself, it'll be 50 francs, I expect. She hadn't dared look, but had jumped out of bed all the same and quickly tried to be as nice as she could to him, brushing his collar, pulling his cloak to rights, handing him his umbrella, opening the door for him and calling after him in the corridor to ask whether he had forgotten anything. When she came back and unfolded the note, it was 100 francs. He's made a mistake, she thought, or else he's crazy.

As she tells me the story, she's still under the influence of the terror the man inspired in her at the time. Then she enacts another comedy for me. She puts on my white silk scarf like a coif and drapes my ulster over her shoulders like a nun's habit. She looks charming. The scene is a convent school during the silent period. The girls are busy with needlework and behave as outrageously as they can, so as to force Sister Miletia to speak. Now she's acting Sister Miletia, whose silent gestures get more and more infuriated, and now she's herself, as the mangy sheep among her more demure classmates, the one who regularly succeeded in getting Sister Miletia to speak. The show concludes with the cry of the Sister, who is now trembling with fury: 'Voulez vous sortir!'[75] The cry wells up tonelessly, groaning from the hollow chest, as though someone were shouting up the staircase from below. I'm rolling about the bed in fits of laughter. Henriette says, with a hint of sadness: Rachel never made you laugh like that!

The night, or rather the day, passes more peacefully than I had feared. I'm only wakened once by her heart-rending cough. Whenever she coughs, there's a strong odour of decay about her. I had doubted her story about spitting blood. Now she shows me the large, dark red stains on her handkerchief. I tell her it's from her nose. A ray of sunlight illumines her face. It's possible perhaps, isn't it? She blows her nose as hard as she can, but no blood comes.

While we are sitting in the Café d'Harcourt, a slender masked figure dressed as a man comes in. I nudge Henriette: That's Rachel. She starts to tremble. Indeed, I'm afraid myself that it might be Rachel. But when the costumed figure has reached her seat and removed her mask, it turns out to be an elderly woman.

14 DECEMBER 1892

We get up very late. I give Henriette her 40 francs, and in return she promises not to bother me again until January. She would like to celebrate New Year with me. I go for something to eat in the Restaurant de la Bourse, and then go on to the circus.

15 DECEMBER 1892

Get up early, work, go to the Louvre after lunch, and as I'm coming back home I see a man in a top hat leaving the house. It's Herr Muth. I call out to him, and regret it the same instant. He comes up to my room with me and tells me a long story about having been away for three days, without having had any memorable experiences during that time. As we go off to dinner, he begins a story, but then skips round to my left side, because, he says, he can tell his tale better from there. He had met a servant-girl in Compiègne, a German girl who had previously had a place in Paris. Her employers there had expected her to bathe an eleven-year old boy every day. Later she fell ill, and now she's subsisting on coffee and bread.

After dinner we stroll under the Odéon arcades, where I buy Pierre Loti's *Aziyadé*.[76] Then we go to the Café d'Harcourt. Not a single girl among those present finds favour in Muth's critical eyes. He has some fault to find with every single one. One is too fat, another too skinny, one is too gloomy, another too cheerful. Isn't that a monster, for instance, he whispers in my ear, as another girl comes through the door beside us. The girl in question turns round full-face and laughs at me: it's Clarisse. After seeing her from the front, Muth reckons she's not so bad after all. Unfortunately, she has put her hat on askew. This, however, makes no difference to his principles. What could such a creature mean to him? He felt no sexual desire, and there was nothing else to be had there, after all. I quote Goethe's poem 'Connoisseur and Enthusiast' to him,[77] which he accepts with a smile, although it upsets him profoundly, especially the second part, where the scene is moved to the picture gallery. After a while Fernande comes in and says hallo, asking where on earth I've been, nobody ever sees me. I'd told Rachel I'd gone away on a trip. I tell her I'd looked for Rachel a number of times but had never found her. She should give her my best wishes. After she's gone, I tell Muth that in the *quartier* they reckon the lady's a *gugnotte*.[78] – What was a *gugnotte*? – A lesbian. – He'd seen that the moment he set eyes on her. He'd just been on the point of telling me. I say, it's high time we left, otherwise I'd run into Rachel. We leave and then separate; back in my room, I go to bed and read *Aziyadé* and then go on to have three wet dreams during the night.

16 DECEMBER 1892

Worked.

17 DECEMBER 1892

Worked. In the Luxembourg in the afternoon. Evening in the Café Rouge.

18 DECEMBER 1892

Worked. After dinner I go up the Boulevard St Michel and run into Rachel. She takes my arm, now she's got me, she won't let me go again. She had come round on Monday. My key had been in the lock, but the door had been bolted. She had knocked, but no one had answered. Fernande had asked her why I was nowhere to be seen, she had told her I was away on a trip, only so as not to have to say I was avoiding her and going with other women. Had I already had dinner? – Yes. – Then we would go for a walk. That was healthy. In front of a large residence on the Boulevard St Germain she says I should buy it for her some time when I happened to be in funds. I say it isn't fine enough for her. I'll set her up in a house on the Champs Elysées. Would she care for a carriage and a couple of footmen to go with it? – And what sort of horses, Russian or English ponies? – She'd leave that for me to decide. – The immaculate roomy kitchen in the basement with its gleaming copper pots and pans impresses her no end. If she had to, she says, she would settle for this house. It's bitterly cold, and, however agreeable it is to walk, I'd rather be sitting with her in some bar or other. But she drags me along ruthlessly. In a side street in front of the Palais Bourbon she points out the apartment where she had lived with her lover for a year. She used to take *bébé* for a walk in the Champs Elysées every afternoon. She would never live so well again, that was for sure.

The Seine is abnormally high. From the Pont de la Concorde she points out the great rolling waves that come swirling towards us in the moonlight like an endless shoal of gigantic fish. We walk on to the grand boulevards, look at the flower shops, and drop into the Café de l'Univers on our way back. I'm rather concerned that she may attract unwelcome attention as a *grisette*.[79] To avoid this, I don't allow the conversation to flag for a moment, and as nothing better occurs to me, I mention that I've been told that Fernande is a *gugnotte*. So we start talking about Daudet's *Sappho*, about which she shares my opinion. I then tell her about Pierre Loti and his flirtation with pederasty, and so finally we get round to the difference between French and German literature. In this way everything passes off well enough. A gentleman and two ladies opposite, it's true, do pass various remarks, but we for our part don't spare them either. The younger of the two ladies, English in type, with a bright, hearty laugh, earns Rachel's unqualified approval. On the way home I ask her if she wouldn't care for a glass of something, but she's afraid I might meet someone I know. She buys herself a pound of chestnuts at the corner and we go up to my room, where I make some tea.

As usual, Rachel strips to her vest straight away, and sprawls on the divan. We carry on chatting until two o'clock. She begins to dance a cancan and climbs on to my shoulders, and, heavy as she is, I carry her round the room. She's enough to make one's mouth water, and, unusually for me, I'm pretty much in love with her. We get stuck into each other, she inflicts a number of love-bites on me, and in spite of my false teeth I manage to leave a suggestion of the same on her thigh. When we get into bed, she draws the curtains as close as she can. She does this on account of the glandular scars beneath her chin, which have got noticeably larger. Whether they are open sores, I can't tell. I act as if I didn't notice them. Exceptionally, I find I'm more potent than otherwise, but afterwards I fall asleep instantly, with a 'bon soir, ma petite femme',[80] to which she replies with a 'bon soir, mon mari', and I go on snoring without interruption until three in the afternoon.

19 DECEMBER 1892

Rachel tries in vain to make me get up. In the end she has recourse to the whip, and snatches the blankets away. Ultimately she even tries to put on my socks. Crouching in front of the flickering fire in her vest and a silken petticoat with her hair let down, she is a perfect picture, a charming Mignon,[81] half French, half gipsy. Lying in bed, I can see the scarlet flames mirrored in her dark eyes. The firelight flickers up and down her bare arms. She puffs the smoke from her cigarette into the blazing coals as she tells me about the *Damnation of Faust*, trilling the passages she has managed to memorize. After I've got dressed at last, we go to the Café Cligny and arrange, when we part, that we'll meet again there the day after tomorrow, at twelve o'clock at night. I go to dinner, and afterwards listen to the band in the Café Scribe. I go to bed betimes, so as to be able to get up early.

20 DECEMBER 1892

Work until twelve, have breakfast in the Palais Royal, and set off to call on Mme Gotthelf. She's not at home, but should be available at eight o'clock. I visit the Neo-Impressionist exhibition in the Hotel Brébant, and then go to the Café de la Terrasse, where Herr St. approaches me. Frl. Hüny has given me a ticket for a subscription ball in the Hôtel Continental. Herr St., who is also going, suggests we should meet in the Café de la Terrasse. When I call at Mme Gotthelf's at five o'clock, she has still not returned. She should be at home tomorrow at ten. I go home, do some work, and don't sleep a wink all night.

21 DECEMBER 1892

Am up and about by nine, put *Schwigerling* under my arm, and drive to Frau Gotthelf's. Her husband receives me in the drawing-room. He's short and stout, with a puffy red face, pouting lips, and a rather furtive look. He invites me to come more often. His brother-in-law, Lewis, told me he was a monster, gets drunks every day, comes home and beats his wife and children, doesn't contribute a sou to the household expenses, and had allowed the youngest of his children literally to starve to death. I read the first act to Frau Gotthelf in the dining-room. Then it's time for lunch. She shows me two pictures she recently received from Sacher-Masoch, and advises me to send my *Spring Awakening* to Sacher-Masoch.[82] He might be able to do something for my *Schwigerling* as well. She also advises me to call on Frl. Read,[83] who is François Coppée's most intimate friend. She asks me whether she should have her portrait painted by Morgenstern. I stupidly advise her not to, doubting whether he's really up to the task yet. We arrange to meet at nine o'clock in the Café de la Terrasse.

I go to dinner, and then to the editorial offices of the National, in order to get hold of my ballet, if I can. But M. Leblanc has just left. I go home to work, but Herr Muth soon arrives. After a few desultory remarks, he reveals himself to be a chauvinist, and I grow heated. We end up with a pointless wrangle about the words 'sensuous' and 'randy'. Then it's time for me to go for dinner. In the Café de la

Terrasse I meet Morgenstern and his partner, Herr Freund, with whom he proposes to make a tour of the South of France. He has been engaged for the coming month in Rency, Lyons. Herr Freund was a sculptor in Berlin, then became a lightning sculptor, travelled all over the world with his act, amassed a fortune of 50,000 francs, married a Parisian girl and started a business in Paris. The Parisian girl had a lover, however, or rather, a loveress, a bosom friend, a *cicisbea*, who moved in whenever Herr Freund went away on a business trip. He was tipped off, caught the two ladies *in flagrante* and got a divorce. His business was no more successful than his marriage, however, and he had squandered the last of his fortune a few weeks previously.

After a while, Frau Gotthelf comes in with her entire family. Herr Gotthelf is sitting playing cards in another corner of the café. The conversation has a soporific effect, especially on me, as I haven't slept for two nights. Morgenstern goes off to the circus, the whole party breaks up, only to settle down again at Herr Gotthelf's table, to await Morgenstern's return. After he's come back, Frau Gotthelf urges him to recite the poem about the pencil sharpened at both ends. He does so with some reluctance. She then asks me whether I won't recite something or other. I assure her that I have absolutely no talent of that sort. People start cracking Hebrew jokes, and the whole party laughs at them. When I swear I can't understand them, old Gotthelf says: Don't give us that. As the party is breaking up, Frau Gotthelf invites us all to come and visit her on Tuesday evening.

Morgenstern and I go into the Café Wetzel, where he tells me how he attended the wedding of some circus performers when he first came to Paris. There are two ladies sitting next to us whom we are treating. Suddenly Morgenstern leaps up: There's Leitner and Holtoff![84]

Leitner and Holtoff are the two strongest men in the world and have been engaged by the Casino de Paris as a counter-attraction to two American brothers, also the strongest men in the world, who are due to appear shortly at the Folies Bergères. Leitner has a young lady with him. Holtoff sits down at our table. He is a handsome fellow with the unassuming childish self-esteem peculiar to a strong man. He tells us how they had to use their fists to ward off the women as they left the Casino de Paris. They had pounced on them by the score. ... Pretty, these Parisiennes, weren't they? – He comes from Elberfeld, was a commercial traveller, like Leitner. He says they had an accident yesterday, one of the horses had fallen off the gangway – and if the beast falls on top of you, then it kills you! – They talk about Freund. That's a fellow for you, says Holtoff, he squeezes blood out of the director's fingernails. You have to, you know. If the director doesn't need you, then he shits on you. But if he needs you, then he'll cut you down from the gallows. – All at once a lady falls on Holtoff's neck, a prostitute of superb elegance, in immaculate gloves and the most exquisite gown, glittering with real diamonds. She is in raptures at having seen him, having him, being able to sleep with him. She got to know him at the Folies Bergères two years ago, and had recognized him at first sight. Not that she's crazy otherwise about men qui font les poids.[85] Her supreme joy is the sharpshooters. She tells us about an American marksman at the Folies Bergères; every time he pulled the trigger a shudder ran through her body. – Mais il est un joli garçon, she says to her friend, pointing at Holtoff. Je jouirai, oh, je jouirai.[86] She puts her hand in Holtoff's, where it vanishes, like the butt of a pistol. At the same time she agrees with her friend that he hasn't got a large hand, considering that he's an athlete. The ladies extend their respect for Holtoff to Morgenstern and myself. We address each other with the greatest deference imaginable. When one of them asks what I do for a living and I reply that I'm nothing but a writer, she consoles me, saying that it's a respectable calling. The women at the tables round about, who had been talking with us as equals, now regard us with timid admiration, as creatures of a superior breed whom you couldn't very well invite to step outside with you.

We're on the point of leaving when someone leans over me from behind and grasps my hand. It's Adèle. She's badly dressed and looks a bit drunk, or rather a bit crazy. She asks about my friend. I say he's in America, in New Orleans. Since I'm about to pay, I give her a franc, whereupon she clears off. As we're saying goodbye to Holtoff's lady-friend outside, I wish her a restful night. She taps me on the mouth with her fan: how dare I wish her any such thing! I walk as far as the Boulevard Sebastopol with Morgenstern, leap into a cab there, fall asleep, and am wakened by the cabby in front of my hotel.

22 DECEMBER 1892

Get up about nine in the evening, dine and go to the Circus; I'd promised Morgenstern I'd go. After the show I go to the dressing-room with him and find myself face to face with Mister Daniel. Mister Daniel is the clown in the Cirque d'Hiver. I ask him what's happened to the Lee brothers. They've gone to Berlin. Morgenstern takes me to a tavern in the Rue Riche that's frequented by circus performers. In the front bar a dancer from the Folies Bergères is sitting by the counter with her legs spread apart, puffing the smoke from her cigarette up at the ceiling. In the little parlour at the back we find the big cat trainer, Tescho, from the Folies Bergères practising on the mandolin. Morgenstern and he begin by greeting each other in every living language, but make do with German when it comes to the conversation. Tescho was born in Mainz. He used to be an acrobat but changed over to training big cats two years ago, and is therefore a rival to Durow, who wanted to buy his cats from him. Thus the conversation turns to the Durow–Rubini court case. Frau Rubini, a Paris agent, negotiated Morgenstern's contract in Rency. That irked Durow, and he started calling Morgenstern Rubini, instead of Rudinoff. He sends his footman round to Morgenstern to ask whether he isn't perhaps called Rubini. Morgenstern rams the man's nose up against the programme, where his name is given, and also claims he punched him in the face. Shortly afterwards, Mme Rubini comes into the circus, hears about the quarrel, and brings a suit against Durow in court. It's generally agreed that Durow is suffering from megalomania, having himself addressed as Prince Durow and getting the young people at the matinées to shout: Vive Duroff!

Herr Valende, who puts on an act with trained mastiffs at the Folies Bergères, enters in his heavy fur coat and fur cap, with a riding-crop under his arm. He once owned a roundabout, but is now a wealthy man, tours during the summer with a company of his own, in which Tescho is also engaged, and has recently acquired a number of lions. So the conversation turns to etchings. He bought an etching yesterday in which Hercules is wrenching open a lion's jaws. I mention just in passing that it was probably Samson, but no one believes me. Two young men come in with a very pretty girl. In the Folies Bergères they appear as an act with one young man and two pretty girls. I'd seen them a number of times without ever suspecting this deception.

The whole company, except for Valende, decides to go to Charly's. Tescho, Morgenstern and I drink another gin at the bar and then we, too, go to Charly's. When we arrive at this dive, we hear the strains of a mandolin, the strumming of a guitar and the sound of singing coming from inside. In the front room men and women from the circus are standing jammed together. We push our way through with some difficulty and get into the second room. The first person to meet my eye is Mlle Campana, the prima ballerina from the Folies Bergères, this angel who has so often moved me to the verge of tears with her superhuman gracefulness, this entrancing butterfly with her blossoming cheeks, her dazzling teeth, and the positively beatific gaze of those nobly set eyes. Her complexion is somewhere between ashen and muddy, her eyes are pitifully weary, her cheeks deeply sunken, her dress as unbecoming as may be, with a suggestion of a humped back. She is sitting next to a faded gentleman, and has a tall flower basket filled with confectionery in front of her. She seems to recognize me, which would be no wonder, since I invariably sit in the front row. Tescho, Morgenstern and I commandeer a small table in the opposite corner, and order stout with lemonade. In her gestures, in her speech and movements, incidentally, Mlle Campana displays the same gracefulness as she does on the stage. Singing to guitar accompaniment goes on uninterruptedly from the adjacent room, and a jockey from the big race is dancing a negro fandango in a circle of his friends. The landlord, Mr Charly, is in fact a German, but looks typically French. He has a charming little wife, a born Parisienne, whom anyone would take for an Englishwoman. Mlle Campana coughs constantly. It is the short, feeble, laboured cough of the consumptive. The disease can in any case be seen clearly written on her face. At two o'clock, when everyone gets up to leave, she passes close by me a number of times, but I can't summon up the nerve to speak to her.

Tescho pushes off home with his mandolin, while Morgenstern and I make for the Café Wetzel. As we're passing the Restaurant de la Rotonde, I tell Morgenstern about the adventure I had there one evening with ——. It was on one of the last evenings before his departure for the New World. We were coming out of the Café Wetzel, had strolled in the wake of some girls, and had thus

Toulouse-Lautrec, a sketch of the American clown 'Chocolat' who enjoyed enormous popularity in Paris during the 1890s.

discovered the upstairs premises of the Restaurant de la Rotonde. We ordered a bottle of wine there, and in no time at all an old whore joined us for a drink. I requested her in the politest possible terms, however, to go back to her seat. Chocolat, the clown from the Nouveau Cirque, provided the entertainment for the entire company. He performed all sorts of tricks, got all the women to slap his face and kiss him at one and the same time, and tried to find a kind of middle way between the pasha and the eunuch. —'s interest was captured by a noble beauty who reminded him of the actress Heese in Milan, and who also took the above-mentioned liberties with Chocolat.

When she left, we followed her, — spoke to her, we went into the café together, and took our ease in a *chambre séparée*. Our fair guest at once undressed, and the waiter trembled as he served the champagne – from sheer emotion, he claimed. —, who had rapidly commandeered the girl's charms, introduced me to her as his father. I was very weary from our various preceding exertions and felt no desire to share the spoils with him. I simply asked for permission to watch the proceedings.

For this purpose the gas had to be turned down, and, as it was already broad daylight, the curtains drawn. A blurred, tangled huddle of bodies emerged on the divan in front of me, to the accompaniment of various grunts and groans, with only the girl's naked shoulders being clearly distinguishable. — cried: Now! – I turned up the gas, and the act of love was consummated in the full glare of the lamps. When we had all simmered down a bit, the girl showed us her right hand, with the little finger missing. She had lost it as a small child during the war of '71, in the course of a brawl involving the Germans who were billeted in her parents' home. In the most glorious morning sunshine we drove her back in a cab to her apartment after Weinhöppel had given her money for a pair of new gloves.[87]

Morgenstern doesn't know — well, but had once acted with him in a play by Gumpenberg that had been put on at a soirée of the Modern Society.

In the Café Wetzel Adèle at once accosts me again, asking me once more about —. After I have assured her firmly that he is in America, she asks, with an appreciative glance at Morgenstern's imposing physique, whether he's also a friend of mine? – Yes. – Then I should tell him that he might take —'s place in her affections. I pass this on to Morgenstern, who is going to think about the offer. Morgenstern, incidentally, has taken a great liking to the Café Wetzel. There's an extrtemely good-looking half-caste sitting next to us, or rather an octoroon, with a somewhat flattened nose, prominent lips, and a pair of languishing pitch-black eyes. Her soft little hands are heavily laden with rings, which creates a splendid effect in contrast to her dark skin. She is from the island of Djerba, and came to France as a child. Her dress is immaculate and tasteful. We talk about the fact that we have met fairly often in the Moulin Rouge, and also once in the Restaurant de la Rotonde and, when the café closes, she invites us to accompany her to the Restaurant de la Rotonde. We accept, although both of us assure her in advance that she can't count on us in any other way. In the upper room of the Rotonde more or less the same company is assembled as I found when I went there with Weinhöppel. We have scarcely ordered a bottle of wine when the same old whore as on that occasion sidles up to our table and asks very humbly whether she may join us in a drink. As we have company anyway, I pour her a glass. Chocolat is not present, alas. One of the gentlemen present sits down at the piano and strikes up a waltz, whereupon everyone gets up and dances. Morgenstern, who is also keen to contribute something to the entertainment, starts imitating bird-calls, but gets little response. The solemn beauty who once accompanied us to the Café Figaro is sitting at a table behind us, together with two gentlemen. I ask Marguerite, that's our half-caste's name, whether she knows her. – Oh, indeed, she'd often spoken to her. Then I ask her whether it's true that the girl lost her little finger in the war of '71. But Marguerite knows nothing of any little finger. It is indeed astonishing how adroitly the girl manages to conceal her defect. Marguerite immediate rushes across to her. I tell her not to do anything silly. No, no, she just wanted to tell her something, but then she asks the girl point-blank to show her her left hand.[88] The girl refuses. I can hear her stammering various lame excuses. I can see an appalling row in the offing, so I go across without further ado, take the half-caste by the arm and lead her back to our table. After a while the entire party breaks up. Our ladies asks us to escort them. If Weinhöppel had been present, the half-caste would at least have been in luck. But Morgenstern is still thinking about his 200 francs, and I haven't the slightest inclination or desire to make new acquaintances in this sphere. As we're leaving the restaurant, I earn another look of heartfelt gratitude from the pretty girl with the missing finger.

As Morgenstern and I are going back along the Chaussée d'Antin, I tell him how I once had trouble on a similar occasion, in the company, in fact, of a certain Langhammer from Berlin. – Langham-mer? says Morgenstern, as though thunderstruck. – Not the famous Langhammer, I say. – Karl Langhammer from Berlin? – From Berlin, 7 Sigmundhof. 7 Sigmundhof! I know him, I know him. There's only one Langhammer in Berlin. – Then he tells me how they had been at school together, how they had met again, quite by chance, as extras in Ibsen's *Wild Duck* at the Residenztheater, i.e. he, Morgenstern, had already acted a few small parts, how they had then collaborated in illustrating a people's Bible, with him, Morgenstern, doing the figures and Langhammer the landscapes, and how he'd completely lost sight of him since then.

We talk about Langhammer's appearance and his childishly frank character, his inoffensive nature – it's the same man, beyond any doubt. I'm in close correspondence with him at the moment, because I've asked him to retrieve my *Schwigerling* from Entsch and to place it with another agency he recommended to me. Morgenstern asks me to give him the news about him, Morgenstern, when I next write, but, of course, to show his circus performances in the proper light, so that Langhammer wouldn't imagine, for instance, that he, Morgenstern, had betrayed his ideals. In connection with Langhammer's splendidly childish nature, Morgenstern tells me a fantastic story which Langhammer allegedly told against himself with the greatest glee. Langhammer used to keep company with women and had bought condoms, so as to be safe from infection. It had then been a fairly simple matter, as he hadn't all that much money, to wash the condoms out at home, to inflate them, and then to hang them up to dry. His mother, so he went on, had once asked him what he used those skins for, and he had told her he needed them to put his paints in.

As we part, Morgenstern asks me to take breakfast with him on Monday at noon.

23 DECEMBER 1892

Worked.

24 DECEMBER 1892

Buy myself a white tie and get into my ball outfit late in the afternoon.[89]

4 SEPTEMBER 1893

... notice two wonderfully good-looking American girls, octoroons, travelling with all their goods and chattels, a small foretaste of the beautiful wide world. In Olten, alas, I lose sight of them. In Basel I manage to get myself a good seat and snore pretty well all night in the company of three apathetic gentlemen.

5 SEPTEMBER 1893

I ask my opposite number for a light and offer him a cigarette. He's a partner in the Stein silk firm in Zürich. I ask him about Clara Weiner. He says she turned out to be a wicked person, so that Herr Stein had left her to his friend Herr Pollak. The countryside round Paris in the mild morning light dazzles me with its paradisial charm. At the Gare de l'Est I take a cab, unfortunately neglecting to take my trunk with me straight away, and go to the Hôtel Mont Blanc, 63 Rue de Seine. I rent a large, bright room on the second floor, quiet and looking out on to the courtyard, have a wash and take a tram back to the station in order to pick up my trunk. The life of the streets delights me in a manner which I didn't experience on previous occasions. Everything seems to float in a light which doesn't dazzle you. I can distinctly feel the relief after the harsh, blinding light of Zürich. I have breakfast at Duval's on the Boulevard St Michel, and then call on Mme Herwegh.[90] She is obviously delighted to see me again. Mlle Read had called on her and said how very pleased Mme Nemethy had been by my visit in Bregenz. I reply that I wish Nemethy would finally delight me with a translation.[91] After a while a workman with an intelligent face and dressed in a white overall comes in and Frau Herwegh entrusts him with the lace shawl her daughter sent from Argentina. The workman has been trying to sell it, 80 francs is the minimum price. I have the chance once more to admire the delicate workmanship which I presumably won't ever again see. I'm itching to put the 80 francs down on the table. After he's gone, Herwegh shows me an example of his immense dexterity. By dint of incredible ingenuity he had repaired a decanter for her, but it had cost 6 francs, so that she had been obliged to ask him to keep it for the moment. Then the lament about her extreme penury starts. I take this opportunity to make clear my bizarre situation, and then simply let her carry on. After a while Marcel[92] turns up with the news that Carnot is dead,[93] his mother should reserve a window with Mme Closange, because by tomorrow there wouldn't be one to be had. He looks in poor shape and has got a great deal thinner. He still hasn't found a publisher for his father's biography. His mother launches into a brief funeral oration for Carnot, whereupon Marcel and I take our leave and go off for a glass of beer. In the café he picks up the nearest newspaper. Carnot is in a better state than before, the rumour was some trick on the stock exchange. I ask him to come to the Folies Bergères with me in the evening. But he feels rotten. He thinks he's got pleurisy. I advise him to rub his chest with iodine, amongst other things. He finally asks if he could screw, in the circumstances. I say it's up to him. If he ate sensibly, it couldn't do any harm. He then asks if I can help him edit the letters from the time of his father's engagement and the correspondence between Herwegh and Lassalle.[94] I tell him I'm much too busy, and the main thing was to make sure of a publisher in Germany. Then we part and I go home and lie down on the bed. After I've dined in the Brasserie Pont Neuf I go to the Folies Bergères, but find the place hasn't re-opened yet and go on to the Olympia. I'm so tired that I'm afraid I'll collapse, but I manage to stay on my feet until after 12 o'clock. There are one or two attractive dances on the programme, an adorable india-rubber lady; the ballet is unspeakably poor. After the performance is over I stroll along the boulevards to the Brasserie Pont Neuf, where I'm almost overcome with weariness. On the way home, at the Carrefour Buci, a pretty girl walks past. I set off after her. A few steps further on she has reached her hotel. Est-ce que vous montez?[95] The door closes behind us. I climb the stairs in total darkness. She has a nice room. She points out that the candle won't last long. After we've dealt with the commercial transaction we lie down on the bed. She's called Margot and claims to be a model. She is sweet, wholesome and pretty, so that I cannot resist instantly savouring her aroma with my tongue. Just as I start doing this, the candle goes out. That doesn't put me off at all. I have rarely found a blossom of such pure flavour and such delicious structure. Every now and then her body twitches, then she lies quiet again. These spasms recur periodically. Then it seems as if an electric current is flowing through her entire body, and I hope to achieve an ejaculation. While I'm in full song, I feel a bug bite on the left side of my neck but take no notice. Finally I can't carry on. I may have spent about twenty minutes thus. My tongue is numb, the girl is tired, and so we get down to the business of love. As she's washing afterwards, she remarks that bed bugs are a real nuisance. I say, if you had a candle I would get dressed and go home now. She says she'll ask Marie to lend her a candle. She goes out and comes back with a lighted candle.

Marie is standing in her nightdress at the open door of her room and I ask her not to stand on ceremony but to come in. As I'm getting dressed the two girls sit there in their flimsy nightdresses, one of them on the edge and the other on the end of the bed, chatting about the evening's events in the restaurant, where a customer had smashed a marble table. They have both lighted cigarettes, and I try in vain to decide which of them is the cuter. As a parting gift Margot gives me some wax vestas, so that I shan't tumble down her seven flights of stairs, and I go back to my hotel and go to bed.

6 SEPTEMBER 1893

When I wake up I notice that I've had a wet dream; that won't make a particularly good impression on the staff. I wash myself with soap and with a certain sense of zeal for physical and mental hygiene, wash my penis as well and toss myself off in my enthusiasm. Then I go to lunch, take a cab and drive to Frl. Hüny's. As I get out of my cab I see her sitting at an upstairs window wearing a light blue blouse. She receives me courteously. I can hardly speak because my tongue is fearfully sore. It's at least a centimetre longer than it was. I've acquired a lisp and can hardly close my lips. Frl. Hüny tells me that she's been in Switzerland, only for a few days, in search of a secretary. Steinherz is leaving her. He has been taken on as sole correspondent for the *Wiener Zeitung*, of which Hermann Bahr is editor-in-chief. Schuppi was also in Switzerland, as was Frau Breslau,[96] whose mother died recently. She tells me about a woman who dabbled in sin, who had pursued a number of men, ruined others, and whose letters Huysman had used in his *Là-bas*.[97] She strongly recommends me to read *Là-bas*. She tells me she once commissioned Marcel Herwegh to write articles for her on musical events. He might have earned 60 francs per month with four articles, but he had passed the job on to his mother, who had then concocted something about '48, which she had paid for but couldn't use. I leave her and go home, write to Director Müller, to Donald, etc. and go to see Frau Herwegh after dinner. At my suggestion Dietz in Stuttgart has made her an offer of 130 francs for her pamphlet, which he wants to use for newspaper articles. She's turned it down, she reckons her pamphlet is too good for the purpose. I tell her that the articles would after all at least be an advertisement for her pamphlet, and the 130 francs would be more or less a free gift. She asks me to write to Dietz again. I promise to do so, although I find it embarrassing. I stay with her until midnight and then move on to the Brasserie Pont Neuf, where I take up my drama again at the point where I broke off three months ago. After a couple of hours I'm still not inclined to go home. I can't get Raimonde out of my head. I simply can't believe that she's gone to Brazil. So I go to Barrat's, find my former seat by the window is still vacant, and sit watching the people round me. The girls have uninteresting faces that I don't recognize. Two of them come up to my table and ask me for a cigarette. They wouldn't bother me any more, as they know I always like to be by myself. The mandolin player has been replaced by a crude fiddler. The guitarist is also new. Only the baritone with the big nose is still the same. No sign of Raimonde. I listen to a number of Italian arias and then go to bed about four o'clock.

7 SEPTEMBER 1893

After breakfast I buy *Les Soirées de Néstor* and read Huysmans' short story 'Le sac au dos' in a café. As I'm leaving the café I see a delightful apparition, a girl with intelligent, expressive features and unusually luxuriant ash-blonde hair. She has a slender figure, bears herself like a queen and is 19–20 years old. She has a paintbox in her hand. After I've recovered from the shock, I go home, write until eight, have dinner and stroll along the boulevards. On the Boulevard St Michel I see two girls coming out of a shop. One of them bowls me over with her childishly slight, slender build, her bright little child's face and an irresistible jolly glint in her eye. I accompany the pair of them home, and spend an hour alone with my little doll. She lives in a tiny little attic with flowered wallpaper and a view of the starry firmament, too high up to have anyone opposite her. She is as slender as a long-stemmed rose. She tells me about an aunt she has in the Faubourg St Antoine. The aunt has a child, and the child has a doll, a marvellously beautiful doll. She played with the doll whenever she went there. She had dressed it from head to foot, and had spent the whole week sewing. I ask her if she has ever sat as a painter's model. No, that was too tiresome. She couldn't keep still. I tell her she should sit for ladies, that was less demanding. You got tea and cakes. I give her Breslau's address, she should go along some time, 40 Les Ternes.

She does in fact remind me of everything delicate and delicious by Breslau that I've ever seen. But she doesn't seem to be very keen. Making love is less bother. She shrieks a little all the same, and then she's a child again and laughing at my beard. The second time the enterprise fails. I can't seem to find my way in. I get on a bus and go to the Opéra and have an ice-cream in front of the Café de la Paix. An unbroken stream of prostitutes of both sexes parades past on the pavement. The *petits* . . ., boyishly dressed, with their neat black straw hats and that mysteriously grave look on their youthful faces have never before made such an impression on me. At midnight I go to the Brasserie Pont Neuf, work until two and then go to bed.

8 SEPTEMBER 1893[98]

After lunch I buy myself Maeterlinck's *Princesse Maleine*,[99] take a seat in a café and read it through in one go. It shows me how the thing should not be done. I sit with old Mme Herwegh until midnight. She is very ill. She vomited all last night as the result of a rotten supper at Mme Schweitzer's. I bring the conversation round to Krafft-Ebing,[100] and she tells me that the Princess Metternich could only make love to women. She had given Thérèse a villa, where she indulged in orgies with her and other lesbians. She had also presented the leading tailor in Paris with a villa; he, for his part, only made love to men. At that time there had been a ladies' house in Paris where men were admitted as spectators and where the ladies indulged in their caresses *coram publico*. She, old Mme Herwegh, had never been there, for she detested anything that was against nature. As I'm leaving the Brasserie Pont Neuf at two o'clock there's a girl in a flowing cape walking in front of me. I think it's Marie Louise, but it turns out not to be her. I go to Bovy's, prompted by an unconscious need to have news of Raimonde. The only familiar face in the little dump is Marie Louise. She asks me for a glass of milk and tells me a girl had poisoned herself yesterday with sublimate on the terrace of the Café d'Harcourt. Raimonde was still in the *quartier*. She was *dans la purée*.[101] This fills me with vast satisfaction. I ask Marie Louise if she's still on morphine. No, not for ages. She's reading *La Faute de l'Abbé Mouret*.[102] There then follows a fairly long discussion on Zola, whom she doesn't care for, by and large. It's getting on for four when I go home and to bed.

9 SEPTEMBER 1893

As I'm sitting at lunch I see the beautiful painter crossing the boulevard in the company of an unprepossessing individual and, it seems to me, vanishing into the Café Soufflet. I think to myself: You too, after all. I quickly settle my bill and walk over to the Café, but she isn't there. After working for an hour I go and sit in the Jardin du Luxembourg. There's a crowd of ten-year-old girls playing all round me, all of them with bare legs. I feel as if I'm in the seventh heaven. They're elegantly dressed, with yellow bootees and short black socks. Their movements as they clamber over the benches are innocent and of a dream-like grace. As they run and jump they stamp their feet so vigorously that their short skirts fly up into their faces. I light one cigarette after another and think about Raimonde and the beautiful painter who I suppose is out here painting somewhere in the open. After dinner I go to the Olympia, where I am even more delighted by the india-rubber lady and the czardas dancers than I was last time.

After working until after two in the Brasserie Pont Neuf I go back to Bovy's and find a cute, prettily dressed little girl whom I'd like to see home. But she's not willing. She says she has the *chaude pisse*,[103] her lover had thrown her over because of that and she was dreadfully frightened. In her profound anguish she allows me to go on kissing her for ages. Then I wish her a speedy recovery, go home and carry on working until seven.

10 SEPTEMBER 1893

After working in the afternoon I go to the Moulin Rouge in the evening. The hall is crammed to bursting point. Liszt is conducting a symphony on the rostrum, he goes off and comes back as Offenbach. In this way he runs through the entire history of music. I observe a pair of dark eyes trained on me from the midst of the crowd. In front of me, wedged in among the standing spectators, Kadudja is sitting with her friend. Fortunately it's impossible to push my way through to their table. After the end of the performance a quadrille starts up in the hall, danced by about a score of couples, all of them mediocre *balleteuses*, however. I stick by Jeanne la Folle, who is cavorting about solo in a huge black plumed hat, a dark close-fitting dress and yellow bootees. Kadudja and her friend ask me for a beer, I put them off until tomorrow. They leave me in high dudgeon. Finally, in order to while away the time until midnight, I fling myself into a comfortable cane chair in the vestibule, having first selected a pretty opposite number, a girl with dark curly hair and the solemn features of a great tragic actress. After a while a pretty Creole girl sits down beside me, claims she's an operetta singer, she doesn't know Paris at all well, and did I want to sleep with her. I tell her she's too expensive for me. – It wouldn't cost 100,000 francs. – With her looks she couldn't very well ask for less. – I should give her what I could afford. – I couldn't afford anything, she was much, much better off than I was, etc., etc. We part the best of friends, I make my way to the Brasserie Pont Neuf, work until two and go to Bovy's to get some word of Raimonde, if I possibly can. The only familiar face I see is Nini, without Lulu, in fact. One of the customers claims to have received money from her once, which she hotly denies. In all her life she'd never given a man money, and hoped she would never need to as long as she lived. In the meantime a girl I once took home about six months ago accosts me. I no longer recall her name. On that occasion she was dressed in black; now she's wearing a brand new light coloured dress with a blue silk bodice. At that time she stank to high heaven, and picked up a book the moment we got into bed together, *La Fille Élisa* by Edmond de Goncourt,[104] that little Germaine had brought me. She read it right through by first light, and then scampered off. As her vest was grubby, I lent her one of my sprigged night-shirts, which she was desperately keen to take away with her. I must have told her at the time that I'd make her a present of a ring instead. She has a round, pallid little face with chubby cheeks and a pretty chin, a delicate snub nose, full lips, narrow eyebrows slanting outwards and an uncommonly appealing moist dark eye. As she's elegantly dressed and wearing gleaming yellow glacé gloves, I presume that she has got into the habit of washing. She's not living in the Hôtel Voltaire any longer, either, but in the Rue St Sulpice, on the first floor. I ask her if she would like a drink. – No, she wasn't thirsty. And so we go off together. I've never seen such a neat, cosy little room. It is hung in sprigged yellow cotton, rather like my night-shirt on that other occasion. The vast bed-curtains that take up almost half the little room are made of the same material. The girl with her pretty yellow dress with the blue bodice fits so perfectly into this case that I feel myself secluded in this little room, cut off from the whole world, from sin, extravagance and peril. She asks me whether I would like a Chartreuse, takes a cut-glass decanter from the mantelpiece and pours out two glasses. The Chartreuse has the colour of liquid gold and has more or less that effect as it courses through our veins. As we drink we talk about her colleagues. Whether Lulu and Nini are lesbians, she wouldn't know, it was possible, why not? It's true that Lulu had her own furniture, but she lived in a tiny little hole, a single room, where she had installed her few sticks of furniture. She told everyone all the same that she had her own furniture. Lulu was definitely the dominating partner, the brains, while Nini had to play the poodle and could only accept the men that Lulu allowed her. – Had I slept with Lulu? – I say, no and add stupidly that she hadn't wanted to. – Then she starts to talk about Raimonde. She was a lesbian! – She had seen me with her in the *grand comptoir*[105] on that memorable night. – How much had I given Raimonde? – To make up for my blunder about Lulu I say 15 francs. – Pas plus que ça?[106] – No, and she had to whine and wheedle to get that. – How did I like Raimonde? – I shake my head and say, c'est une belle femme![107] – At this, she starts on a list of Raimonde's female lovers, la grande Susanne, then the little girl she was with at the *grand comptoir* that time, the one I was with chez Barrat, etc. She couldn't understand how you could go to bed with a woman. – It was the sweethearts of other women who came to her to squander the money their women were forced to give them. That was how she knew about it, and wouldn't want to keep a man as long as she lived. – I say, it's nice, after all, to have somebody to yourself, someone that belongs to you, that you can dominate. At that she laughs out loud. It was the men who dominated the women they got their money from. The women were prostrate on the ground at their feet. They were nothing but slaves. We're on the point of going to bed when I notice a pack of cards lying on the table. I ask her whether she tells fortunes by the cards. We sit down facing each other once again and she tells me a great deal about a letter, about a dark widow, about my two sisters, my mother, about money that I'm going to get from a blonde gentleman, etc. The procedure takes about half an hour. Then we go to bed at last. I find my way into a narrow gorge, beyond which a blissful paradise stretches out endlessly. Since I can't block the entrance again right away, I spend a sweet spell of time relishing its flavour until this rapturously sweet indulgence has restored my strength for a second felicitous expedition into the inner regions of that dark tellurian realm. Then I relish the fine, broad bed and the blissful dreams that hang in the bed-curtains. My fair one asks me to take her to les Halles, we would un peu vadrouiller.[108] She has only just begun to feel wide awake. Groaning, I get dressed. Then we drink another Chartreuse and stroll through the grey dawn light in the direction of les Halles. She says she only wants une soupe au fromage in the *grand comptoir*,[109] there was sure to be a great crowd of people there. In the room at the back there are only three or four solitary *grisettes*. My beauty orders a soup, I order a bottle of wine and we tuck in silently. Then the waiter comes up: Des écrevisses? – Une douzaine de Marennes? – Un demi poulet?[110] – She shakes her head, the waiter walks away. That softens my heart. I tell him to bring a dozen oysters. As we're swallowing them, I say we should go to Barrat's afterwards and drink a coffee. So we go to Barrat's, where I gulp down five or six coffees at one franc a cup. The lamps have been put out. Opposite us the band are sitting and eating their supper. My beauty asks me how I like the woman. I say she has l'air trop cocotte.[111] She belongs on the boulevards. Then she asks me if *she* doesn't have l'air trop cocotte. I say something flattering, whereupon she asks me if Raimonde doesn't look like a tart. – Mais c'est une belle femme,[112] I say, which she admits. As I still haven't consumed enough coffee, I say we should go to the Chien qui Fume, because the coffee's cheaper there. So we walk through avenues of cauliflower and beetroot in the first sunlight of the day to the Chien qui Fume, where I once more order a helping of oysters and a bottle of full-bodied wine. We sit at a window on the first floor and have the whole bustle of the Halles market before our eyes. We agree there's no finer sight than watching people really hard at work. The talk turns to Napoleon I: my sweetheart is crazy about him. She's read a book that deals with all the mistresses at the French court, from Diane de Poitiers on. She lets herself go in more detail about Mme de Pompadour and Mme de Maintenon, and especially about the Beauharnais family.[113] Then we talk about the Lucullan delights in the various restaurants *au quartier* and *à l'autre côté de l'eau*,[114] about fine vegetables, asparagus and strawberries, and I order a bottle of champagne. The girl seems to come from a good family. I can see no sign that she's anything but equal to the situation. She's from Falaise in Normandy. I know the dump well enough from

Maupassant's short stories to be able to check up on her. She says she's got a wealthy married sister there who comes to Paris every winter, but she never sees her. She expects to come into money herself when she comes of age, 30,000 or 40,000 francs. She would immediately buy herself dresses and probably run through it within a year. There's not the slightest hint of any desire to abandon her career. She says she's no longer at home in Falaise, where people go to bed at nine in the evening and rise at seven in the morning, where they don't go to a café all the year round and don't go out on the tiles a single night. I look at my watch and say to myself it's probably stopped. I ask the waiter, for God's sake, half past eleven already! Now we've really got to have a sumptuous lunch. We go back to the *grand comptoir* and partake of a lunch consisting of croûte en pot, a poulet mayonnaise, a bowl of salad and some gigantic pears. We decide to take coffee in the *quartier* and take a cab to the Boulevard St Michel. In the Source she suggests a game of Faro. She wins a trifle that I quickly get back from her. Once she's back to 5 francs she stops the game and asks to be paid. I put her off until tomorrow, but she goes on pleading until I give her the 5 francs, on condition she buys me a coffee in the Vachette. That's because I haven't as much as a sou in my pocket. So we go to the Vachette, where I take infinite satisfaction in getting her to pay for my coffee. Then we set off home and part company at the Carrefour de l'Odéon. As we're parting, it occurs to me that I haven't asked her what her name is. I go home and find a parcel from Director Müller on my table, a letter from Auntie Plümacher and one from Mama. I lie down on the bed and sleep until seven, go to dinner and afterwards to Frau Herwegh, bankrupt in soul and body. As I'm sitting opposite her, I hear an intermittent belly rumble, but can't for the life of me make out whether it's her belly or mine. Suddenly she breaks off and says she has to ask my advice on a very difficult matter. That restores my composure. I'm prepared for any kind of assault and calmly wait for whatever's coming. She asks me what I think about her asking my mother to advance her 200 francs until New Year. She would be in a position to return it at New Year. She didn't know my mother, it's true, had never set eyes on her, but did I think she would give her the money. Surprising as this suggestion is, I don't let it floor me. I say it would no doubt be the natural thing for her to leave this mission to me. But she has no confidence in that solution. She says she would write herself, and would have done so already, if she hadn't been reluctant to do so without my knowledge. That didn't seem to her practical, in any case: what was my mother's address? Judging by my description, my mother must after all be a very simple woman, she must have frightfully come down in the world, but if only she had a kind heart. She wouldn't do it for her own sake. It was for the benefit of Marcel, whom she would dearly love to send to the seaside for a few days before the start of the season. She wouldn't, of course, write to my mother that it was for Marcel's sake. She would write as if she needed the 200 francs for herself.

1 JANUARY 1894

At twelve o'clock I'm in the Café d'Harcourt and meet Alice, who was in Brussels for three weeks. She is rather pale, but still as lovely as any queen. I go to the Café de la Source, drink a couple of glasses of grog, go home, copy out a number of scenes and read through the third act. Then I go to bed, read *La Joie de vivre*.[115] The waiter brings in my boots and wishes me good morning. I promptly fall asleep again. At eleven o'clock the waiter brings me a letter from Mlle Read, in which she writes that she feels so *disposée à parler avec moi même de ce dont on ne parle jamais*.[116] *Pressée* is written on the envelope and heavily underlined. I go on sleeping until about three.

I have an appointment at six o'clock with Gaston Fero in the Duval St Michel, but am determined not to go all the same. Why should I ruin my entire evening with this pompous, crazy ass, when I can find a better use for it? I go to lunch round about four in the afternoon, and come back home, only to find that my room has not been tidied. I go to the Café Vachette and read the papers, then back home again. The room has still not been done. I lay a fire in the fireplace and write until eight, go to the Duval St Michel for dinner and afterwards go on writing until midnight. Then I go to the Café d'Harcourt, talk with Rachel, Bertha, Germaine, Lucie, Susanne etc. for a couple of hours, and am back in my room by two. It still hasn't been tidied. I put the bed more or less to rights, lie down and read until about five before falling asleep.

2 JANUARY 1894

I order chocolate in bed at nine, write until three, go to my little restaurant for lunch, then to the Café Vachette, and about five to Mlle Read. I'm prepared for every sort of emotional outburst. I've been reckoning that she means to ask my advice as to whether she should give Mme Herwegh the 500 francs that Herwegh wanted to borrow from her. She drags in some fat volumes and shows me her life's work. She goes to the Bibliothèque Nationale and digs out all the newspaper articles that have ever appeared on Barbey d'Aurevilly and pastes them into thick exercise books. She presents me with a photograph of Barbey d'Aurevilly and Mme Ackermann's poems,[117] gives me Heine's will and various other items to take away and read, and hands me Mlle Rousseil's pamphlet on her behalf. Mlle Rousseil was here yesterday, she had shown her the album I gave her, and Mlle Rousseil very much regretted that she wasn't represented in it.[118] After chatting for an hour, I go home and write.

At twelve o'clock I meet Gaston Fero in the Café d'Harcourt. His health is improving, at least he feels in good spirits and is once more resuming his relations with the various monsters he had left pining for him for the past six weeks. Rachel comes up and wishes me a happy New Year. Finally, Alice also comes along, and I make an appointment to meet her tomorrow. My stout Christ child is nowhere to be seen. Shortly before two, Gaston Fero expounds the following theory: if he's lying in bed with a girl, he lets her wait first of all. That was the surest way to size them up. If she takes the initiative herself, then that's a sign that she lacks the sense of shame that is innate in women. That was a much more reliable criterion than the fact that she was elegantly dressed. If a woman was elegantly dressed, he instantly sensed the *grande dame*, and that he found off-putting, whereas that innate female sense of shame had to be there, even in a prostitute. He was the consumer, he was the one who footed the bill; therefore the girl had to wait until he made a move, if she hadn't lost all sense of shame.

We part at two o'clock. I work for another hour, fall asleep over my work, wake up stiff with cold, and go to bed.

3 JANUARY 1894

Get up about three, lunch, and go to the Bon Marché in the bitter cold in order to buy myself a travelling rug. I meet Mlle Douglas at Mlle Read's, together with Mlle Marie Lefond, and a taciturn lady whom I don't know. The conversation once more revolves around Mme Block, who shot herself in Balltricette after abandoning her husband and ten-year-old daughter in the expectation that Dr Privier, a professor at the Sorbonne, would marry her. She had joined the Dames de France, and that was how she had come to fall in love with Dr Privier. In spite of the divorce, her husband had provided the means for her to live in an apartment in the Rue des Écoles that was furnished in the most luxurious taste. But since Dr Privier would not, or could not, marry her, she had shot herself in Balltricette. Everyone agrees that she was a woman of outstanding beauty, and the only thing they don't excuse is the fact that she had abandoned a ten-year-old daughter for the sake of her lover.

A young girl of impeccable bearing, but with a thoroughly boring face, comes in and talks to Mlle Douglas about Schumann as compared with Schubert, a conversation in which I join with pleasure. In the end I'm left alone with Mlle Read and Mlle Douglas. The three of us huddle up to the empty fireplace, where the fire has gone out, and Mlle Read, with a foot-warmer at her feet, prattles on like a prayer-wheel. I hand her back Heine's will and go to dinner at Boulant's, meet M. Montreuil there and have a more satisfying discussion than ever with him about the plays of Couturier,[119] whom I once met on the stairs at Mlle Read's, and whose *L'Inquiétude* she had given me to take away with me: that's the play that opened two days ago at the Théâtre Libre. I go home, write the final three sentences of the fourth act,[120] and take the manuscript to old Mme Herwegh.

The old lady receives me with undisguised delight. We haven't seen each other for three days. She brews me a grog and offers me some dates. Then we wish each other a Happy New Year. She points proudly to a huge pile of firewood lying by the hearth. She feels like an Indian widow. I should take a good look at it, in ten days time there would be nothing left. If Mlle Read didn't show up by then with her money, she didn't know what she'd use for firewood. She shows me two letters she received for New Year, one from Mme Street, and one from Mme de Rousseau. She'd not yet had any word from Mme Ménard. Perhaps she'd come with her daughter and visit her. True, she was in poor health, but she did have her own carriage. Mme Ménard was very robust by nature, but during the Commune[121] they had arrested her husband, and she had missed her period because of that. As a result she was suffering from anaemia in the head and neuralgia. She certainly couldn't have any more children. Her daughter's engagement to Georges Hugo would in any case give her plenty to think about.

The old lady is looking forward to the *Figaro* article about herself and Orsini in fear and trembling, but not without some pride. There would be a frightful row with her son Horace, but Mme Street would claim to be her best friend. Mme Lewenoff had been to see her yesterday and had asked after me. She'd told Lewenoff I'd celebrated New Year with her. Lewenoff had then said: 'And he doesn't come to see me!' Finally she tells me stories dating back seventy years to her time in boarding school. We part about twelve and I go to the Café d'Harcourt.

Gaston Fero is sitting in the darkest corner. He says he's leaving soon anyway, he's got something on. I suggest he shouldn't let me keep him. Then Alice comes in and asks me if I'll take her with me. I take her across to Steinbach's, we polish off two dozen oysters, drink a bottle of wine, then her friend Emma comes and tells us about the Folies Bergères, about Émilienne d'Alençon, whose beauty utterly fascinates her. We go back to the d'Harcourt and Emma starts looking for a man. At last she's found one, a hangdog fellow, a real cut-throat. She comes back to us, points him out and asks whether she should take him on. He'd offered her 10 francs, but she'd be sure to take the money in advance, whatever happened. Before she goes off with him, she comes back to say goodbye. Bibi is sitting next to us, with his clean-shaven rascal's face and dented hat, pulling all sorts of faces and turning up his eyelids. About two we take a heated cab to drive home because of the beastly cold, but the window-panes are missing.

I light a fire, Alice divests herself of her charming dress, I also get undressed down to my silvery grey tights, and we sit in front of the fireplace, talking and smoking. She lets down her thick, dark blonde hair, which falls round her like a shawl as far down as her hands. Her great luminous blue eyes, the imperious Olympian grandeur of her features, the splendid cut of her fresh lips, her plump fresh white arms, the delicate lace chemise with the blue ribbons, all this is of a sumptuous perfection such as I have never witnessed in any other woman.

I take her legs on to my lap, spread them open a number of times, and then bend down between them and excite her with my tongue. Even though she hasn't washed beforehand, there isn't the slightest taint to the taste. I enjoy the delicacy that's offered to me for its own sake, as a creature of purely physical pleasure, as a gourmet, without being in the least sensually aroused. She has laid her legs over my shoulders and digs her heels into my back in order to spur me on. With her hands she holds me fast by the hair. Her ample body begins to shudder, writhes and heaves up; at the climax she whinnies like a foal. I shove my lower jaw back into place and notice that I've torn a ligament in my tongue and am lisping like any Jew. After the tempest in her body has subsided, she goes into the *cabinet de toilette* in order to wash, a need which I for my part don't feel.

After we have chatted on for an eternity we go to bed. I ask her whether she's a Socialist or an Anarchist. She says she's a je-m'en-foutiste.[122] She has had un petit pucelage[123] for the last fortnight and enjoys me with the intelligence, circumspection and precaution of an artist in her profession. We fall asleep by candlelight under a new Scottish travelling-rug that I bought in the Bon Marché today and that I've spread over my blankets on account of the severe cold.

4 JANUARY 1894

Alice gets up at one o'clock. It's pitch-dark in the room. The heavy curtains don't let in a single ray of light. I strike a match and set up fresh candles. Then she gets dressed quickly. Every garment is simple and elegant, smart and spotless, from her neat laced bootees to her black velvet cape trimmed with fur and her grand feathered hat. Her appearance is imposing without straying into the realm of the colossal. Her eyes radiate an Olympian *joie de vivre*. I wallow in bed until three o'clock, then go to lunch in the bitter cold and on to the Café Vachette, where I read Mlle Rousseil's pamphlet.

It's a mixture of hatred of Mme Tissandier and her enthusiasm for classical antiquity, complaints about bad food at Mme Tissandier's, about sleepless nights spent on the chamber-pot, cheek by jowl with quotations from Tacitus, letters from President Carnot, from Lessings, from Gounod, poems by Armand Sylvester, alongside vehement accusations against Mme Adam, who is alleged to have killed her first husband and to have had three children by Père Dédor, whom she calls a Judas, then a description of the wretched plight of the Jews expelled from Russia whom she had visited in Paris with the aim of offering them comfort, together with an account of Mme Tissandier's situation at the Odéon, which she calls a flea-pit, an assertion that Mme Tissandier eats raw calves' feet, whereas she herself has to live on beefsteak when appearing in tragedy, and, in the middle of all this, squabbles about old clothes, about vests that Mme Tissandier gave her and that are said to have been torn, then her defence in court, larded with verses from *Phèdre* and *Athalie*,[124] reviews by Richeque and Serery, whom she calls an old Silenus, the story of her youth and the youth of her mother, who sold flowers in the street, some poems of her own about Alsace-Lorraine, excursions into the country undertaken by Mme Tissandier in the company of a wealthy gentleman, the connection with the house of Rothschild, on which both of them had sponged for all they were worth. Etc., etc.

For dinner I go to the Maison Fara, where the maid tells me the gentlemen still came from time to time, and had indeed been there that same evening. I write at home until twelve and go to the Café d'Harcourt. Alice wishes me good evening and enquires when I got up. Emma is very pleased with her hangdog customer of yesterday. Il était très gentil.[125] My little Christ child arrives at the last moment, turns sentimental but cordial, orders a warm bouillon and makes me promise to see her home once more before I go to London. I go back to my room and go to bed about four o'clock.

5 JANUARY 1894

I have chocolate brought in at eight o'clock, write until two, go to lunch and then to a café, where I nearly freeze to death for three hours, and then call on Mlle Read. Present: la belle Mme Ritter, the Professor from the Lycée Condorcet, Mlle Douglas and Mlle Read. Mme Ritter gets up, she must get home, her mother has scalded her hand. The Professor also takes his leave, he is very busy, he's been working on his doctorate for the past ten years. I then ask Mlle Douglas for her impression of Rousseil's pamphlet. She asks Mlle

Read how she could have such stuff printed. Mlle Read says we have no idea how much she had to cut out beforehand. I say it's a shame that a single word had been suppressed. The conversation turns to Forain,[126] and Mlle Read gleefully narrates a number of his crudest dirty stories. She is not in the least deterred by the arrival of Mlle Chevet. Mlle Chevet brings the conversation round once more to Mme Block, and I take my leave. As I'm going Mlle Read recommends *Les Liaisons dangereuses* to me,[127] a book that contains the strongest meat she had ever come across, and she had a pretty strong stomach. Bourget had drawn her attention to it.[128] He reckoned it to be one of the most significant products of the preceding century. Apart from this, she asks me for the third time to write something in her album.

I go to dinner, and then to old Mme Herwegh. She asks me to read to her, and I'm just on the point of beginning, when Marcel arrives. He has to write something or other for his concert and behaves so boorishly that I find it hard to give him a civil answer. The old lady is afraid there will be a scene and does her best to restrain me by all manner of flattering little attentions – dates, marzipan, rum, cigarettes, and her good-natured, nervous smile. After he has finished his letter he goes on bragging for a while in the most shameless fashion and then takes his leave. The old lady and I stand speechless by the fireplace. She asks me to speak my thoughts aloud. I tell her there's no point, and when she insists, I confine myself to the comment that he treats her in a way that beggars description. She hadn't asked me for my opinion with a view to defending him or, if possible, erasing the vile impression he had made on me. He meant no ill, etc., etc., he took after his father, his father had been just the same. Then she asks me to carry on all the same and read her another act.

I read as badly as may be, nevertheless the old lady seems deeply impressed. In connection with the description of my heroine, she proceeds to tell me the story of how Marcel shot himself. She, Mme Herwegh, had an old friend with whom she'd been on the best of terms for some thirty-odd years, a Mme de la Nux. Mme de la Nux had a son, who had married a fifteen-year-old girl, a Mlle Livaro, when he himself was only seventeen. They had known each other as children, and they went on behaving like children even when they were married. The first child arrived after a year. The father gambolled around the room with it, as if he himself were a child.

Within a year he was totally insane and had to be put in a lunatic asylum. The young woman, by then aged seventeen, gave herself to a wealthy gentleman and, within a few years, promised to marry him, if he paid for a divorce from her husband in the lunatic asylum. After the divorce had been granted she no longer wished to keep her promise and married an elderly gentleman who was not of an amatory disposition, less on account of his years than for other reasons. She claimed he had a fistula. She was in any case terrified night and day that her former lover would take occasion to kill her. In spite of all this, she was on the best of terms with old Mme Herwegh. She called her *la mère idéale*,[129] and the old lady seems to have been very fond of her as well. But when Marcel was playing together with the girl at a soirée, Mme Herwegh remarked to her old friend Mme de la Nux: I only hope for God's sake that she doesn't fall in love with Marcel! That would be the end of him. Old Mme de la Nux claimed that her former daughter-in-law had been the sole reason why her son had gone off his head. That didn't stop her, however, from communicating Mme Herwegh's fears to her former daughter-in-law. The following day the young woman meets Marcel in the street and asks him: Voulez-vous être mon amant?[130] And Marcel replies: Oui. Old Mme Herwegh claims, incidentally, that she had already been flirting with him. She then brought him to the point where he shot himself. A button stopped the bullet penetrating his body. Marcel thought nevertheless that he'd been hit, and fell to the ground. The bullet was found stuck deep in the lining of his coat. He then went to his mother. And so, says old Mme Herwegh, my child came back to me. It was only thanks to the efforts of old Dr Lallier that he'd been saved from death. Before that, incidentally, he was said to have twice poisoned himself with morphine, and here, too, it was thanks only to Dr Lallier that he survived. The young woman had then got divorced from her impotent husband after he had squandered her entire fortune. She resumed her maiden name, and a year ago Mme Livaro had written a letter to Mme Herwegh from Nice.

Old Mme Herwegh fetches her correspondence file from the desk and reads me the letter. Mme Livaro finds herself bereft of the means of subsistence and is thinking of taking a post as 'dame de compagnie'.[131] The letter is cordial and sincere, but somehow rather childish. She is trying to restore the old bonds of friendship. It's so long since she heard from her *mère idéale*, and she asks for news.

Mme Herwegh had replied, if her son was still alive, then it was no thanks to Mme Livaro, but thanks to old Lallier, and the only request she would make of her was that she should stay well away from her and her son. She still has her letter here: Marcel had forbidden her to send it. She had then asked her old friend Lallier, who had also advised her not to reply. Three months after writing to old Mme Herwegh, the young woman had married a young officer – ten years younger than herself, in fact – who had just returned from Tonkin, since he couldn't stand the service there. She was now living in Algiers with him.

It's past one o'clock when I leave the old lady. I drop in briefly at the Café d'Harcourt, and then go to bed.

6 JANUARY 1894

I wake at nine, have a chocolate brought in, fall asleep again and don't wake up until six in the evening. I go to the Odéon and a number of other bookshops in order to buy *Les Liaisons dangereuses*. They tell me everywhere that the book is banned by the police. In a second-hand bookshop in the Rue Soufflot I find a marvellous copy at last, the first edition, bound in leather and gilt-edged, for 10 francs. When I come out into the street again, the sky to the north is red. I go in the direction of the glow. It looks to me as if there's a fire in the Théâtre des Variétés, but it turns out to be on the other side of the boulevard, quite close to the Folies Bergères. There are no flames to be seen, but a couple of streets are as bright as day from the reflection in the sky. After watching for a while, I take a seat in the Folies Bergères and enjoy the enchantingly beautiful legs of Émilienne d'Alençon, which are unveiled by degrees in the *Ballet des 42 arts*. By the time the show is over, there's no sign of the fire, although the pumps are still working. The hoses lying the length of the street are in very poor repair and squirt water up the ladies' skirts as they step over them, which occasions screams on all sides. I go into the Brasserie Pont Neuf and go to bed dog-tired at two o'clock.

7 JANUARY 1894

I call on old Mme Herwegh late in the afternoon. She's read the third act through once more and thinks it's frightful. But above all, she says, a question addressed to the fates. Can you lend me 10 francs? I give her the 10 francs and am just on the point of starting the fourth act when Marcel arrives, in a state of great excitement as usual, to sort out the tickets for his concert. A disgusting squabble starts between him and his mother, with him cursing his brother at intervals and expecting me to laugh at his jokes. His mother tells him deliberately, and with a certain air of solemnity, that she has bought her ticket for his concert herself. He urges her to accept it as a gift from him. She replies that she's making it a New Year's present to herself, he should allow her that pleasure, she'd always bought her own ticket on previous occasions, and with that she hands him the 10 francs she's just borrowed from me: he's to go straight away and use the money to send out the invitation cards. He embraces her, gives her a kiss, and takes the 10 francs. In all probability anyway he's already that morning discussed with her where the money to send off the cards is to come from. She will have replied, no doubt: 'Wedekind's coming this evening. I'll try to see whether he's got any money.' And now they're putting on this act for my benefit. As he says goodbye, I only just manage to shake his hand with a show of friendship, but he's hardly gone before I feel a fearful nervous fit coming on. I've lost the power of speech, I can't open my mouth, and I fall flat on the floor. I feel it would help if only I could let out a scream, but I can't. The old lady grasps the situation instantly, fetches eau-de-Cologne, rubs my temples with it and remains perfectly calm. I pull myself together then, but about a quarter of an hour elapses before I regain the power of speech. When the old girl sees I'm getting better, she tells me a silly story about a man with a funny name, and gradually manages to make me laugh. She behaves just like Mali did six years ago after that dreadful disaster. Only that Mali's eyes were filled with tears as she laughed.

I say goodbye, mooch around by the Seine, ending up in the Café d'Harcourt. Marie Louise is sitting next to me and asks me if I'm a morphine addict. Germaine comes in and shakes hands with me. Marie Louise asks if I've slept with her, she reckons she's got syphilis. She'd passed it on to an officer and he'd had to have treatment for three months in Fontainebleau. I say, perhaps she caught it from me. After all, she'd told me at one time that Henriette had syphilis. She says the entire *quartier* knew that Henriette had syphilis, and that's what she'd died of, after all. At two o'clock I go home to bed.

8 JANUARY 1894

Wake up early, at eight o'clock, but feel absolutely whacked. After lunch in a café I write to Hartleben.[132] In the evening, after dining in the Rue Viodema, I call on old Herwegh once more. On the way there I'm gripped by an unholy dread, my agitation mounting with every step I take. I have a feeling that it needs only one word to bring about a repetition of yesterday's attack. If Marcel is there, or if he turns up while I'm there, I'm determined to beat a hasty retreat. All day long I've felt so battered in body and soul, as if I'd been given a thorough thrashing. As I knock on the door, I'm well aware that I look frightful. 'At last, at last!' cries the old lady when she sees me, and asks how I got on yesterday after I'd left. After I've reassured her, she says she's just finished reading the fourth act and thinks it's frightful. Mlle Read had been to see her and had brought 100 francs. She had asked her to check the French in the fourth act along with me, she'd be ready to do that any time, I only had to fix a morning. Then she gives me back the 30 francs she still owes me. Then someone else had called on her, had brought her *marrons glacés*, and had invited me to tea on Thursday evening. I make a guess that it was Mme de Lewenoff, but it was in fact Mlle Hüny. I had written to her yesterday asking her to send me back Hauptmann's *Weavers*. We run through the French passages in the fourth act together and chat about this and that. About twelve I take my leave and go to the Café d'Harcourt.

Alice and Emma wish me good evening. Being very bored, I offer Alice some refreshment, but tell her straight away that I won't take her back with me, because I had some kind of nervous fit yesterday. She, on the other hand, asserts that she's in very good form, since she'd slept from two o'clock last night until seven this evening – and by herself, too! She asks me to escort her to Chez Balzac, she absolutely must find someone, she simply couldn't go to bed by herself tonight. By two o'clock I've had second thoughts, and am only worrying about how to save the expense of a cab. I manage to do this by keeping her guessing until we get to the Boulevard St Germain. There I say I'm sorry there isn't a cab, otherwise we could take it.

In my room I light a fire, she gets undressed, and I read the letter from Frl. Hüny that I found in my letter-box, a four-page epistle. An old friend of hers had been run over, etc. Alice's plump and dazzling arms arouse my lust. I run my tongue up and down them; she states, ça me fait jouir.[133] She is even more responsive on her back, along her spine. Otherwise, our intercourse is a shade low-key. She no longer has the sublime respect for me that she had on the first day of our acquaintance. She orders me to bring the wash-basin over to her, to fetch a towel, without troubling to make it seem like a graceful performance. I get into bed and warm the nest, still thinking about the fit I had yesterday. When she's at last lying by my side, I first of all stimulate her with my hand to the point of distraction before I take pity on her. But then she takes her pleasure like a wild beast. While she's washing she asks me when she was last with me. I take out my notes and look it up: it was on the third of January. She asks me if I keep a diary, and is dying to read it. As that's not possible, she asks me to translate. This I do as best I can, but she thinks I'm making fun of her. It seems barely credible to her that I can write down such filth. Certain details convince her, however, that my notes are authentic. She says, moi aussi je vais faire mon journal – écrire des cochonneries – je fais un minet – il me fait muni – ça fera du bon, ça![134]

I don't take my hands off her all night. Even when we're sleeping, I carry on with the exercises. Whenever I stop, she wakes up and asks me to go on, she can't sleep otherwise. I wake up at one o'clock in the afternoon and take her, but she's still asleep, and doesn't wake up until she's well and truly in my embrace. She stays in bed until four in the afternoon. At one point I dream that she's gone, but when I wake up she's still there. I promptly show that I deserve her presence. At four o'clock she gets dressed, by candlelight, of course, and leaves, after presenting me with a little bouquet, of which I hereby attach a sample.[135]

I get up at six, go to the Café Vachette, reinvigorated and refreshed in body and soul, write to Mlle Hüny, dine on the Avenue de l'Opéra. I spend the evening in the Olympia. While I'm sitting in the aisle below the stage in a comfortable cane chair, a girl in a dazzling gown with a diamond necklace comes up to me and asks me to give her something. I say, Oh, je suis tellement pauvre![136] – She twists my moustache, plaits my beard into a pigtail and asks me for two sous: Ça me portera bonheur.[137] I give her a couple of sous. She then showers me with kisses, so that I very nearly pass out, and goes on her way.

I read the papers in the Brasserie Pont Neuf until two o'clock.

On 10 January 1894 Wedekind had his photograph taken in Paris, 'so as to know some time in the future what I looked like when I had a thousand francs in my pocket.'

10 JANUARY 1894

It's the tenth already, and I still haven't paid my hotel bill. I pocket a thousand franc note, the second last one, and change it at the Crédit Lyonnais. Then I get myself photographed so as to know some time in the future what I looked like when I had a thousand francs in my pocket. Late in the afternoon I call on Mlle Read. Mlle Read has Demoiselle, Barbey d'Aurevilly's cat on her lap and once more tells the story of the death of her grey cat, which expired recently, linking it with the state of health of her mother, who has been suffering from nose-bleeds for the past three weeks. The cat's demise had been astutely predicted by Dr Seligmann: the eyes are dilated, the tongue looks bad. There's something amiss in the brain, that's for sure. Either she'll die or get better. She'd spent the whole day in her bed, and the other six cats had taken it in turn to go and enquire how she was. They had shaved her chest and applied a poultice. At midnight she crept up to the blazing hearth, fell down and died after vomiting two spoonfuls of water.

Opposite me is sitting Dr Letourneau; Alexander Herzen's youngest daughter,[138] not yet sixteen, had shot herself in Florence for his sake. The talk comes round to Mlle Rousseil's pamphlet; the doorbell rings, and Mlle Read asks us to lower our voices for a moment, as it may be the lady herself. It's the lovely Mme Ritter. She's in a state of dreadful anxiety. She has just made five calls and had been asked everywhere she went whether Vaillant had been condemned to death or not.[139] If he was condemned to death, then he would be a martyr, and nobody's life would be safe. Mlle Douglas, who is otherwise terrified of every puff of wind, is in favour of executing him. The conversation becomes so boring that I take my leave.

After dinner I call on old Mme Herwegh. I meet Gaston Fero at midnight in the Café d'Harcourt. He has resumed his rake's progress that had been so rudely interrupted. He has found a girl by the name of Jeanne, a face of true Grecian loveliness. Fortunately, she isn't present. He won't go back to his Susanne. She dresses too respectably for his taste. She's well on the way to spoiling herself by turning into a *grande dame*.

11 JANUARY 1894

Get up at half past eight, and am at Mme Herwegh's by half past nine. Mlle Read arrives immediately afterwards and the three of us once more go through the French in the fourth act.

Mlle Read sits on the sofa like a princess on her throne, with the old lady on her left and me on her right. I feel very gratified by the understanding and helpfulness of the two ladies. The final scene and the figure of little Kadega in general meet with their unqualified approval. After we've finished work, the conversation turns to Dr Letourneau, and hence to Alexander Herzen and his daughter Nathalie, who is said to resemble her mother, Herzen's first wife, in every respect. Herzen was the illegitimate son of a Russian magnate, but acknowledged. His wife was the illegitimate daughter of his father's brother, but not recognized by him. Her mother was a milliner from Stuttgart. After the June rising he was expelled from

Paris and went to Geneva together with his wife, who was far gone in pregnancy.

Old Mme Herwegh had said to her husband at the time that he should get out as well, since he was threatened with the same fate. She couldn't go with him, as they hadn't the necessary money. Herwegh had spent two years feeling sorry for Herzen on account of his utter nonentity of a wife, but in Geneva he fell in love with her, and the three of them rented a villa on the Lake of Geneva. They then moved on to Nice, followed by Mme Herwegh, who had already begun to smell a rat. In Nice, Herzen and Herwegh discussed whether they should swap wives. Herzen doesn't seem to have started an affair with Herwegh's wife, although he calmly watched the goings-on between his wife and Herwegh. What he did in fact, together with Charles Edouard, was to throw parties for his friends in the local brothel, for which his wife adored him. She proved capable of retaining the affections of her husband and her lover, until a friend of Herzen's once tackled him at a dinner regarding his wife's behaviour. That same night Herzen had a show-down with his wife and instructed Frau Herwegh to inform her husband the following morning that he proposed to challenge him to a duel. Frau Herwegh replied that he was welcome to take a shot at her husband, if that would give him any satisfaction. On the other hand, she could tell him in advance that her husband would never shoot at him. He then demanded that she should leave Nice, together with her husband. So she travelled to Genoa with her husband, acting the part of Sister of Mercy and consoling him as best she could over his disrupted liaison.

Herwegh had no appetite and wouldn't eat anything, and Frau Herwegh said to herself, she wouldn't eat anything either. He had come to an agreement with Herzen's wife that they would live apart for a year so as to expiate their guilt, then they would get divorced, she from her husband and he from his wife, and they would get married. Before their departure for Nice they had planned to stab themselves to death together, a resolve which Herwegh's wife had also frustrated. She has the dagger to this very day.

The Herzens left Nice shortly afterwards, however, and were reconciled, although Herzen's wife was once again heavily pregnant – by Herzen, in fact, Frau Herwegh claims. Herwegh didn't stick it for long in Genoa. He went to Switzerland, to Zürich and Lauffenberg, where he lived for three years in a state of total destitution.

In Genoa his wife soon acquired a circle of admirers among the Italian emigrant community. This was the time when she got to know Orsini, Garibaldi, Count Pepoli, Mazzini, Fabrici etc. She fell in love with one of them and, as she felt insecure, she wrote to her husband to tell him about it. Herwegh wrote back, saying that he had forfeited his claims to her. She was free. She says this struck her as frightfully cruel. At the same time Karl Vogt came over from Nice to tell her that the Herzens had left, she could move back to Nice. She handed over to him her son Horace, then aged ten, and followed him to Nice a few days later.

Scarcely had she arrived back in Nice when the Herzens moved in again and rented an apartment just across the road from her. Herzen's wife was confined shortly afterwards, and died in childbirth. Old Mme Herwegh still remembers how she heard a coffin being made for her behind the shutters of a joiner's workshop just across the street. Herzen then convened a court of honour consisting of Mazzini, Karl Vogt and others, so as to have Herwegh declared dishonourable and a false friend. What was more, he had articles published in the Nice papers in which Herwegh, the man on whom an entire nation had once gazed with pride, was represented as a depraved individual. Then he sent his Herr Hauf to Zürich with instructions to slap Herwegh's face at a public meeting.

One day Charles Edouard arrived on an errand for Herzen with a letter Herwegh had written to Herzen saying that he was no longer in love with his wife. She was ugly, too classical for his taste. Frau Herwegh told him that the business he was engaged in was a despicable affair, and showed him the door. She never saw him again. He's living in Paris and had a play put on this winter at the Déjazet Theatre: it was called *L'Agente* and ran for more than two hundred performances. She says he reckoned it a point of honour to go to bed with a different woman every night. When he came back from Algiers, she had once picked up his wallet and found a condom in it. She says she can understand how one might embrace a man in this way or that way, but if he suddenly said, 'Excuse me a moment', then every illusion went by the board. She had never experienced anything of the kind in her own marriage. As a sixteen-year old youth Charles Edouard had been a police informer in Warsaw, and had to run for it because he had started an affair with the wife of the chief of police. He went to Berlin, where Frau Herwegh got to know him while she was still a young girl.

After his wife's death Herzen left Nice and went to stay with his best friend, who lived in London. One day he said to this friend, I'm an evil man, I've taken your wife. The friend retorted, you can keep her, and fetched a girl off the streets that same evening. Herzen married his conquest, who was a friend of his first wife. He had five children by her. By his first wife he had a son and a daughter, the afore-mentioned Nathalie, who were said to have had sexual inter-course with each other, even as children. His eldest daughter from his second marriage grew up in this company, and when she was seventeen she fell in love in Florence with Dr Letourneau, who had long been married at that time. Letourneau replied to her written advances with the idea of bringing the girl to her senses. Then he fell seriously ill and was confined to bed for three weeks. When he had recovered, he learned on the occasion of his first visit to friends that the girl had in the meantime shot herself.

Herzen's son, who is now a professor in Lausanne, has his father's memoirs in his possession. During a fit of financial embarrassment he proposed to publish them, but Dr Letourneau stopped him: the memoirs were not to be published prior to the death of Frau Herwegh. Old Mme Herwegh had learned this many years ago from her friend Nicoline, who was a close friend of Dr Letourneau, and at whose house she had once met him.

After Herwegh had spent three years herding swine in Switzerland, he asked his wife to come back to him. At the time she had said to herself: I can do this only if I can be sure that not a single reproach will ever cross my lips. She reckons to have fulfilled this self-imposed condition. And so she came to Zürich in the fifties, to join the society of Liszt, Wagner, Bülow, Countess Hatzfeld, Semper,[140] Moleschott, Lassalle, etc. This is the story of those affairs of the heart that Mme Herwegh told me some weeks ago,[141] saying a woman either comes to terms with it all, or else keeps her mouth shut. I would understand why she couldn't write her memoirs, in spite of all the offers and encouragement she was given.

I escort Mlle Read home, go to lunch, spend the afternoon in a café and by nine in the evening am at Mlle Hüny's, where I meet Dr Felix Vogt and a girl who is studying medicine. The conversation is as dull as may be. Felix Vogt is dreary, clumsy, ugly, brash and fatuous.

The party breaks up at eleven, and I suggest to the medical student that we walk back to the *quartier*. She is an East Prussian, with thick dark hair, sturdily built, very agreeable, with expressive eyes. She writes medical reports for Mlle Hüny. We talk as if we had known each other for ten years – about the prostitution of under-age children and about syphilis. She lives a long way past the Panthéon. After seeing her home, I go to the Café d'Harcourt. My little Christ child asks me to drink an Américain with her. Alice is sitting opposite us with some friends. Suddenly a young workman comes in and shouts, 'Vive Vaillant! Vive l'anarchie!' The students clap and egg him on, although no one actually joins in. The landlord pushes him gently out of the door, not without a certain deference.

12 JANUARY 1894

After working in the morning, I go to Mlle Read's in the evening. Mlle Read and Mlle Douglas are arguing about love. Mlle Read is arguing that you can feel something emotionally without in fact having actually experienced it. You could surmise it with the help of your intuition, you could visualize it, if you had read a great deal. Mlle Douglas argues that the image will never conform to the reality, it might be similar, but it wouldn't be an accurate likeness. It was *toujours à coté*.[142] She should give her the name of one great actress who had lived a chaste life. It was the same with poets. All of them had simply written down during the day what they had practised the night before. Mlle Read asserts that she had in fact been in love, once when she was only twelve, and again when she was fifteen. Mlle Douglas asks her what sort of love it was, then. She claps her hands together over her head, Mlle Read needn't imagine things. She had no more been in love than the armchair she's sitting in. Mlle Read says she did have that feeling, what did you read novels for, then, you can experience any sort of emotion, if you have the potential, if the feeling is lodged in your heart. She would act Phèdre every bit as well as someone who had had ten lovers.

Mlle Read is forty-eight years old, Mlle Douglas is fifty-two. I egg both sides on as best I can. As I'm leaving, Mlle Read tells me that Mme Nemethy will be in Paris the day after tomorrow. She had written to her from Munich.

After dinner I mean to work at home, but fall asleep and go to bed by eleven o'clock.

13 JANUARY 1894

Get up at five in the morning, work all day and call on old Mme Herwegh in the evening. I'm so worn out that I go to bed by twelve.

14 JANUARY 1894

After dinner I go round to old Mme Herwegh's. She reverts to her Herzen story. Following the June insurrection,[143] Herzen travelled alone to Geneva and Herwegh followed on with Herzen's wife. Countess d'Agoult[144] said to Mme Herwegh at the time that she should beware of that woman; d'Agoult had had an affair with Herwegh, and when she saw that it was breaking up she allied herself with Mme Herwegh.

Mlle Hüny has given Felix Vogt one of her complimentary tickets for the concert. The old lady hadn't slept a wink all night because of that. Felix Vogt wrote an uncomplimentary review of Marcel the day before yesterday. She calls him: That Caliban! That swine! But I don't want to offend the swine. If the Muses and Graces ever appeared in order to bring him inspiration, then it was backsides first – and straight into his beastly mouth, at that! We talk about Mlle Rousseil and her corpulence, and the old lady says: She has a sort of flesh that calls for love, or rather, the kind of flesh that craves copulation. And she carries her own mattress around with her. She tells me about Lassalle, he had drawn a pension of 12,000 francs from the Countess Hatzfeld. He had specified all kinds of legacies in his will. Herwegh had got 2,000 francs, Colonel Rüstow an annual pension of 300 francs. Rüstow should have stopped the duel at all costs. He hadn't done so because he was having an affair with the Countess Hatzfeld himself.

Until two o'clock in the Café d'Harcourt.

15 JANUARY 1894

In the afternoon I put the fourth act under my arm and take it to Mlle Read, who has promised to read it once again. The drawing-room is in semi-darkness. A slender figure next to Mlle Read rises and offers me her hand. It is Mme Nemethy. Mlle Read is sitting huddled in an armchair next to the fireplace, looking very unwell, and with a streaming cold. The conversation turns to the concert, and I feel blissfully satisfied when Nemethy says Marcel should really get a job playing in an orchestra. He played without feeling, and she'd sooner have any gipsy fiddler than him. That might just pass muster in Paris, but in Germany no one would take the slightest notice of him. I take my leave, get changed, go to dinner and then to old Mme Herwegh. She asks me if she looks 'convenable'.[145] I tell her she is elegant. She has pinned to her hat-ribbons a brooch that the Marquise Tollney gave her. She says she can't keep up with fashion any longer, she has no choice but to create her own fashion. She gives me the money for the drive wrapped in a piece of paper. That was more convenient, because you didn't have to rummage around to get the right amount. She had already told me the day before yesterday that she would pay for the cab one way. After scuttling into the bedroom a couple of times with a candle, she asks me to unfold the paper, she thinks she has put in two francs too much, it was a Republic coin. I've long since unwrapped the money, so I empty my pockets, there is in fact a 2-franc piece, but it isn't a Republic minting. Then she says she must have put it somewhere else, she knew precisely what money she had, she had meant to take it with her for any unforeseen eventuality. She's very much afraid she may get an attack of diarrhoea during the concert, and so she wraps her last candle-end in a piece of paper. She hands it to me, I'm to put it in my pocket, but asks me to give it back to her, unwraps it and lights it again. She's going to have a last try at home after all. In the meantime I should fetch the cab.

I fetch the cab and wait by the doorway. During the drive she tells me that five or ten tickets have been sold. Marcel had given another 150 to Duchemin to distribute last night. In the vestibule of the Salle Frand she asks the staff about the arrangements, so that she'll know her way about in case of an emergency. The hall is already half full, all complimentary tickets, an inelegant audience. After we have taken our seats in the second row, Dr Beluge, Mlle Riocii, M. and Mme Duchemin come up to offer the old lady their good wishes. Then Marcel comes on and plays a pretty sonata by Sinding.[146] I've done my very best to welcome him with my applause. The old lady had bitterly reproached M. and Mme Duchemin after the last concert because of their lukewarm response, and now they seem to have responded, too. Otherwise, a devout silence prevails. Then Henri Falke and Mme de Lewenoff followed on two pianos. Mme Lewenoff, in a deeply plunging neckline and in a brightly spotted dress, behaves like a demented cook. The gigantic grand piano flutters like a sheet of newspaper beneath her touch, recoiling at every note she strikes. She threatens to break its legs. After she has expressed her thanks for the non-existent applause with an ungracious curtsey, and accepted from Herr Falke a huge white paper poke allegedly containing roses, a second cook takes the stage and sings a couple of songs, devoid of voice and taste, of which, fortunately, no one understands a word.

Before Marcel comes on for the second time, Mme Herwegh seizes me convulsively by the arm and says: 'When he comes on again, let yourself go a little. Do me that favour.' So I let myself go a bit, overcoming the disgust I feel at the sight of him and the dreadful impression left by the singer. After the final number M. Ménard d'Oréant appears in the company of his wife, the lady who missed her period because of her anxiety about him during the Commune, and they congratulate Mme Herwegh. Then I escort the old lady into the foyer, express my admiration to Mme Lewenoff, talk to her younger daughter, then Mlle Read turns up and, as we're on the point of leaving I encounter Mme de Rousseau's wonderfully beautiful eyes. In front of the hall the old lady asks me if I've said good evening to her. I say she will scarcely have noticed me. She replies, I'd better go and do it. I say I've got nothing to say to her. Very well, then, we'll leave it, she says, but she changes her mind as we're going down the steps, and sends me back. I'm to say I'd only just learned that she was present, and felt I had to wish her good evening.

So I go back to the cloakroom and say this to her. She remembers my visit very well and opens her fabulous, inscrutable eyes as wide as she can to meet my gaze. She is indeed more of a goddess than a human being, and yet getting on for fifty, if not more. She is George Street's mistress and has an eleven-year old daughter by him, a tall, slender child, ready to make her debut in life any day now. The girl's physique and expression are a legacy from her grandmother, Mme Street. Down in the vestibule I find myself once more face to face with Mme de Rousseau. She deliberately turns her gaze back towards me and lets me run straight into it. Then she appears once more at the door of our cab, leaning in to greet us, still in that same fabulous, dreamy fashion.

On the drive home the old lady tells me that another five tickets had been sold at the box-office. The deficit would amount to 300 francs. When she heard her son playing like that, then she felt she could fetch him the stars from the heavens. I go into the Café d'Harcourt and since I can't find a seat anywhere else, I sit down beside that cute little Madeleine who spent the night with me a couple of times last summer. I ask her to give me an introduction to her friend in London, Dr Fox, 123 Oxford Street, but she says he'll barely remember her. Then she shows me her new brooch, which is supposed to have cost 200 francs, and a diamond ring for which she had paid 400 francs. She had 1,800 francs in a savings bank. I ask her if that was a legacy from her father. She says no, she had earned it herself. The legacy from her father she had invested in shares and drew an annuity of 2,000 francs from it. Together with what she earned over and above that, she could live in fair comfort.

Then Gaston Fero comes in. He's back on top of his form once more. He quite likes the look of Madeleine, only she shouldn't be so respectably dressed. Anyway, I'd probably ruined the price already, as far as he was concerned. Yesterday one of the girls had pulled a small revolver from her corset while she was talking to some gentlemen. He had gone to the manager and asked him to stop her doing that.

17 JANUARY 1894

Go to Mlle Read's in the evening, the conversation revolves around the concert, an enthusiasm that doesn't quite ring true. Mme Fourgeuse shakes my hand in the friendliest manner. Then la belle Mme Ritter comes in, very poorly, she is leaving in the next day or so. She is outraged that Peladon has bought the castle of Les Beaux.[147] A lady who supported him had given him the money for it. Now a subscription list had been opened to establish a home for the Rosicrucians in Les Beaux. Les Beaux is an ancient property belonging to the Templars, set in beautiful countryside. It upsets her dreadfully that this charlatan should practise his mumbo-jumbo in this paradise. Since he's made Paris and Marseilles too hot to hold him, he's settled in Nîmes. He has already had his photograph taken in a monk's habit.

I take my leave, get changed, go to dinner, and afterwards to old Mme Herwegh to let her know that I'm spending the evening somewhere else. On the day before his concert Marcel had played at

Mme Ménard d'Oréant's. Mme d'Oréant has written to ask how she might express her gratitude in material terms. Thereupon he had dictated a letter to his mother, saying it was impossible for him to evaluate his own performance. The old lady is very upset, wondering whether Mme Ménard won't perhaps feel offended and send nothing at all in the end. She reads both notes to me and asks me insistently for my view.

After I have managed to prise myself free, I take a cab and drive to Mme Nemethy. She has not yet finished furnishing her quarters. A little fire is flickering in the hearth. She takes a seat between me and the lamp and we talk about Strindberg.[148] She tells me he wanted to marry her. She had gathered this subsequently from letters he had written to Ola Hansson.[149] He had been in dire straits and thought that she might rescue him. She says the manager of the Vaudeville has asked her for a translation of a play by Strindberg. He would like to put on something by him. Strindberg had made no impression on her personally. He had no influence whatsoever on women, but, on the other hand, enormous influence on men. He had persuaded a number of them to get divorced from their wives. She believes that the charges he makes against his wife in his confession are totally unjustified.

We start talking about my *Spring Awakening*, and she gives me the address of a publisher in Paris to whom I might offer the translation.

Then the talk turns to Marcel Herwegh. She says he had behaved in a boorish manner at her house. One of her friends had wanted to box his ears. Countess So-and-so, who was very poor, had lent him 10,000 francs, and when she asked for the interest, he spread rumours to the effect that she had wanted him to marry her daughter and was furious with him because he hadn't. He had promised to marry another woman, if she would give him an advance of 300 francs. He had suggested to Nemethy herself that she should hand over her entire capital to him, he would invest it in California at 8 per cent. If she didn't care to risk the whole lot, then she might at least trust him with 20,000 francs. He had told her he was giving his mother 2,000 francs a year; if he were only to get married, his children could expect a large fortune, etc. etc. Then she goes on to tell me the story of how he had once shot himself in the presence of a lady, had fallen down, and how the bullet had afterwards been found in the lining of his coat, and asks me if I believe that his father had been poisoned, as he claims.

It is a very welcome relief to be able to speak my mind freely about him. She asks me – with a piercing look – whether I go to see him. She's afraid I might have seen her photograph in his apartment. I say, Heaven forbid. After all she's told me, I'm only sorry that I was so annoyed with him. He's beginning to interest me. At eleven I get up and go to the Café Vachette, write to Frau Breslau, who has asked me to tea on Friday, and stay in the Café d'Harcourt until two o'clock.

18 JANUARY 1894

Get up very late and drive to Langen the bookseller at 112 Boulevard Malesherbes without breakfast.[150] I give him my book. He asks me how old Nemethy is. I say I've never asked her and take my leave. I spend an hour or two in the Grand Café and the Café de l'Univers, and then go to call on old Mme Herwegh after dinner.

Mme Ménard has just sent her 300 francs for her son, together with a charming note addressed to her personally. Full of pride, she plants both elbows on the table and gives me a challenging look. Then she reads me out a letter to Mme Schweizer, in which she actually states in so many words, if the Muses and Graces had ever approached Dr Felix Vogt, then it had only been for the express purpose of shitting in his mouth. Then she tells me once more, as it happens, the story of how Marcel had shot himself and the bullet had been found inside the lining of his coat. Marcel had spoken to old M. de la Nux at the concert; the old man had told him he had cursed his daughter Jeanne, because she had married a doctor against his will. The doctor had treated her with a course of thrashings. Now she was lying in hospital without a sou, and in *la misère noire*.[151] Mme Herwegh, who had always been fond of Jeanne, had written a letter to old de la Nux that Marcel mustn't know about, asking him to tell her his daughter's address. She would like to visit her and comfort her, if she could. Then she tells me that Jeanne had once taken language lessons from her, Mme Herwegh, together with a doctor, and about three years later had suddenly adopted a young boy of about three who, even at that time, had borne a striking resemblance both to her and to the doctor. She had an irresistible suspicion that the doctor on whose account her father was now cursing her was the same man as this particular doctor. The lady in whose apartment Marcel had shot himself was, incidentally, not old de la Nux's daughter, but only an acquaintance of hers, as was Phégine, who later became Count Morny's mistress, and when the Count tried to get rid of her, visited him one evening in his bathroom.[152] Count Morny was sitting in his bath, Phégine standing behind him, opposite the mirror. She said 'Bon soir', and shot herself through the heart.

In the Café d'Harcourt until two o'clock.

19 JANUARY 1894

At five o'clock I take a cab and drive to old Mme Herwegh's. She's already fit and ready to go. I conduct her downstairs and we drive to Mlle Read. We come face to face with a priest on the stairs. We enter, I can't see a thing, of course, and Mlle Read asks: Who's going to introduce the ladies? In the meantime I've made out Mme Nemethy and introduce her to old Mme Herwegh. Unspoken mutual disappointment. The old lady launches out into dogmatic praises of Marcel's soulful playing, while I tell Nemethy about my visit to the bookseller Langen yesterday. I get her to promise to complete the translation at once, if Langen nibbles at the bait. She asks me not to talk about Langen elsewhere. He was just starting out in publishing, he seemed to have lots of money, and if that became common knowledge he would be swamped with writers. Then she tells old Mme Herwegh that she'd like to invite Marcel to visit her soon. She so longed to see him again. She asks me for the old lady's address and for Marcel's address. I give her both, without thinking that I told her the day before yesterday that I didn't know Marcel's address. She gives me another piercing look. Then she tells the company she can't make up her mind whether to become a hermit or a nun. She felt so frightfully alone. She couldn't stand being here at home. In Schliersee she had had Ola Hansson's three-year old son with her all day long. She would so much like to have children. Mlle Read says, you could adopt one of course, but that was a ticklish business, too. It's on the tip of my tongue to say, if you need a pair of boots, you get someone to make them for you.

On the way home old Mme Herwegh tells me that old M. de la Nux had written to say there wasn't a word of truth in the story about his daughter's misfortune, it was true she had married the doctor, who had to get divorced for the purpose, but she was well in every respect, wasn't being ill-treated by her husband, and wasn't in

The publisher Albert Langen.

hospital.

I get changed, go to dinner and then drive to Mme Breslau's. I find her in the company of her sister and her companion. Once again I suffer the nerve-racking effect of her blustering, off-putting, uncouth manner. Her way of talking seems to me like the flourishing of a keen, glittering blade in front of my eyes. She herself gives the impression of a winded, highly strung racehorse that's been pulled up trembling and panting for five minutes and can barely wait to break into a headlong gallop again. Personally, she totally lacks all those qualities she depicts in her paintings: she stands in glaring contrast to her art. She lives neither in a respectable apartment, nor in a gipsy encampment, but in a wilderness. In conversation she is intractable. She accepts no train of thought other than her own, and if I tell her that Mt Pilatus is higher than the Rigi, nothing on earth will prevent her

from explaining to me that Mt Pilatus is not the highest mountain in
the world by a long chalk. Her sixteen-year old sister is a caricature of
her, with eyes that bulge hysterically from her head. She talks about
prostitution with the crude objectivity of the sexless. There's not a
trace of the sixteen-year old girl to be found in her. Mme Breslau
shows me into her studio, plumps down on her knees, and rummages
about in her portfolios. She shows me a number of charming pastels,
at the sight of which I nearly burst into tears, given the coarseness
that prevails around me. In spite of their supreme charm and
profundity, the faces, especially the children's faces, have the same
strained look about the eyes that I have myself sensed all evening.
They look as if they were staring into the sun, or as if someone were
flourishing some bright, keen instrument in front of their eyes. On the
easel is Bjørnson's oldest daughter as a young girl, the one who is at
present married to Ibsen's son.[153] Mme Breslau points out the
contrast between this Norwegian girl and the charming Parisiennes
around us, the robust bone-structure, the large hands, the barbaric
furtiveness in the expression of the eyes. As I leave the ladies I feel as if
I'd been pricked with a thousand needles. I feel profoundly unhappy
about all the coarseness I have absorbed and emanated. As I take my
leave, I feel like a lion-tamer leaving the cage backwards, unable to
take his eyes off any of the beasts until the cage-door is safely shut. I
go into the Café d'Harcourt, intending to drink as much beer as
possible, and to have myself petted as much as I can at the same time,
but I don't manage to say a single civil word to any of the girls. Alice
comes up and asks me: Qu'as-tu donc? – Tu as l'air tellement
malheureux. – I heave a sigh and say to her: Oh, tu ne sais pas d'où je
viens![154]

20 JANUARY 1894

I stay in bed until two, as if shattered by yesterday's ordeal. I think to
myself: I must have struck Mme Breslau like a Byzantine brought up
in a harem. When I get to old Mme Herwegh's in the evening I can
still sense a nervous excitement in myself. I speak more loudly than
usual, in an incoherent fashion; I find it hard to retain a grasp of my
own ideas until our conversation ultimately assumes its normal
informal character. I let fall the word 'pederasty', and the old lady
asks whether the passive partner doesn't suffer dreadful physical

Frank Wedekind as the lion-tamer and Gertrud Eysoldt as Lulu in
Earth Spirit, Berlin 1902.

injuries. I'm in the middle of explaining this to her when she
interrupts me. Her doctor had called on her this morning and she had
questioned him about buggery, but he hadn't been exactly forthcoming. It was she who had taken the lead in the conversation.

Marcel has been telling her lies again. Mme Nemethy, he says, has
ugly hands and bites her nails. When I assure her that the opposite is
the case, she peevishly breaks off the discussion. Then I tell her the

story of my love affair with Frl. Juncker,[155] our sustained mutual balancing act between love and execration, and go off about one o'clock to the Café d'Harcourt in excellent spirits.

21 JANUARY 1894

After lunch I take a cab and drive to Albert Langen the bookseller, 112 Boulevard Malesherbes. He's expecting Knut Hamsun any moment and will take him to see Nemethy. He doesn't want to publish my *Spring Awakening* before Hamsun's *Hunger*,[156] which he trusts will be a great success in Paris. We talk for about an hour, then I take my leave and go to the Café de l'Univers, where I read the first fifty pages of Hamsun's *Mysteries*,[157] which Langen gave me to take away with me. Then I change, dine, take a cab and drive to Mme Nemethy's. I stay with her until after midnight. Hamsun and Langen weren't there. I've never spent such a pleasant evening with her before. We talk about all sorts of things, and I come to the conclusion that she's a helpless child and is exploited and ill-treated on all sides. As I leave her, I toy with the idea of marrying her, as Strindberg had once done. I brought her my manuscript and asked her to keep it until I get back. In the Café d'Harcourt I meet Gaston Fero and arrange to join him for dinner at six o'clock the day after tomorrow.

22 JANUARY 1894

In the afternoon I go to old Mme Herwegh to fetch my books. She can't get over the thought that, when she was young, everything about her was beautiful, without her being a 'beauty' *in toto*. She enumerates her charms for me, beginning at the top and working her way down: hair, not very abundant, but soft as silk, brow narrow, nose exceptionally delicate, lips ideal, but her beauty had come to a full stop at the chin. Then her figure, svelte, hands and feet positively works of art. I take my leave until nine o'clock, buy half a dozen pairs of socks and dine on the Boulevard Sebastopol.

I find her in a dejected mood in the evening. An appreciative review has appeared in the *Matin*, but not appreciative enough. Marcel is put on the same level as Mme de Lewenoff. The review is from the pen of that goose, Mme de Rousseau. If her lover, George Street had been at the concert, wicked fellow as he was, he would have been enough of a musician to be able to tell the difference between Marcel and that bourgeoise, Mme de Lewenoff. I say I've never heard anything said of George Street other than that he was a charming *garçon*. She retorts that she'd once remarked to his mother, it was a pity her son was not as great as he was tall. He had once imagined in fact that Marcel had insulted him, so Marcel had written him a comic letter: he does like to joke. Thereupon George Street had simply cut him dead. Marcel Herwegh then came to his mother in a state of great excitement, burst into tears, and said if George Street carried on like that, then he would send his seconds to call him out in the end. She got on the omnibus, went to Mme Street and demanded to know how her son dared behave in that way towards Marcel. She admits that George Street is an excellent music critic, but he's a petty-minded creature and anything but a generous soul. You only had to recall how he'd behaved towards his mistress, Mme de Rousseau, who had never cost him a sou, quite the reverse, and to whom he'd been constantly unfaithful after the first fortnight. But how could it be otherwise, with a mother like Mme Street, who had a son by Prince Napoleon,[158] from whom she kept on getting money. In the end it had got too much for the Prince, and he'd said to his secretary, that woman has cost me quite enough as it is.

At twelve o'clock I go to the Café d'Harcourt. Alice and Emma sit down beside me. Alice is more charming than ever in a new dress. She asks me: Tu m'emmènes? She offers me 'un pucelage de quatre jours'.[159] I say I've just come back from visiting my mistress. Alice is travelling to Brussels tomorrow. Without having laid a finger on her I feel very much in the mood. I drown my feelings in beer and go home to bed.

23 JANUARY 1894

Get up at eight o'clock and pack my suitcase. After lunch I drag two parcels of books to Mlle Read and say goodbye to her. Then I call briefly on old Mme Herwegh. I find her together with her doctor, telling him the story of how Haydn narrowly escaped castration. As a boy, Haydn had a remarkably fine voice, so that a group of enterprising individuals took charge of him and got him to sing in public. When he was twelve years old and they were afraid that his voice would break, they decided to take him to Rome and get him castrated there. They talked about a promising future which would only be open to him if he were to study in Rome. The unsuspecting youth told his father about this, and he, realizing at once what they meant to do with his child, snatched him away from his teachers' hands just in time. It was thanks to this accident that Haydn retained his reproductive faculty. She gives me a recommendation to take with me which Marcel has written to Mme Trübner. And to go with it a phial of *eau de mélisse*[160] to sprinkle on a lump of sugar if I feel sick. Dr Beluge makes to leave, thinking I have to discuss Herzen's affairs with the old lady. I ask him to stay where he is and go back to my hotel.

Gaston Fero arrives punctually at six. I give him a poem that's lying on the table by way of a souvenir; he's not keen to accept it, however. He needs a lot of persuading before he finally makes up his mind to put it in his pocket. Then we drive to the Gare St Lazare, register my luggage, and go to dinner. The conversation is virtually non-existent. I tell him, shortly before Nietzsche died, he wrote a letter to Strindberg which Nemethy has translated and which is to appear in *Le Figaro* during the next few days.[161] He replies that it's a shame that you have to spend so much on postage if you write letters. In the Grand Café, where we sit together until the train is due to leave, the elegance of the place upsets him. At the station I commit to his care Alice, Rachel, Germaine, Marie Louise, Raimonde, Madeleine, Lucienne and my little Christ child, he's to take my place with them all. He can't believe I'm serious. When I assure him that I am, he lowers his head glumly: I've ruined the prices for him. I shake his hand and lean back in my corner. The train moves off and I think he's long since gone, when he wrenches the door open once more and shouts into the compartment to ask whether I've forgotten anything.

An Englishman is sitting opposite me. At the other end of the compartment there is another Englishman, who is sitting facing a French lady, over whose knees he at once spreads his travelling-rug, although he doesn't fall into conversation with her until we get to Dieppe. He whispers a few cryptic words to her. She tells him in reply all about her sea-sickness. She's done the journey seven times, and has vomited on all seven occasions. She would vomit this time as well, that was for sure. This doesn't stop the Englishman having her luggage taken on board along with his. On board, however, he at once takes possession of a sheltered corner, apparently his customary place, wraps himself in his travelling-rug and doesn't crawl out of it until we get to Newhaven. As I feel sick in the cabin, I pace up and down the deck, gulping down a hefty dose of *eau de mélisse* from time to time, as I dog the footsteps of a little French girl, a waitress or the like, whom I had already noticed on the platform in Paris. I start up a conversation with her about wind and weather and follow her up on to the bridge. There she vanishes from my sight for ever more. I suspect that she has slipped into the mate's cabin. But since all the other ladies have disappeared as well, my heart is set at rest, and I go on striding into the wind all by myself. Apart from the sleeper in his customary place, I'm the only passenger on deck. I'm in the very best of spirits, never having changed my domicile with such a light heart and so free of moral scruples. The abundance of kindness, affection and helpfulness I have encountered in Paris these last months may be the main reason for my sunny confidence. At five o'clock I clamber down into the cabin, stretch out on a bench and, in spite of my fearful hunger, fall asleep instantly.

LONDON

JANUARY–JUNE 1894

24 JANUARY 1894

The steward shakes me by the shoulder. We've arrived. I open my
suitcase at the customs and reserve myself a seat in the compartment.
After a while I see my suitcase being wheeled up again and being
discussed by all and sundry. It's not closed. I close it and get back into
the compartment. Then a ticket-collector comes in, asks me to go
with him, and leads me to the luggage van. He points out that my case
isn't closed. I close it again, but it's no good, it stays open. The ticket-
collector gives me to understand by signs that I should turn it round
the other way. I turn it round and go back to my compartment.
Opposite me is a young Englishman returning from Genoa. The
windows are covered with frost.

At seven o'clock in the morning we arrive at Victoria Station in
bitter cold. I drink a hot coffee, take a cab, and drive to the Hotel
New York. Mr Marlin has been dead for two months. Fortunately
the new owner speaks French. I take a room, drive back to Victoria
Station and fetch my suitcase, drink another coffee in the hotel, and
go to the British Museum. I find masses of material for my Divine
Birth.[1] Then I take lunch in a café and start looking for the way to the
Tower. I get as far as St Paul's Cathedral, but I'm so worn out that I
go into a bar and then drive home in a cab. I order dinner for seven
and then fall asleep. After dinner I go to bed. I dream of Mlle Read, of
Nemethy, Alice, Marie Louise and my old lady.

25 JANUARY 1894

I go to the National Gallery and am furiously annoyed by the glass over all the pictures. After lunch I get on the Underground at Charing Cross and travel to the Tower, look round the museum, the most boring and tasteless I have ever seen, travel under the Thames via London Bridge and come back home through the underworld, dine at seven o'clock and take the omnibus to the London Pavilion. Apart from a couple of authentic English children, I find nothing new and very little that's congenial. I spend some time in a bar amid a pack of frightful whores, and go to bed at twelve o'clock.

26 JANUARY 1894

Stroll round the streets and buy the Daily.

— 1894

At dinner I recount how I was in the Middlesex Music Hall in Drury Lane a few days ago.[2] My neighbour to my left tells me it's the commonest theatre in London, and my neighbour on the right says it's reckoned to be first-class of its kind. My opposite number, Mr Mess from Frankfurt, asks me to take him with me if I go out somewhere again. Did I mean to go somewhere that evening? I say I had intended to go to a music-hall in Whitechapel. He is wildly enthusiastic, but takes so long to get his overcoat on that it's too late to go. In the meantime we are joined by a young man from French-speaking Switzerland, and we go together to the Middlesex Music Hall. The two gentlemen show not the slightest understanding for the place. The dances bore them, they don't like the music. The child performers are too young, the audience too rowdy, they can't make out the tunes, they can't see the costumes, and they don't sense the hundred-year-old atmosphere that surrounds them. One takes out a local Pruntrut newspaper,[3] the other deplores the fact that he can't 'make the acquaintance' of anyone around him.

On a raised platform in the centre of the pit, with his back to the stage, sits the chairman, surrounded by his staff, and with a little square mirror in front of him in which he can keep an eye on the stage. He rises at the conclusion of each act to announce the next number in a brief address to the ladies and gentlemen, and calls for

order in the gallery when the audience gets too rowdy. The programme carries the following notice: Since it is Mr J.L. Graydon's
wish that the entertainment presented in the Middlesex Music Hall
should always be free of any feature liable to give offence, he invites
the respected audience to notify him of any offensive words or
actions on the stage which may be liable to misinterpretation, or
which may have escaped the attention of the management, and will
be grateful to anyone doing so.

The audience expresses its approval by whistling, and its disap-
proval by hissing. During the intervals, someone in the gallery
invariably strikes up the chorus of the preceding song, the whole
audience joins in and sings it until the curtain rises once more. The
hissing and whistling sound as if a hundred railway engines were
starting up. The greatest applause is earned by a dancing-girl of
about four years of age dressed in a brief white princess frock, with
bare legs, short white socks and little shoes in gilded morocco leather.
She sticks a monocle in her eye and sings the Monte Carlo song,
showing her scanty white lace knickers up to the waist at each beat of
the drum. As she withdraws into the wings, a veritable battle-cry goes
up, a howl such as you might hear in a Kaffir kraal, a bawling,
screeching and whistling as in a menagerie when the meat appears in
front of the animal cages.

The first part of the programme includes a vulgar farce in which
the police are beaten black and blue. A serious drama in two acts
rounds off the programme. A wealthy villain and a poor lad quarrel
over a girl. The girl chooses the poor young man, who enlists for
service in the Asian war. Even on his first appearance the villain is met
with such a storm of hissing from the gallery that the chairman is
obliged to intervene. The villain also makes his way to Asia and
becomes a chieftain of a Khirgiz tribe. As he enters in his Khirgiz
costume at the beginning of the second act, a number of rotten
oranges are hurled at him from the gallery. Every word he utters is
greeted with universal derisive laughter. When he finally contrives to
capture his rival's wife and is leading her to execution, the entire
audience showers him with abuse. The girl, a pretty, slender creature,
had worn a plain grey dress with a broad white shawl in the first act:
Marie Antoinette. Now she makes her appearance all in white, with
her dark ringlets hanging down, a white belt round her waist, and her
hands tied behind her back with a rope. As she stands there

motionless, reciting in a fine contralto voice a long tirade on the subject of her inviolable virtue, a solemn silence reigns. The spectators in the gallery crane their necks to the point where you can see a dozen faces ranged one above the other. At the approach of the English army a thousand voices give vent to whistles. The poor lad, who has in the meantime become a captain, is attacked simultaneously by a dozen Khirgiz tribesmen, whom he fells one by one. Before each new encounter the audience encourages his heroic valour with shouts and whistles in any number of different keys, whenever a new adversary staggers and falls to the ground. By the time the hero confronts his enemy with drawn sword, the corpses are lying so thick on the stage that the duellists hardly know where to tread. After a brief skirmish, the hero seizes his opponent by placing his left arm round his waist, and thrusts his sword through his clothes with his right. The English army leads in the girl, with her hands still bound, whereupon a howl of applause goes up once more. After her husband has managed to slash through the rope with his sabre, she addresses a couple more tirades to the audience, and the curtain falls.

BERLIN

21 DECEMBER 1905–1 JULY 1908

21 DECEMBER 1905

Conclusion of an actor's contract between the Max Reinhardt management of the Deutsches Theater in Berlin and myself, valid from 1 October 1906 until 31 March 1907, at 1,000 marks per month. Reinhardt, as manager, has the right to declare the contract extended for a further year on the same terms.[1]

15 MARCH 1906

Tartuffe rehearsal, Max Reinhardt directing. After Herr Reinhardt has strenuously rehearsed me in the part of Tartuffe for two solid hours, Felix Hollaender[2] comes up to me in the interval with a draft contract which was never even mentioned up till now. He asks me to come into the office and assures me that the same contract has been signed by all the authors working for the Deutsches Theater. I needn't hesitate, then, to sign it as well. The contract requires the undersigned 'for the period of five years to submit all his dramatic works in the first place for performance in the Deutsches Theater'. No obligation in return for this undertaking is stipulated in the contract. There is not even a period for the performance of the individual plays laid down.

Weary and confused as I am following my exertions, I sign the contract.

After the rehearsal has lasted for another hour, Herr Hollaender invites me to lunch at Borchardt's, together with Reinhardt, the manager, and Herr Levin.[3]

Tilly Newes and Frank Wedekind on their wedding-day in Berlin, 1 May 1906.

19 JUNE 1907

Herr Reinhardt asks me at the Deutsches Theater whether I'm willing to extend my acting contract with him for a further year. I state my agreement.

1 OCTOBER 1907

I've been waiting in vain ever since the 19 June for written confirmation of the extension of my contract that we discussed, but arrive punctually in Berlin all the same, having spent the past three weeks on preparations for the first scheduled performance.

8 OCTOBER 1907

After waiting a week for notification, I go to the Kammerspiele Theatre, where I take part in rehearsals and ask Herr Hollaender whether my acting contract is to be regarded as extended or not, since

Frank and Tilly Wedekind on their way to rehearsal at the Berlin
Kammerspiele.

nothing has been concluded in writing. Herr Hollaender gives me a
firm assurance that the contract has in fact been extended by our oral
agreement of 19 June.

4 NOVEMBER 1907

After taking part in all the rehearsals scheduled since 8 October, I go
to the office to collect my salary. The accountant informs me that he
has no instructions to pay me. I report this to Herr Reinhardt. Herr
Reinhardt tells me: 'I'll put the matter right at once.'

5 NOVEMBER 1907

I go to the office to collect my salary. The accountant tells me he has still had no instructions to pay me. After that I make no further effort to get my salary, and in fact have still not received it.

8 NOVEMBER 1907

Herr Reinhardt sends me a written offer to extend my contract, albeit on modified terms, but I don't agree.

14 NOVEMBER 1907

I inform Herr Hollaender that I will relinquish my salary for the current winter season (6,000 marks), if I can have back the author's contract I signed on the 15 March during the *Tartuffe* rehearsals. Herr Hollaender replies that this is not his decision, but Herr Reinhardt's.

15 FEBRUARY 1908

In response to my claim that the contract existing between us, dated 15.3.06, is unfair, Herr Max Reinhardt denies responsibility, since it had not been agreed to by him, but by Herr Hollaender; in the presence of Herr Direktor Andreae,[4] however, he repeats the firm assurance that he will pay me an appropriate emolument in return for my services during the remaining three years covered by the contract.

8 APRIL 1908

Herr Reinhardt refuses categorically to agree to any sort of payment for the obligations contractually imposed on me by the author's contract of 15.3.06, but makes me an offer by word of mouth to guarantee my publisher's claims on the Deutsches Theater up to a specified limit during those three years.[5] I entreat Herr Reinhardt to give me back the disputed contract, for which he has not paid me a single penny. My association with the Deutsches Theater will not be affected in the slightest thereby; on the other hand, my sense of personal grievance will be removed by the return of the contract. I try to make Herr Reinhardt understand that I haven't spent twenty years

The producer Max Reinhardt (1873–1943) in his early years.

fighting for my freedom only to become ultimately an unpaid employee of the Max Reinhardt management, and to end up with fewer rights than any other writer one cares to name. I try – utterly in vain – to convince Herr Reinhardt that the existing contract between us is impossible between individuals who have a social relationship with each other, and that no decent man would insist on the fulfilment of such an unfair contract.

Herr Reinhardt retorts that he cannot cancel the contract without the consent of the shareholders of the Deutsches Theater. In reply to this manifest untruth I declare that I will make applications to the shareholders of the Deutsches Theater.

From contracts with other authors submitted to me, I note that

Frank and Tilly Wedekind at the Deutsches Theater in Berlin.
A caricature by Lida von Wedell.

barely one of them corresponds to the contract which I signed, and that I have simply been swindled by Herr Felix Hollaender's assurances of 15 March 1906.

22 APRIL 1908

Herr Max Reinhardt submits a written contract to me in which a guarantee to meet my publisher's claims is stipulated, on condition that I appear in the Kammerspiele and the Deutsches Theater for performance fees that are a third of those I am currently being paid by other theatre managers.

1 JULY 1908

In view of the possibility that Herr Max Reinhardt was speaking the truth on 8 April, I am collating from my diary notes all the dates recorded in these pages for submission to the shareholders of the Deutsches Theater, together with a request that they empower Herr Reinhardt as manager to cancel the unfair and humiliating contract, so that after my three years of artistic activity in Berlin, I do not have to leave the city with a sense of personal humiliation. I tell myself in all due humility that a man does not labour to achieve artistic distinction, only to be faced with such an accumulation of loathsome experiences by reason of being an artist. If the Deutsches Theater should not see its way to cancelling the contract, then I would simply feel obliged to stop writing plays for the next three years. In this case it would be pretty well out of the question for the Deutsches Theater ever again to receive a stage work of mine after the lapse of that period.

MUNICH

16 FEBRUARY–23 FEBRUARY 1918

FOLLOWING his marriage to Mathilde (Tilly) Newes on 1 May 1906, Wedekind lived in Berlin until 1908, and it was there that *Spring Awakening* was first performed at the Kammerspiele under Reinhardt's direction. Because of the continuing dispute with Reinhardt and his continuing fondness for Munich, where his plays were being performed with increased frequency, Wedekind moved there in September 1908. His first daughter Pamela was born in Munich on 12 December 1908.

16 FEBRUARY 1918

With Friedenthal at Benz's.[1] Afterwards with him in his apartment. We drink 'Brüderschaft'.

17 FEBRUARY 1918

Torggelstuben,[2] alone. A fit of weeping on account of my rupture.

18 FEBRUARY 1918

Morena telephones.[3] I invite her to dinner in the evening. Tilly telephones.[4] Agree to meet her tomorrow evening. Dictate Tilly's two letters from January 1906. Tea with Lion Feuchtwanger. Frau Dr —. Call for Morena at the Continental.[5] Spend the evening with her in the Odeon Casino. Drink a bottle of wine at home. Read Tilly's letters.

Frank Wedekind lived in this house, 50 Prinzregentenstrasse, Munich, from 1908 until 1918.

19 FEBRUARY 1918

Fanny K. stays in bed.[6] Sore throat. With Schaumberger[7] in the club during the afternoon, black sausage and plum brandy. Go to Tilly's for tea. She's staying at the Müllers, who are on tour in Augsburg. I get her to read her letters. We go to the Odeon Casino for dinner. A cheerful evening. Go home. She sleeps in my room. ☿ on the divan.[8]

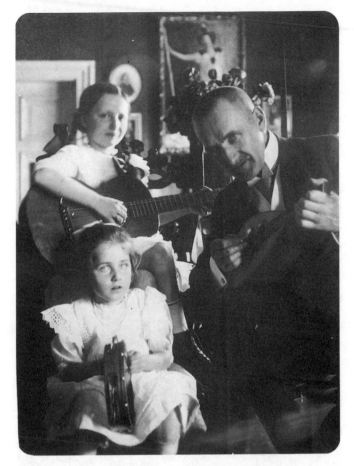

Frank Wedekind with his daughters Pamela and Kadidja.

20 FEBRUARY 1918

♂ in bed. Tilly gets up at ten, plays with Kadidja, goes to Müllers at twelve o'clock. I have lunch with Pamela. Learned my part in *Herakles*.[9] Walk. Buy this diary. Club with Schaumberger. Dinner in the evening with Anna Pamela. Torggelstuben with Friedenthal and Dr Albert.

21 FEBRUARY 1918

Learned *Herakles*. Coffee in the club. I discuss the production and stage-sets for *Herakles* with Stollberg at the Schauspielhaus.[10] Dinner

One of the last photographs of Frank Wedekind, taken in 1918.

with the children in the evening. I cut out a doll for them, complete with costume. Torggelstuben with Friedenthal. We draw up a cast-list for *Herakles*. On the way home he tells me so much about myself that is true that I feel quite relieved.

22 FEBRUARY 1918

Learned *Herakles*. Torggelstuben, alone. In my room with Dr Kaufmann from the Kammerspiele.

23 FEBRUARY 1918

Learned *Herakles*. With Frau Dressler, who informs me that Anton returned from England last night.[11] To tea with Hans Carl Müller. To the Kammerspiele with Tilly. *A Winter's Tale*.[12] My rupture is giving me trouble.[13] I become abusive, go away, and then come back. We part in peace. Torggelstuben with Mühsam[14] and his girl-friend.

To Tilly[15]

A hostile fate tears us apart
With cruel, rapacious power,
However fond the loving heart
We share one mortal hour.
So, Tilly, one more kiss, dear lass!
For what must be, will come to pass.

For you are young, your blood will surge
In search of pleasures fair,
So do not heed compassion's urge
To share my dismal lair.
So, Tilly, one more kiss, dear lass!
For what must, be will come to pass.

I'm old, infirmities abound,
I brood too much, it's clear.
It's not my way to hang around
With ailing souls, I fear.
So, Tilly, one more kiss, dear lass!
For what must be, will come to pass.

APPENDIX

Extract from the Paris diaries for 8–10 September 1893 published in *Die Fürstin Russalka* (*Princess Russalka*), Paris, Leipzig, Munich, Albert Langen 1897, pp. 91–103.

8–10 SEPTEMBER 1893

I wake up about four. The curtains are still drawn, the room is in pitch darkness. I light the candles and begin to get up gradually. I feel rejuvenated after yesterday's exertions: a peculiar mobility in the joints, my head clear and my body twenty pounds lighter. I can feel my specific weight . . .

As I go out into the street, the evening sun is playing on the top floor windows. I go into my little restaurant, buy myself Maeterlinck's *Princesse Maleine* by the Odéon, and read it through in one sitting in a café. – If he had given his phantoms rather more flesh, they would undoubtedly have stayed alive longer. – I dine at the Palais Royal and work at home until midnight.

As I'm coming out of the Brasserie Pont Neuf, there's a girl with a flowing cape walking in front of me; she reminds me of Marie Louise, but it isn't her.

I go to Bovy's, because I have a subconscious urge to hear some news of Raimonde. The only known face in the little dump is Marie Louise. She asks me for a glass of milk and tells me that a girl poisoned herself with sublimate yesterday on the terrace of the Café d'Harcourt. Raimonde was still living in the *quartier*. She was *dans la purée* with debts of 40,000 francs. – This fills me with vast satisfaction.

I ask her if she's still on morphine. No, not for a long time now. She flings open her cloak and points out that she's got rid of her burden. She had been in hospital for three weeks on account of the miscarriage, and they'd got her off morphine. She does indeed look a great deal better. She's stopped using make-up, sleeps like a new-born baby at nights, and is not obsessed by morbid ideas when she wakes up. She still reads in bed before she goes to sleep. She's reading *La Faute de l'Abbé Mouret* at the moment. She would never have believed that Zola could write such a lovely book. She had previously begun *L'Assommoir*,[1] but she finds it boring and in bad taste. She could write that sort of thing herself, if only she had the time!

In the meantime I'm being pestered by a girl to whom I once gave a louis d'or six months ago. I can't think what her name is. At that time she was in black, now she's wearing a brand new light-coloured dress with a blue silk bodice! I had given her one of my delicately sprigged shirts, whereupon she picked up a book, Edmond de Goncourt's *La Fille Élisa*, that little Germaine had lent me, read it right through by daybreak, and scampered off. She'd have liked to take the shirt with her as well. I must have promised to give her a diamond ring instead.

She has a pale, round little face with chubby cheeks and a pretty chin, a delicate snub-nose, generous lips, slim slanting eyebrows, and an uncommonly appealing pair of liquid dark eyes.

Since she's dressed with the utmost elegance and is wearing gleaming glacé gloves, I assume that she has also gained in personal terms. She's no longer living in the Hôtel Voltaire in the Rue de Seine, either, but in a first-floor apartment in the Rue St Sulpice. I ask her whether she would like a drink. – No, she wasn't thirsty.

I've never in all my life seen such a neat, cosy little room. It is hung with yellow, delicately sprigged cotton, as if my nightshirt from our previous encounter had been used for the purpose. The vast bed-curtains that take up half the room are made from the same material.

The girl in her corn-yellow dress with the blue bodice fits so perfectly into this dainty container that in the narrow space between door and window I feel as if I were set apart from everything by boundless ethereal spaces, from the world, from sin, from extravagance, dangers and duties alike. She asks me if I would care to drink a Chartreuse, takes a cut-glass decanter from the mantelpiece and fills two little glasses. The Chartreuse is the colour of liquid gold and has more or less the corresponding effect as it flows through the veins. As we drink, we talk about her 'colleagues'.

She doesn't know whether Lulu and Nini are in love with each other; it was possible, why not? Lulu, it was true, had her own furniture, but she lived in a hole, a single room where she'd installed her few bits and pieces. She told everyone, all the same, that she had her own furniture. Lulu was definitely the dominant partner, the brains, whereas Nini had to act the poodle and could only go with the men that Lulu allowed her to go with. – Did I know Lulu?

I say, no, adding incautiously, it wasn't for want of trying.

Then the talk turns to Raimonde. – Oh, yes, she was a one! – She saw me with her that memorable night *au grand comptoir*. – How much did she cost you, then?

To make up for my *faux pas* concerning Lulu, I say – 15 francs.

Pas plus que ça?

No, and she had to whine to get that much.

How did I like Raimonde?

I shake my head solemnly and say: C'est une belle femme!

She then recites a list of all Raimonde's lovers – la grande Susanne, little Lucie, who was with us then *au grand comptoir*, that pretty Lucienne, who was with us at Barrat's – she couldn't understand how someone could go to bed with a girl!

I say, she probably kept lovers herself.

Oh, là là! Those were friends of other girls who came to her to spend the money they were given by the girls. That's how she knew. No, she wouldn't care to have a lover in her life.

I say, it's nice all the same to have someone who belongs totally to you, someone you didn't have to bargain with, someone you could be kind to, someone you could give yourself to solely for love.

She bursts out laughing, it was the men after all who dominated the women they took money from. The women lay on the floor at their feet, they were nothing but slaves.

As we're talking in this way, I catch sight of a pack of cards on the table and ask her if she tells fortunes from the cards; she asks me if she should tell my fortune – dire la bonne aventure,[2] the whole business takes a good half hour. We sit down facing each other and she tells me a great deal about my mother, my two sisters, and a pile of gold I'm to get from a fair-haired gentleman, in whom I instantly recognize my publisher.

An hour later my sweetheart suddenly gets very merry and suggests we might go down to les Halles for a bit, un peu vadrouiller. It was so warm outside and so stuffy here in her room.

My objections count for very little. I manage to get to my feet, we quickly swallow another Chartreuse, and stroll through the grey light of dawn across the Pont Neuf in the direction of les Halles. She would just like to have une soupe au fromage *au grand comptoir*. There was sure to be a great crowd of people there anyway.

There is neither a crowd nor music. At the back of the restaurant there are a few solitary *grisettes*. My fair companion orders the soup, and I order a bottle of wine, and we consume both in silence. Then the waiter comes up to us. Des écrevisses? Une douzaine de Marennes? Un demi poulet? She shakes her head three times, and the waiter goes away. This well-nigh reduces me to tears. I call him back, he should bring us two dozen oysters, and as we're swallowing them I say we'll go on to Barrat's for coffee.

At Barrat's the lights have already been put out. Across from us the members of the orchestra are sitting eating supper. My fair one asks me how I like the woman. I reply that she looks too much like a tart. She asks me then whether *she* doesn't look too much like a tart? I say something flattering, and she asks me whether Raimonde doesn't look like a tart? – Mais c'est une belle femme! I say, which she grants me: 'Tu l'aimes à la folie!'[3]

I've drunk four or five cups, and could do with still more. But the coffee is too expensive here, it costs 1 franc a cup. So I suggest we go to Le Chien qui Fume. She doesn't know the place. I tell her it's quite close by, so we make our way in the first rays of the morning sun through dense ranks of cauliflower, carrots and turnips, clamber up the spiral stairs to the saloon, take seats by the window, and have the entire bustle of the market before our eyes. We agree there's no finer sight on God's earth than the sight of people really putting their backs into their work.

In order to do full justice to our observations I order oysters again instead of coffee, and a bottle of really strong wine to go with them.

The great Napoleon provides the topic of our conversation. My little angel adores him. If she were a man, then Europe would have to look out! – We talk about the Duke of Leuchtenberg,[4] she raves about his lovely eyes, and I describe his magnificent tomb in St Michael's Church in Munich. She reckons that he was Napoleon's brother-in-law, I believe he was his step-son. Neither of us is very sure about it.

She recently read a book, the author's name escapes her, which dealt with all the mistresses at the French court, from Diane de Poitiers down to the fair Thérèse. So we talk about Dubarry, Maintenon, Madame de Pompadour, Madame de Sévigné, Madame de Staël, about Adèle Courtois, Soubise, Cora Pearl, Giulia Barucci, Anna Deslions, and finally end up happily with Pope Joan.[5]

Then the talk turns to culinary delights, to the various restaurants in the *quartier* and *à l'autre côté de l'eau*.[6] The small restaurants with fixed prices were no good. You got a full-scale dinner, true, but you weren't satisfied if you were working. I'm bound to agree with her, having had the same experience. Like me, she can't digest anything but green vegetables. Apart from asparagus, she prefers Brussels sprouts to everything else. Cauliflower she finds too tasteless. She has the same tastes as I have. We talk about fresh strawberries, pineapple; gradually we become one heart and one soul. When she goes outside for a moment, I ask the waiter to bring a bottle of Pommery.

Mild sunshine lies over the Halles. In front of our window there's a great scurrying hither and thither, like an ant-heap. The lofty, gaudy barricades of turnips and cauliflower have already vanished – possibly they've already been eaten. I feel an ineffable sense of well-being.

The girl seems to me to come from a good family. I can detect nothing which suggests otherwise. She sits down opposite me again and raises her glass to her lips in a manner which could not be bettered even in the best social circles. She comes from Normandy, from Falaise. I know the dump well enough to be able to check up on her. She, too, has read Maupassant's *Maison Tellier*,[6] but she steers the conversation away from that topic. She says she still has a wealthy married sister in Falaise who comes to Paris every winter, but she doesn't ever see her. She expects to come into some money herself when she comes of age, something like 30,000 or 40,000 francs. She'll start buying dresses and probably get through the lot in three months. There isn't the slightest indication that she means to retire into private life when this happens. She says she doesn't belong there any more, in Falaise, where they go to bed at eight in the evening and get up at seven in the morning, where they never go to cafés, either in summer or in winter, and never spend a night on the tiles. I suggest that she should choose me as her special friend when she comes into her money. I point out my good points, my cheerful nature and my practical experience in handling women. She laughs and says I'm wealthier than she is. I shake my head and say I don't expect to come into thirty or forty thousand francs. Very well, then, she'd agree, provided I'd squander all I had together with her; I need only put it on the table. I prefer not to take up this offer, for fear of impairing my credit-worthiness.

I look at my watch and say, it's stopped. I ask the waiter. Heavens above! It's gone half past twelve. My fair companion is no less taken aback. Now we simply must have lunch.

She tries to arrange her hair in front of a mirror, but she can't see herself. The mirror is smothered in inscriptions from top to bottom: there isn't room to stick a postage stamp. Nevertheless, she asks me to give her a diamond. I give her my shirt-stud, but it won't write. I say, I'll have to get it newly ground some time.

Because of the glaring sunshine we walk through the Halles, across the flower market, in fact. Roses, from the most delicate snow-white to the deepest burning red, are piled up roof-high on both sides. I inhale their heady perfume greedily. It affects me like a powerful stimulant. It's pleasantly cool in the *grand comptoir*. The waiter, who remembers us from some ten hours back, very nearly falls flat on his face in his profound respect. We both feel the need of some refreshment, but we order lunch more or less from a sense of obligation. We agree on a poulet mayonnaise, a huge bowl of salad, a basket full of peaches and juicy pears, and a light white wine. Coffee we'll take in the *quartier*.

Peeling a peach with her dainty fingers, my beauty asks me how she actually looks. I say, of course: Bewitching! In fact, she smacks just a little of the dissecting room. But the moist brilliance of her eyes is just the same as ever, and also the fresh scarlet of her lips, which does surprise me.

'You've put on some lipstick, haven't you?'

'No, that's genuine. I always have lips like this.' And she proves it by rubbing them vigorously with a damp handkerchief. That needn't necessarily make them any paler, I think to myself, but what does it matter after all.

We drive back to the *quartier* over the Pont Neuf in an open cab. Paris flaunts herself in her finest glory, or perhaps it's just that I'm unduly receptive? The glittering blue Seine, with its countless billows of steam, its dingy tugboats, its long, white, gleaming barges, the trees on the boulevards with the last of their leaves trembling in the noonday breeze, gaudy streamers from last year's carnival still fluttering here and there from their branches – all this combines to raise my spirits, and seems to me to have been created by God for that express purpose.

In the Café de la Source my sweetheart proposes a game of Faro. She wins a trifle, which I get back from her in two further hands. Then she wins 5 francs, stops the game and demands to be paid at once. I promise to pay the day after tomorrow, but as she refuses to yield, I finally stump up, bearing in mind that for her time is money, whereas the opposite applies to me, but on condition that she stands me a coffee in the Café Vachette. In fact, I really don't have a single sou in my pocket.

We stroll into the Café Vachette. The waiter, who sees me here every day, sitting in my lonely corner, enquires with redoubled politeness what I would care to order. I refer him to Madame. Madame feels genuinely embarrassed. She stammers with downcast eyes: Two coffees. – With cognac? the waiter asks me. – That depended on Madame. – With cognac, of course! Madame hastens to add.

We both feel a bit done in. After I've finished my coffee I ask her to buy me another. She's still clutching the 5 francs, she hasn't put them in her pocket, and as the waiter walks past, she orders me another coffee.

It's half past three, I haven't much time to lose. We walk as far as the Carrefour de l'Odéon together, and there we part. I watch her for a while as she walks away. As she turns the corner at St Sulpice with her easy, springy stride, it suddenly occurs to me that I've forgotten to ask her what her name is. I go into my hotel, draw the curtains, and lie down on the bed fully dressed.

PS. Reading through these lines again, I suddenly notice something about them. The odd thing about such leaves from a diary, if they are genuine, is that they contain so little in the way of actual events. The moment events intrude on life, then the pleasure, the interest and the time for a diary all evaporate, and the human individual rediscovers the spontaneous innocence of the child or the animal in its wilderness.

NOTES

AUTOBIOGRAPHICAL NOTE

1 On 21 October 1878 the German Reichstag passed a law against the 'dangerous aspirations of Social Democracy'. Enacted initially for three years, the law was repeatedly renewed until its repeal on 30 September 1890. This legislation drove many liberals into exile – in Zürich, amongst other places.

2 *Erdgeist*: drama by Wedekind, written 1892–5, first performed in Munich on 29 October 1898.

3 Wedekind was accused of *lèse-majesté* in 1898 because of a poem about the German Emperor's visit to Palestine which was published in the satirical magazine *Simplicissimus*. He sought refuge in Switzerland, but returned voluntarily to Germany in June 1899 to be tried in Leipzig. He was convicted, but the prison sentence was commuted to confinement in the fortress of Königstein. After serving some six months of his sentence he was released on 3 March 1900.

4 *Der Marquis von Keith*: drama by Wedekind, written in Zürich in 1900, first performed 11 October 1901 at the Berlin Residenztheater.

5 *Der Kammersänger* was a one-act drama by Wedekind himself. The typescript of an English translation by Ashley Dukes (*The Court Singer*) is among the Wedekind papers in the Munich City Library.

LENZBURG CASTLE 9 FEBRUARY–25 MARCH 1887

1 Artur Kutscher, who wrote the most comprehensive biography of Wedekind during the 1920s, dates these entries 1888, but 1887 seems the most likely year. The original manuscript has been lost, and the text here is based on the first publication in *Die Fürstin Russalka* (Paris Leipzig Munich, 1897), pp. 104–19.

2 *The Armourer*: an opera (*Der Waffenschmied*) by Albert Lortzing (1801–51).

3 Probably Bertha Jahn in Lenzburg, later dubbed 'the erotic aunt' in reference to an experience dating back to 1883.

4 Mother: following the death of her parents in Chile, Emilie Wedekind, née Kammerer (1840–1915), had married a singer and publican, Hans Schwengerle. In 1860, while performing in a variety theatre in San Francisco, she made the acquaintance of Dr Friedrich Wilhelm Wedekind. They were married in 1862. Wedekind and his father had broken off relations after coming to blows in October 1886, and Wedekind's father died suddenly on 11 October 1888. Wedekind was incautious enough to tell the story of this estrangement to Gerhart Hauptmann, who promptly turned it into a drama, *The Reconciliation (Das Friedensfest)* subtitled *A Family Catastrophe* (1890).

5 Spanish: 'safe retreat'.

6 Orsina is the virago mistress in Lessing's drama *Emilia Galotti* (1772).

BERLIN 24 MAY–4 JULY 1889

1 Dr Heinrich Welti, music critic and writer, whom Wedekind had known ever since his schooldays in Aarau. His fiancée was the singer Emilie Herzog.

2 Julius Hart (1859–1930) was a poet, critic and editor; he had written for the *Tägliche Rundschau* since 1887.

3 *Pillars of Society*: the drama by Henrik Ibsen, first performed in 1877.

4 Elias Tomarkin, bacteriologist in Zürich, had been a friend of Wedekind since his student days there.

5 Erkner: at that time the last station on the Berlin suburban railway, where Gerhart Hauptmann lived from 1885 to 1889. The Villa Lassen was the house he had rented from Nicolaus Lassen.

6 Marie Hauptmann, née Thienemann, whom Hauptmann had married in 1885, and her sister, Pin Thienemann.

7 The painter Hugo Ernst Schmidt.

8 'Papa Hamlet': a short story celebrated as one of the first examples of Naturalism in German literature. It appeared under the pseudonym of Bjarne B. Holmson, but had been written jointly by Arno Holz (1863–1929) and Johannes Schlaf (1862–1941).

9 Karl Henckell (1864–1929): lyric poet whose acquaintance Hauptmann had made in 1888 during his stay in Zürich. Wedekind had also got to know him at that time. Hammi was the nickname of Wedekind's brother Armin, whom Hauptmann had also met in Zürich. After concluding his medical studies, Armin had married Emma Frey in March 1889.

10 Otto Ludwig (1813–65); his story 'Zwischen Himmel und Erde' has often been reckoned a model of German literary Realism.

11 Hauptmann's children Ivo (9 Feb. 1886), Eckart (21 Mar. 1887) and Klaus (8 July 1889) were born in Erkner.

12 The play in question was *Vor Sonnenaufgang (Before Sunrise)*, which appeared in the middle of August.

13 Wedekind possessed no more than a copy of the certificate of American citizenship that had been issued in Zürich. He repeatedly had problems on

this account. He quoted his lack of valid identity papers as one reason for leaving Germany at the time of the *Simplicissimus* prosecution, and he was obliged to move from Berlin to Munich for the same reason – ironically, on Independence Day, 1889!

14 A disease of the spine, a consequence of syphilitic infection.

15 'I wasted the day.'

16 An opera by Gaetano Donizetti (1840).

17 Hanover was Wedekind's birthplace, where he spent the first five years of his life.

18 Kletzengarten: a beer-hall in the Fürstenstrasse, Munich, a favourite haunt of Wedekind and his friends.

19 Wedekind's cousin Minna von Greyerz.

20 'like little devils'.

21 Scene in a boarding-house: the opening scene of the comedy *Die junge Welt (The Young Folk)*, published in 1891, first performed in 1908.

22 Helene Lange (1848–1930) was a pioneer of the German feminist movement. In 1887 she had proposed a reform of girls' schools.

23 Jules Michelet (1798–1874), essayist and historian. The reference is to his study *L'Amour*, first published in 1859.

24 Uncle Erich: brother of Wedekind's father, Dr Friedrich Wilhelm Wedekind, who had died on 11 October 1888.

25 Farce by H. Wilken and O. Justinus (1887).

26 i.e. a prostitute.

27 Franz Moor: the villain in Schiller's tragedy *Die Räuber (The Robbers)*, 1777.

28 Adolf Stoecker (1835–1909) was preacher to the Berlin court and cathedral from 1874 to 1889, and a Conservative member of the Reichstag.

29 Major thoroughfare running west into the Tiergarten.

30 The soprano Emilie Herzog (1859–1923) had made her début at the Munich Hofoper in 1880 and moved to the Berlin Hofoper in 1889. She sang a number of times at the Bayreuth Festival. There seems to have been some uncertainty about her marital status, perhaps because the theatre management were against her marriage. One source says she married Heinrich Welti, the Swiss musicologist, in 1887.

31 *The Lady from the Sea*: drama by Ibsen (1888).

32 *Torquato Tasso*: drama by Goethe (1790).

33 The monumental altar dedicated to Zeus and Athena which had been excavated and transported to Berlin on the initiative of the Berlin museums during the years 1878–86. It has been on display in the Pergamon Museum since 1930.

34 Feuerbach's *Symposium*: a well-known painting by Anselm Feuerbach (1829–80). Reclam translation: i.e. of Plato's *Symposium* in an edition by the German publisher Reclam.

35 Speeches of the Greek orator Demosthenes (384–322 BC) defending the freedom of Greece against Philip of Macedon.

36 Zenobia: the theme of a number of dramas, including one by A. Wilbrandt under the title *The Master of Palmyra* (1889).

37 Frau Pansegrau: Wedekind's landlady while he was living at no. 28 Genthinerstrasse. Wedekind adopted her name for a character in his play *Die junge Welt (The Young Folk)*.

38 Donald: Wedekind's youngest brother (1871–1908), whom he encouraged in a literary career. Although he never completed his own education, Donald tried to make a living as a private tutor in the United States. He committed suicide on 4 June 1908. A volume of his short stories was published in 1985 under the title *Der gefundene Gürtel (The Discovered Girdle)*.

39 Wedekind's brother William Lincoln, born 16 May 1866, also pursued a somewhat vagabond existence in the United States, claimed his share of the family estate in 1889, married Anna W. Kammerer of New York in that year and later went to live in South Africa.

40 Stendhal's work *De l'amour* came out in 1822, but the German translation did not appear until 1888.

41 recruits: i.e. a loan of money. Wedekind uses this expression in the letter to his brother. It may be a recondite reference to Lessing's play *Minna von Barnhelm*, where it is used by a ne'er-do-well French officer.

42 Mieze: Wedekind's sister Frieda Marianne Erika, who was making her name as a singer at the Dresden opera.

43 Mali: Wedekind's other sister, Emilie. Both in manuscript and in typescript Wedekind consistently writes 'Mali', but his elder daughter, the late Pamela Wedekind, insisted that Emilia's pet name was 'Mati' (from Swiss *Maitle*, 'girl, maiden').

44 Julius and Heinrich Hart (1859–1930 and 1855–1906) edited the *Kritische Waffengänge (Critical Encounters)* between 1882 and 1884, a defence of Naturalist aesthetic theories.

45 Carl Hauptmann (1858–1921), dramatist and novelist.

46 Pankow: a village near Potsdam, now part of Greater Berlin and the seat of ministries of the German Democratic Republic.

47 This incident may have inspired the plot of Hauptmann's comedy *Der Biberpelz (The Beaver-skin Coat)*, first performed in 1893.

48 Julius Rodenberg (1831–1914) edited the *Deutsche Rundschau*, which he had founded in 1874.

49 Provencal oil: presumably Hauptmann was struck by the term or by its incorrect pronunciation with a hard c. The incident illustrates the Naturalist writer's obsessional concern to record authentic dialogue.

50 Arnold Böcklin (1827–1901), Swiss painter with a fondness for landscapes featuring mythological figures and dramatically striking atmospheric scenes in glowing colours.

51 The two young gentlemen were Max Marschalk (1875–1957), later Hauptmann's brother-in-law (in 1904 Hauptmann married Margarete Marschalk), and Emil Strauss (1866–1960), best known as a writer of short stories. Strauss describes the meeting in a letter to Margarete

Hauptmann dated 30 April 1947: 'It was in July 1889, possibly even Midsummer's Day, at any rate a Saturday. Max and I had arranged to go on a nocturnal walk, and late in the afternoon we took the train to Friedrichshagen . . . Next day we arrived, tired and hungry, on the terrace of the station restaurant in Erkner, ate what they had to offer, had a good rest and filled in the time writing a postcard to Halbe . . .

'In discussing where we should go from there, I suggested that we should first go and call on Gerhart Hauptmann, who had recently had a good story, 'Bahnwärter Thiel' ('Thiel the Platelayer') in *Die Gesellschaft*, and had published a poem called 'Promethidenlos' . . . we set out in search of him after getting directions from the landlord, and did in fact find the house, which turned out to be a proper villa in a pretty large garden, which caused Max to have misgivings: he wanted to turn back, and seized my coat-tails when I walked on, trying to pull me back.

'I pulled myself free, marched on and said he shouldn't make us look silly, perhaps someone was standing at the window and watching us. He followed me, still protesting, and not without another grab at my coat-tails at the corner – we had to walk round to the back of the house.

'At last I found myself standing in front of a glass door and was able to ring the bell. A dark-haired, graceful, eminently attractive lady (Pin) opened the door; I asked for Gerhart Hauptmann, she went and fetched him. I told him we were on a little walking tour and would like to pay our respects *en passant*, we admired his 'Bahnwärter Thiel', and I knew long passages of his 'Promethidenlos' by heart. He smiled, pleased and embarrassed, which suited him and made him seem even younger. He led us into the drawing-room, introduced us to his wife, his sister-in-law Pin, his brother Carl, his friend, the painter Schmidt, and Frank Wedekind, who was still sporting his democratic moustache and goatee beard. We drank tea, chatted about literature and social issues, with Carl in his reserve officer's uniform flourishing the most radical views, and finally Gerhart Hauptmann read us the first act of the still uncompleted drama, *Vor Sonnenaufgang (Before Sunrise)*. I was enraptured. 'Naturalism' and 'naturalistic ploys' were then, after all, the main thing, as far as we were concerned, and I had never experienced anything like Hauptmann's manner of reading, expressive down to the last detail, devoid of theatrical and rhetorical tricks.

'We set off for the station towards evening in a sort of family caravan. Carl, in his brightly coloured tunic, and Frank Wedekind travelled into town with us; the former told me about a book, *The Metaphysics of Physiology*, which he's working on. Wedekind spoke about a political comedy that he's just sent round the theatres.

'And so the visit turned out rather differently from what I'd imagined; Max was also well pleased and forgave me for my lack of respect towards the villa . . . Hauptmann had invited us to come again; in July, just before the end of term, we went out again and listened to the reading of another act.' (Quoted from Walter Requardt and Martin Machatzke, *Gerhart Hauptmann und Erkner*, Berlin 1980, pp. 54f.)

52 *Promethidenlos (Promethean Destiny)*, an epic poem by Hauptmann, first published in 1885. *Die Gesellschaft (Society)*, the leading journal of the Naturalist movement, founded by M. G. Conrad in 1885.

53 Karl Bleibtreu (1859–1928): critic, novelist and dramatist; a radical pioneer of Naturalism, which he propagated in his manifesto *Revolution der Literatur* (1886).

54 Georg Büchner (1813–37). His work had been edited and published by Karl Franzos in 1879.

55 Emil Strauss came from Freiburg.

56 Charles Secrétan (1815–95), Professor of Philosophy in Lausanne, concerned himself with current social issues such as the abolition of class privilege and the equality of women.

57 Schlesischer Bahnhof, now Ostbahnhof.

58 *Kinder und Narren (Children and Fools)*, later entitled *Die junge Welt (The Young Folk)*, first published in Munich, 1891.

59 Anna W. Kammerer from New York.

60 Olga Plümacher, a friend of Wedekind's mother in her youth, wrote on philosophical topics, e.g. *Der Pessimismus in Vergangenheit und Gegenwart (Pessimism, Past and Present)*. Wedekind was powerfully influenced by her.

61 *The Youth's Magic Horn*, a celebrated collection of folksongs edited (1806–8) by Clemens Brentano and Achim von Arnim.

62 Presumably a dramatized version of the semi-autobiographical novel of that name (1886) by Alexandre Dumas, Jr. (1824–95).

63 Opera by Carl Maria von Weber, first performed in 1821.

64 mich/mir: confusion of the dative and accusative case, a grammatical solecism regarded as a sign of poor breeding! Stöckern: an incorrect plural for Stöcken (sticks).

65 wasch/was: allegedly a vulgar pronunciation of the German pronoun, 'what'.

66 Probably 'Marianne. Eine Erzählung aus dem Bauernleben' (Marianne: A Tale of Peasant Life').

67 A suburb of Berlin with an elegant rococo palace.

68 Probably a publication connected with Helene Lange's attempt to establish a high school for girls in Berlin in 1889.

MUNICH 5 JULY 1889–4 FEBRUARY 1890

1 Franz Bennat, musician by appointment to the royal court.

2 Fritz Hilpert, a cellist.

3 Paul Heyse (1830–1914): one of the most successful writers of the second half of the nineteenth century, invited to Munich by King Maximilian II in 1854. Heyse was awarded the Nobel Prize for literature in 1910.

4 Emma Klingenfeld, an acquaintance of Ibsen's from the literary circle, 'Das Krokodil'.

5 Franz Muncker (1855–1926), lecturer in German literature at the University of Munich, became assistant professor in 1890 and Professor in 1896. In 1890 he married Magdalena Kaula, a celebrated teacher of singing and the piano.

6 Young men who had completed their secondary education served a reduced term of one year.

7 Charles-Paul de Kock (1793–1871) was a very popular writer of stories and dramas satirizing middle-class life.

8 Hafis: probably a reference to Goethe's cycle of poems *Der west-östliche Divan*.

9 Prince Rupert (1869–1955): Crown Prince, the eldest son of King Ludwig III of Bavaria.

10 Meta von Salis-Marschlins (1855–1929): educator and philosopher, and a pioneer of women's rights.

11 Carl Güttler, subsequently Professor of Philosophy.

12 Operetta music by Alexander Bisson (b. 1848), libretto by Antony Mars (b. 1861).

13 Ernst Julius Engelmann (1820–1902), resident in Munich since 1853.

14 Part of a general radical rising throughout most of Europe in 1848, a 'Year of Revolutions'.

15 Gottfried Semper (1803–79), Professor of Architecture in Dresden since 1834, designed the Dresden Opera House. After the rising in May 1848, he emigrated to Paris and then to London.

16 Irma von Troll-Borostyáni (1849–1912): a leading feminist writer of her day. Apart from 'The Equality of the Sexes and the Reform of Education' (1888), she wrote on problems of prostitution: *Prostitution and the Law. An Appeal to the German People and their Representatives* (1893) and *The Crime of Love. A Socio-pathological Study* (1896).

17 A retired cellist.

18 Wilhelm II had ascended the throne on 15 June 1888.

19 Karl von Piloty (1826–86) became director of the Munich Academy in 1874, having made his reputation with vast historical canvasses. He was Franz Lenbach's teacher.

20 Feuerbach's *Iphigenie*: the painting exists in two versions, from 1862 and 1871 respectively.

21 Franz von Lenbach (1836–1904), portrait painter in Munich, often worked from Hahn's photographs.

22 Lecturer in German literature in Munich.

23 *Fliegende Blätter*: humorous Munich magazine, founded in 1845.

24 *The Gipsy Baron*: operetta by Johann Strauss (1885).

25 No doubt the work referred to elsewhere as *Eppur* (see n. 118).

26 Buchholz: literary manager of the Munich Court Theatre.

27 After this initial meeting, Richard Weinhöppel became a close friend of Wedekind. He later composed music for the Eleven Executioners Cabaret.

28 The Crown Prince, later Kaiser Wilhelm II.

29 Anny Bark, Oskar Schibler and Moritz Sutermeister: school-friends from Wedekind's time in Lenzburg.

30 A play which sharply attacks conventional morality.

31 *Sieben Legenden* (1872) by Gottfried Keller (1819–91); *Last Love*, drama by Ludwig von Dóczy (1845–1919), which appeared in 1887.

32 Piccolo: Wedekind's private code for his penis.

33 The reference is no doubt to the 'Wohlgemuth Affair', a dispute between Bismarck and the Swiss government. On 22 April 1889 the Swiss authorities arrested a German police inspector, Alfred Wohlgemuth, who had tried to enlist a German Social Democrat exile in Switzerland as an *agent provocateur*. He was deported to Germany on 3 May 1889, and the incident led to the breaking off of mutual residence conventions between the Reich and Switzerland. In view of Wedekind's background, this topical affair must have interested him keenly.

34 Scholastica: restaurant at 25 Ledererstrasse.

35 One of Goethe's 'Venetian Epigrams', suppressed by the author:
Raise not your legs up to heaven, my dear!
Jupiter sees you, the rogue, and Ganymede's worried.

36 Reference to *Psychopathis sexualis* (1886) by Richard von Krafft-Ebing (1840–1902), a specialist in nervous disorders and Professor in Vienna from 1889, who was best known for his study of sexual deviations.

37 *Höllriegelsgreut*: a painting by Karl Wilhelm Diefenbach, resident in Munich until 1892.

38 Presumably the reference is to Galileo's statement to the Inquisition after his recantation: Eppur si muove (But it does move), but the relevance is not clear. Evidently a drama, perhaps connected with the *New Firmament* mentioned previously.

39 A popular singer in the Munich Kindl beer-cellar, at 18–22 Rosenheimer Strasse. This was the largest establishment of its kind in the city, with room for 5,000 guests.

40 Meadows by the River Isar.

41 A working-class suburb on the right bank of the Isar.

42 The Mariahilfkirche.

43 The bastion of Lenzburg Castle.

44 Drama by Ibsen (1879), better known in English under the title *The Doll's House*.

45 The first act of *Kinder und Narren/Die junge Welt*.

46 Probably a mistake for 'Matthäi's'.

47 Dr Julius Elias (1861–1927), literary historian and critic, known for his translations of Ibsen.

48 'Der Fischer', a ballad about an angler seduced by a water-sprite.

49 St Sophia, the principal church of Istambul, which has a prominent dome.

50 Wedekind named his second daughter Kadidja Fanny.

51 Hahn: photographer to the painter Franz Lenbach.

52 Drama by Tolstoy (1886).

53 Hero of Dostoevsky's novel, 'Crime and Punishment'.

54 Eduard Jokisch, painter and engraver.

55 Lili Dressler (born 1857) began her career at the Munich opera in 1883. In 1889 she sang the part of Eva in Wagner's *Meistersinger* at Bayreuth.

56 Hermann Levi (1839–1900), Hofkapellmeister in Munich since 1872. He was associated with Wagner and the Bayreuth Festival.

57 The actor Adalbert Matkowsky (1858–1909).

58 Karl Stieler (1842–85), a highly esteemed composer of songs and poems in the Bavarian dialect.

59 Erich Schmidt: German scholar (1853–1913), who had been director of the Goethe Archives in Weimar since 1885, and Professor in Berlin since 1887. The Goethegesellschaft commissioned him to edit Goethe's works in a popular edition of six volumes.

60 Musicians from the Residenztheater. A list in Wedekind's posthumous papers identifies Kutschenreuter and Brummer as trombonists, Ölgärtner as a violinist, Scherzer as a flautist. Franz Bennat figures in the same list as 'Königlicher Kammermusiker', and Sander as a violinist.

61 Wilhelm I.

62 Cosima and Siegfried: Wagner's wife (1837–1930) and son (1869–1930).

63 Act I of *Kinder und Narren/Die junge Welt*.

64 'Young Germany', a radical literary movement, at one time centred in Zürich.

65 Rambergstrasse: called after the painter Arthur Georg von Ramberg (1819–75), Professor at the Munich Academy.

66 There are two peaks named Mythen in the Alps north-east of Schwyz. The friend in question was probably Moritz Dürr, who committed suicide in the winter of 1885, and who may have been the model for Moritz Stiefel in *Spring Awakening*.

67 By the Isar on the southern outskirts of Munich.

68 Adolf Friedrich von Schack (1815–94), writer and diplomat, lived in Munich from 1855 as a patron of the arts. His collection of pictures includes works by Bonaventura Genelli, Anselm Feuerbach and Moritz von Schwind.

69 Portrait of Titian's daughter.

70 Moritz von Schwind (1804–71), the leading representative of the South German Romantic school of painting.

71 Probably an abbreviation for *Eppur*.

72 Operetta by Robert Plaquette (1877).

73 Heinrich Davideit (1833–94), member of the Court Theatre ensemble.

74 A satirical poem by Karl Henckell on the anti-socialist legislation passed by the Reichstag.

75 Wildenstein: castle in Liestal, Canton Basel.

76 Wildegg: castle in the parish of Möriken, Canton Aargau, built by the Habsburgs in the eleventh century.

77 An old Scottish family.
78 A neighbouring village.
79 Painter and engraver (1741–1807), resident in Rome from 1763.
80 The villain in Schiller's drama *Fiesko* (1783).
81 The procuress: see 17 July 1889.
82 Because of his Jewish origins.
83 Heilige Spitalkirche.
84 Recollection of Wedekind's spell in hospital while he was studying law in Munich (1885). He was treated for a rash on his leg.
85 *Winter's Tale: Deutschland. Ein Wintermärchen*, satirical verse epic by Heinrich Heine (1844).
86 The waitress from whose album Wedekind copied some poems (9 Sept. 1889).
87 *The Trumpeter of Säckingen*, a verse epic by Viktor von Scheffel that appeared in 1854.
88 Wedekind incorporated this grisly ballad practically unchanged in his cycle of poems *The Four Seasons*, published in 1905.
89 The second act of *Kinder und Narren/Die junge Welt*.
90 Rudolph Frische. Apart from Wedekind, Frau Mühlberger, at 21 Akademiestrasse, had as lodgers the painters Heinrich Lefler and Ragau and the singer Nina Ninon.
91 Dr Franz Muncker, see 6 July 1889.
92 Klara Ziegler (1844–1900): leading lady, resident in Munich, 1868–74.
93 Franz Nachbauer (1830–1902), highly esteemed tenor at the royal opera house in Munich until 1890. His son, also named Franz (1873–1926) also went on the stage and had a career as actor and producer.
94 Gabriel von Max (1840–1915) was known for his seductive female portraits. Astarte is a fertility goddess.
95 Suburb of Munich with a large mental hospital.
96 Hans Makart (1840–84), Austrian painter, a pupil of the Munich professor Karl von Piloty.
97 Eugen Blaas (1843–1931), member of a family of painters, professor at the Academy in Venice, specialized in figures from popular Venetian life.
98 *Ehre*, a drama by Hermann Sudermann (1857–1928) which had appeared in 1890.

PARIS 1 MAY 1892–23 JANUARY 1894

1 On 3 May 1892 Wedekind wrote to his mother:
Dear Mama,
   I hasten to send off the signed power of attorney as quickly as possible. It is not correct that I put myself down as Swiss when I signed. Dr Stumm just assumed that this was the case. I congratulate you, and all of us into the bargain, that you have managed to complete the deal after all. We all have reason to be grateful to you. The result, if not brilliant, is not at all bad all the same. It corresponds altogether to what I had hoped for at

best. I could only make a detailed judgement if I knew what you have done about the furniture and fittings. As far as that goes, however, please proceed as you think best. You are the party most interested, because of all the things you purchased.

I hardly dare to ask you what you propose to do now, since I am not in a position to exert any sort of decisive influence on you, because of my inadequate circumstances. If you think of having Mali with you, it would certainly not be a bad thing for you to come here with her, since Mali could learn something here. This, incidentally, would also apply in the first place to you yourself. In Lenzburg you came to the conclusion that you need a certain amount of physical exercise to feel fit. If anyone is in a position to understand that, then it's me, since I never felt particularly physically fit in Lenzburg and always suffered from a lack of exercise, with palpitations, lethargy and so on. I'm absolutely convinced that your health would not suffer here in any way, as far as that goes, since the actual size of the city involves a great deal more in the way of exercise than you can possibly get through manual work in Lenzburg. At the same time you can settle down here very comfortably, and might even after all begin to enjoy life up to a point. Please think this over carefully, thinking as much as possible of yourself, and as little as possible of others. Perhaps this will also be best for those others as well.

Please excuse me if I make so bold as to approach you with well-meant advice at a moment when you have just gained a victory.

I ask you at least not to doubt my good intentions, and remain, with most cordial greetings, your grateful son,

Franklin

2 Habermann: presumably purchaser of Lenzburg castle; Katja: identity unknown; Américain: possibly Bourbon whiskey.

3 Frl. Hüny: the writer Emilie Hüny.

4 Exhibition preview.

5 Otto Julius Bierbaum (1865–1910), poet, novelist and critic, a contributor to *Simplicissimus*.

6 Germain Ribot (d. 1893), painter of genre and still-life pictures.

7 *Kean*: a drama by the elder Alexandre Dumas (1802–70).

8 'She's trying to make me . . . but bites me so hard in the balls that I yelp with pain.'

9 '. . . and painting. She also goes riding.'

10 Probably Fritz Burger (born Munich, 1867), who had moved to Paris in 1891.

11 *Die Büchse der Pandora (Pandora's Box).*

12 'I'd prefer it with!'

13 Hermann Bahr (1863–1934): novelist, essayist and critic who contributed to the journal *Die Freie Bühne* in Berlin. Wedekind first met him in Munich in 1889.

14 'Here are the ladies!'

15 'In heaven you eat cakes and drink white wine.'

16 Review: of *Spring Awakening.*

17 Maximilian Harden (1861–1927): publicist, essayist, critic, one of the founders of *Die Freie Bühne*; Friedrich Lange (1852–1917), editor of the *Tägliche Rundschau*; Otto Brahm (1856–1912), also a founder of *Die Freie Bühne*; Fritz Mauthner (1849–1923), drama critic on the *Berlin Tageblatt.*

18 Walter Paetow, Editor of the *Deutsche Rundschau.*

19 'Give me a little present.'

20 To have sex.

21 '. . . but you've got to get it up. I'm so tight.'

22 'She grinds her teeth.'

23 Jeanne la Folle: a celebrated Parisian cabaret dancer.

24 Kadudja: in his diary Wedekind uses this French spelling, but named his younger daughter 'Kadidja'.

25 'What does that mean?'

26 'Marvellous legs.'

27 'My teeny, teeny little titch!'

28 *Der Liebestrank (The Love Potion)* or *Fritz Schwigerling.*

29 Probably a drink.

30 *Rose et Ninette* was published in 1892, *Sappho* in 1884.

31 Wedekind had admired a family of circus performers, Lavater, John and Stephen Lee, when he saw them in Zürich.

32 Presumably a piece of jewellery, a brooch perhaps.

33 An American acquaintance of Frank and Armin Wedekind.

34 A friend from Lenzburg days.

35 The first version of *Pandora's Box.*

36 Arabi Pasha: Egypt became a British–Egyptian condominium under his rule.

37 Asherah: a goddess who figures in various cults of the Near East. One of her names was Astarte, and according to legend she killed her consort – a theme to interest Wedekind!

38 Hermann Wissman (1835–1905), African explorer, leader of the expeditionary force which put down the Arab rising in German East Africa in 1888. He was Governor of the colony in 1895–6.

39 Emin Pasha *alias* Eduard Schnitzer (1840–92) had been active in establishing the authority of the Reich in East Africa. He was murdered in the Congo.

40 The original Chat-Noir was a bohemian cafe and cabaret in Montmartre.

41 Georg Christian Dieffenbach (1822–1901), clergyman and writer, whose sermons and poems were popular in Germany at the time.

42 The theatrical agent, A. Entsch, who had little success in promoting Wedekind's work.

43 Mihály Munkácsy (1844–1900), Hungarian painter, resident in Paris since 1872.

44 Pierre Loti: the pen-name of the French writer Julien Viaud (1850–1923), whose novels and short stories have an exotic flavour.

45 Friedrich Lienhard (1865–1929), representative of a home-spun school of writers who opposed Naturalism and its urban themes.

46 A German poet and anarchist of Scottish extraction whom Wedekind had met in Zürich.

47 Mlle Campana: prima ballerina at the Folies Bergères.

48 Wilhelm Walloth (1856–1932): known for his historical novels in the Naturalistic style.

49 Annette Elisabeth, Baroness von Droste-Hülshoff (1797–1848), German poetess known for her short stories and ballads.

50 Karl Henckell (1864–1929), pioneer of Naturalism. His *Diorama*, like his other works, advocated radical political reform.

51 A large theatre designed for spectacular performances.

52 *The Damnation of Faust* by Hector Berlioz (1846).

53 i.e. the Lulu drama.

54 Novel by Guy de Maupassant (1885).

55 The penitential approach of the Emperor Henry IV to Pope Gregory VII in 1077.

56 Jules Lemaître (1853–1914), an influential critic of the day wrote theatrical reviews for the *Journal des Débats*.

57 Willy Morgenstern, alias Rudinoff, an old acquaintance from Wedekind's circus days. Wedekind characterizes him briefly as 'illustrator and draughtsman, writer, lightning painter from Berlin . . . Cantor in the synagogue'.

58 Shereshefsky: noted by Wedekind as 'a painter from Kiev'.

59 Dichtelei: a tavern in Munich, a favourite haunt of Wedekind's; Gustav Floerke (born 1846), art historian, author of poems and stories.

60 Donald Wedekind wrote articles and features for the *Züricher Post* and the *Berner Bund*; Nietzsche's *Thus Spake Zarathustra* (1883–5).

61 Anatol Durow (1864–1916), Russian comedian and animal trainer. The anecdote narrated here by Morgenstern in a sort of Russian pidgin German turns on an untranslatable pun involving a Russian (or Jewish) mispronunciation of the word 'grösser' (bigger) and the name of the police chief, Gresser.

62 Novel by Guy de Maupassant (1888).

63 'Who's there?'

64 'Les puces (la danse de douleur), Ballet-pantomime en trois tableaux. Livret par Franklin Querilinth', which was published in 1897 in the collection *Die Fürstin Russalka*.

65 *Fritz Schwigerling*.

66 'Oh, wouldn't you like to take [us]?'

67 Bernhard Pollini, actually Pohl (1838–97), theatre manager in Hamburg.

68 Leblanc: newspaper editor.

69 A boarding-house in Munich.

70 'You won't have to pay a lot, I'll be very nice to you, I'll stoke up a lovely fire, I know all sorts of little tricks, etc.'

71 François Coppée (1842–1908), poet, novelist and playwright who was

regarded by Zola as the first lyric poet of the Naturalist movement.

72 Drama by Paul Herrein (1857–1915).

73 Baudelaire's 'Une Charogne' ('Carrion') from *Les Fleurs du mal* (1857).

74 'Dear friend,

I'm in deep trouble and assure you I didn't expect this. I owe my landlady 35 francs, she won't let me in and my overcoat is still in the room.

I did promise I wouldn't ask any more of you, but you know that I'm ill. What's more, for the past two or three days I've been coughing blood.

I hope I'll soon be done with life. If you could help me this one last time, I'd be very grateful.

The doctor told me that once I started coughing blood it would soon be over.

So I beg you to do me this last favour, I would be so grateful.

Your poor Henriette, who kisses you and counts on you.

HENRIETTE

If it's not too much trouble, could you bring me the money at the café or the laundry, 12 Rue des Carmes – that's where I'm staying at the moment. A thousand thank-yous in advance.'

75 'Out you get!'

76 Published in 1879.

77 Written in 1777, it appears generally as 'Anekdote unserer Tage' ('An Anecdote for our Time') and satirizes the attitude of pettifogging critics in relation, first, to a pretty girl, and then to pictures in an art gallery.

78 Wedekind seems uncertain about the spelling of this slang term, which he had obviously never seen written. The handwriting is unclear and may in fact read 'gugnolle', or even 'guignolle', but the sense is perfectly obvious from the context.

79 A working-class girl.

80 'Good night, darling wife.'

81 A strange, hermaphroditic figure from Goethe's novel *Wilhelm Meisters Lehrjahre (Wilhelm Meister's Apprenticeship)*.

82 Leopold von Sacher-Masoch (1863–95), Austrian lawyer and writer best known for the erotic perversion (masochism) which features in his later works.

83 The writer Louisa Read (born 1844) helped Wedekind correct the fourth act of *Pandora's Box*, much of which was originally written in French.

84 A pair of professional acrobats and strong men. The latter may be the prototype of a character in Wedekind's play *Die Kaiserin von Neufund-land (The Empress of Newfoundland)*.

85 'weight-lifters'.

86 'What a handsome fellow ... What a good time I'll have, what a good time.'

87 After taking pains to obliterate his friend's name throughout Wedekind seems to have given the game away here, and two paragraphs later.

88 In the incident previously narrated it is her *right* hand!

89 Immediately after this entry fifteen pages have been cut out of the diary. The narrative resumes in the middle of an account of the author's journey from Switzerland back to Paris on 4 September 1893.

90 Emma Herwegh (1817–1904) was the widow of the radical poet and revolutionary Georg Herwegh (1817–75). She was forced into political exile more than once and lived at various times in Geneva, Paris and Zürich. Wedekind first met her in the spring of 1893 and they became firm friends. Mme Herwegh lived at this time in student lodgings at 40 Rue des Saints-Pères in the Quartier Latin. She secured Wedekind entry to the Parisian *salons* and introduced him, for example, to the writers Mlle Read and Mlle Hüny.

91 The Hungarian countess Emmy de Nemethy began translating *Spring Awakening* into French but could not find a publisher for it.

92 Mme Herwegh's son (1858–1937), a concert violinist.

93 Marie François Sadi Carnot (1837–94), President of the French Republic.

94 Ferdinand Lassalle (1825–64), a leading German social democrat, founder of the Universal German Workingmen's Association. He was killed in a duel with Count Racowitza, his rival for the favours of Helene von Dönniges.

95 'Are you coming up?'

96 In a letter to his brother Armin (14 March 1892) Wedekind refers to the painter Luise Breslau (1856–1927) as 'the most interesting woman who has ever crossed my path'.

97 Joris Karl Huysmans (1848–1907) was a French novelist of Dutch origin. His *Là-bas* features a kind of devil-worshipping mysticism.

98 The substance of the entries for 8–10 September was adapted by Wedekind for publication in his anthology *Die Fürstin Russalka (Princess Russalka)*, Paris, Leipzig, Munich, Albert Langen, 1897, pp. 91–103. This published version is reproduced as an appendix to the present volume. It offers interesting insight into the adaptation of auto-biographical material for literary purposes. The manuscript diary resumes on 1 January 1894.

99 Maurice Maeterlinck's drama *La Princesse Maleine* was published in 1893.

100 See n. 116.

101 'She was in a real mess.'

102 *Abbé Mouret's Sin*, a novel by Emile Zola (1875).

103 'Hot piss' – presumably a symptom of venereal infection.

104 *La Fille Élisa*, published in 1878, was possibly the most popular novel written by Edmond de Goncourt (1822–96).

105 'The main bar.'

106 'Is that all?'

107 'She's a lovely woman.'

108 'To roam around a bit.' Les Halles was the central vegetable market of Paris.

109 'A cheese and onion soup in the main bar'. This was a speciality of les Halles that was served all night.

110 'Some crayfish? A dozen oysters? Half a chicken?'

111 'Looks too much like a tart'.

112 'But she's a beautiful woman.'

113 Diane de Poitiers (1499–1566) was mistress to King Henry II of France; Jeanne Antoinette Poisson, Marquise de Pompadour (1721–64) was the mistress of Louis XV; Josephine Beauharnais became Napoleon's wife after her husband had been guillotined during the French Revolution; Beauharnais's daughter Hortense married Napoleon's brother Louis.

114 'On the far side of the river'.

115 Novel by Zola, published in 1884.

116 'Inclined to talk to me, even about those things one never talked about.' 'Urgent' is written on the envelope.

117 Jules Amadée Barbey d'Aurevilly (1808–89), French novelist, author of *La Vieille Maîtresse* (1851) and *L'Ensorcelée* (1854); Luise Viktorine Ackermann (1813–90), lyric poet and writer, author of the pessimistic *Pensées d'une Solitaire* (1883).

118 Marie Suzanne Rosalie Rousseil (born 1841) was a celebrated actress of the day who performed at the Comédie Française and a number of other leading theatres in Paris. She also wrote a novel, *La Fille d'un Proscrit* (1878) and published a collection of verse under the title *Dieu et Patrie* (1890).

119 A popular French dramatist. His best-known play was *L'Inquiétude*.

120 i.e. of *Pandora's Box*.

121 The short-lived Communist regime in Paris at the end of the Franco-Prussian war. It was brutally suppressed by Thiers, the head of the provisional government which made peace with the Prussians.

122 'A don't give a damn-ist'.

123 'A minor virginity', i.e. no sexual relations for the past two weeks.

124 Tragedies by Jean Racine (1639–99).

125 'He was very nice.'

126 Jean-Louis Forain, French painter and caricaturist (1852–1931).

127 The celebrated novel by Choderlos de Laclos, first published in 1782.

128 Paul Bourget: French novelist and critic (1852–1935). His best-known novel, *Le Disciple* (1889), is a psychological study of the way in which a determinist philosopher drives his pupil to murder – again a topic likely to interest Wedekind at this time.

129 'The perfect mother'.

130 'Would you like to be my lover?'

131 'Lady's companion'.

132 Otto Erich Hartleben (1864–1905), a writer with whom Wedekind had been on friendly terms since the previous year.

133 'That excites me.'

134 'I'm going to keep a diary, too – write down all sorts of smut – there's my pussy – he's getting me worked up – that's just the thing!'

135 There is a blank space in the manuscript at this point, but the flowers have long since vanished.

136 'Oh, I'm so poor!'

137 'That'll bring me luck.'

138 Alexander Herzen: radical Russian writer and politician (1812–70), a close associate of Georg Herwegh. Herzen was banished from Russia because of his socialist views. He subsequently lived mainly in London but died in Paris.

139 Vaillant and Ravachol were French anarchists condemned to death and executed for attempted assassination in 1893.

140 Sophie von Hatzfeld (1805–81) was the intimate friend of the Social Democratic politician Ferdinand Lassalle; Semper: see n. 95.

141 Affairs of the heart: German 'Herzensgeschichten', a pun on Alexander Herzen's name.

142 'Always off-beam'.

143 i.e. in 1848.

144 Marie d'Agoult, Liszt's mistress and mother of Cosima Wagner.

145 'Suitably turned out'.

146 The Norwegian composer Christian Sinding (1856–1941).

147 Josephin Peladon (1859–1918), French author, first joined the Rosicrucian Order that had been founded by Stanislas de Guaita, but then founded a rival order under the name of l'Ordre du Temple de la Rose-Croix. He used his novels to propagate his mystic beliefs.

148 The Swedish dramatist Johan August Strindberg (1849–1912) held violently misogynist views.

149 The Swedish writer (1860–1925).

150 Albert Langen (1869–1909) opened a publishing business in Paris in 1893, moved it to Leipzig in 1894, and from there to Munich. He founded the satirical magazine *Simplicissimus* for which Wedekind wrote the verses that led to his conviction and imprisonment for *lèse-majesté*.

151 'In a profound depression'.

152 Probably the reference is to the Duc de Morny (1811–65), half-brother of Louis Napoleon and Minister of the Interior in the Second Republic.

153 Bergliot Bjørnson, daughter of the writer Bjørnstjerne Bjørnson (1832–1910), was married to Henrik Ibsen's son, the author and politician Sigurd Ibsen (1859–1930).

154 'What's the matter? You look so unhappy. Oh, if only you knew where I've been.'

155 Wedekind had been friendly with the painter Käthe Juncker since 1890–1. They had first met in Munich.

156 Knut Hamsun's novel (1890). Langen did a great deal to popularize Scandinavian writing in Germany.

157 A novel published in 1892.

158 Eugène Louis Napoleon (1856–79).

159 'Are you going to take me out? ... a four-day virginity' (i.e. four days

without a man).

160 Balsam.

161 Probably Nietzsche's letter of 18 December 1888, in which he reports to Strindberg on the reception of the latter's works in France.

LONDON JANUARY—JUNE 1894

1 i.e. *Pandora's Box.*

2 The text as far as the end of this entry was published in *Mephisto*, 1: 10 (28 November 1896) as 'Ein Fragment aus meinem Londoner Tagebuch' ('A Fragment from my London Diary'). Wedekind was in London from January until June 1894. He had a generally unfavourable impression of England.

3 Pruntrut is a small provincial town in Canton Berne.

BERLIN 21 DECEMBER 1905—1 JULY 1908

1 These notes, headed 'Diary' and designated L 3504 in Wedekind's post-humous papers, come from the period between 21 December 1905 and 1 July 1908. They seem to be the only personal record of this kind that has survived from the period. They are mainly concerned with the dispute between Wedekind and the producer Max Reinhardt and are of interest for the history of the German stage.

2 Felix Hollaender: literary manager of the Deutsches Theater. In 1920 he succeeded Reinhardt as manager of the Grosses Schauspielhaus.

3 Kommerzienrat Willy Levin was one of Reinhardt's financial backers.

4 Probably the banker Dr Fritz Andreae, owner of the banking house Hardy and Co., Berlin, and a shareholder in the Deutsches Theater.

5 Wedekind's publisher at the time was Georg Müller, who had founded the Georg Müller Verlag in Munich in 1903. In 1932 the firm was merged with the Albert Langen Verlag.

MUNICH 16 FEBRUARY—23 FEBRUARY 1918

1 Joachim Friedenthal edited the *Wedekindbuch* that was published in Munich in 1914 to mark the author's fiftieth birthday. He was sub-sequently co-editor, with Artur Kutscher, of Wedekind's posthumous papers; Benz's was a popular name for the Café Luitpold.

2 A Munich restaurant and bar at 8 Platzl noted for its literary and artistic patrons, who included Heinrich Mann, Max Halbe, Oskar Kokoschka and Klabund.

3 Erna Morena, née Fuchs (1885–1962), film actress, married to the writer Wilhelm Herzog (1882–1960).

4 Discrepancy in age, jealousy and different attitudes to life had placed an almost intolerable strain on the Wedekinds' marriage and brought them to the point of considering divorce. At this time Tilly had attempted

suicide. After her discharge from a sanatorium she did not rejoin the family at once but went to live in the Hiltenspergerstrasse with her sister Marthl, who was married to the actor Hans Carl Müller. Cf. Tilly Wedekind, *Lulu. Die Rolle meines Lebens* (*Lulu. The Role of my Life*), Munich, Berne, Vienna, 1969.

5 Hotel in the Max-Joseph-Strasse.

6 Fanny Kadidja, Wedekind's younger daughter, born 6 August 1912.

7 Julius Schaumberger, member of the Society for Modern Living, editor of the magazine *Mephisto*, who had strongly promoted Wedekind since 1896.

8 ♁ is the sign for the planet earth, used in the diaries to denote sexual intercourse.

9 A dramatic poem in three acts by Wedekind, written between October 1916 and March 1917, published in 1917, première 1919 in Munich.

10 J.G. Stollberg, manager of the Schauspielhaus.

11 Anton Dressler, singer and music teacher with whom Wedekind had been friendly since 1896.

12 Marthl Müller acted Perdita and her husband played Florizel in this production.

13 After a difficult appendectomy in 1914 Wedekind suffered a rupture that handicapped him, especially on the stage. On 24 February 1918 he entered hospital for a further operation. Complications set in and he died on 9 March 1918.

14 Erich Mühsam (1878–1934), lyric poet and dramatist, editor of the magazine *Kain* and a member of the central council of the Bavarian Soviet Republic that was briefly set up in 1919. In the *Vossische Zeitung* of 21 July 1928 Mühsam wrote: 'I personally joined the group in the Torggelstuben at a fairly late stage, and I was in fact introduced by Wedekind, who fell into conversation with me following an opening night at the theatre, and went on talking to me until we joined the notables at their table. I had always steered clear of this circle up to that point, precisely because I had assumed that it was indeed an assembly of dignitaries, but I very soon felt at home there, more at home, in fact, than with any other group in Munich's bohemian life. The intellectual standard of the company in the Torggelstuben was far superior to that of the Café Stefanie or other places of entertainment, where people went to read the newspapers, where some used to do their writing, using the facilities simply as a warm place to pass their solitary lives without contracting social ties.' (Cf. *Zu Gast im alten München*, ed. Richard Bauer, Munich 1982, p. 62).

15 Tilly Wedekind dated these verses as written during the night of 23–4 February 1918. It must be Wedekind's last poem, written in an undated pocket diary (archive number L 3476/6/4).

APPENDIX

1 Zola's novel *The Bludgeon* (1877).
2 'To foretell good luck.'
3 'You're madly in love with her.'
4 Eugène Beauharnais (1781–1824), Napoleon's stepson. The tomb in St Michael's Church in Munich was created by Bertel Thorvaldsen in 1827.
5 There is no evidence that Mme de Staël was ever mistress to any member of the French royal family; according to legend a woman is supposed to have served as Pope ('Johannes Angelicus'), either between Leo IV (died 855) and Benedict III (died 858), or else about 1100.
6 i.e. on the other bank of the Seine.
7 A short story about life in a provincial brothel (1881).

INDEX

277